Contributions to Management Science

For further volumes:
http://www.springer.com/series/1505

Christine Falkenreck

Reputation Transfer to Enter New B-to-B Markets

Measuring and Modelling Approaches

Physica-Verlag

Dr. Christine Falkenreck
University of Kassel
Head of International Marketing Research
Mönchebergstr. 17
34125 Kassel
Germany
christine.falkenreck@t-online.de

Dissertation "Impact on Reputation and Reputation Transfer in International Direct Marketing - Empirical Research in Five B-to-B Markets" at the University of Kassel, Germany. Department of Economics, Place of Disputation: Kassel, Date of Disputation, March 6, 2009

ISSN 1431-1941
ISBN 978-3-7908-2356-1 e-ISBN 978-3-7908-2357-8
DOI 10.1007/978-3-7908-2357-8
Springer Heidelberg Dordrecht London New York

Library of Congress Control Number: 2009932424

Cover design: SPi Publishing Services

Printed on acid-free paper

Physica-Verlag is a brand of Springer-Verlag Berlin Heidelberg
Springer-Verlag is a part of Springer Science+Business Media (www.springer.com)

Preface

An increasing number of products and services are not differentiated by inherent features, but by the vendors, particularly their reputation and marketing communication. Consequently, a positive reputation provides competing vendors with a virtually inimitable competitive advantage.

Contemporary research concerning antecedents and consequences of reputation in the domain of marketing is dominated by branding and line extension issues. Organizations' communication efforts and the relation of reputation and the communication media are not fully understood; nor have they been challenged up to now. Moreover, customers' perception of reputation is clearly embedded in their cultural context.

However, contemporary marketing research restricts both conceptual and empirical considerations to Western-type cultures. Frequently, even the differences in Western-type cultures are neglected.

Considering these shortcomings in contemporary marketing research, Dr. Christine Falkenreck investigates the opportunities and limits, and also the potential benefits and dangers of transferring a vendor's positive reputation to product categories never produced or offered by the considered vendor.

Embedding the empirical investigation of both reputation management and reputation transfer in a coherent theoretical framework, which is grounded in the Commitment-Trust theory, is her merit. She derives and validates an integrated model that appears to be valid in all cultures considered in her study. The results of this analysis contribute substantially to our understanding of reputation measuring and managing. These results are not restricted to academic interests and they provided practitioners with a variety of new insights. Thus, this thesis will hopefully be widely discussed in both academia and management practice.

Working with Dr. Falkenreck is an outstanding experience. Hopefully she will continue to engage in scientific marketing research.

Bielefeld, 17 May 2009 Ralf Wagner

Acknowledgements

Like a new product, a thesis follows a development process before its launch. A successful outcome is largely determined by the development process and the people who contribute to it. For this reason, there are a number of persons I would particularly like to thank for their input, help and support during my doctoral research.

First and foremost, this Ph.D. dissertation may never have been written without the encouragement of two key people: Professor Dr. Ralf Wagner, my supervisor at the University of Kassel, and Dr. Annette Speitling, my helpful mentor at the Strategic Marketing Department. I appreciate very much Professor Wagner's insightful advice on the way to conduct research. Many of our discussions not only directly contributed to improving the quality of my thesis, but also greatly motivated me and developed my interest and skills in academic research. In addition, I would like to thank Professor Dr. Marcel Paulssen for devoting his time as a second reader for my thesis.

I am grateful to the German medical devices and pharmaceuticals company that financially supported this thesis, and TforG, the Belgian market research agency, which was involved in the international CATI survey. My particular appreciation goes to my colleagues Lilijana Sesar, Christel Wagener and Theodor Kikenberg, for their friendly help and support during my stay at the Strategic Marketing Department. Special thanks are also due to Jean Cropper, who turned my clumsy language into readable English.

While I was writing this Ph.D. thesis, a vast number of people helped me in various ways. Thanks to my non-marketing researcher friends, Barbara, Eric, and Selli, for reminding me that however important and world-changing I think my work is, in the grand scheme of things, there are many other important things to do.

Last but not the least, I would like to express my utmost gratitude to my dear parents, Uwe and Christel Moll, my little sister Sabine, and my husband, Andreas, for their support during the last 2 years.

I dedicate this work to the best daughters in the world, Thora and Celia, of whom I am very proud.

Christine Falkenreck

Contents

Abbreviations

AMAC	America's most admired companies
B-to-B	Business-to-business
B-to-C	Business-to-consumer
CC	Corporate communications
CR	Corporate reputation
e.g.	(exempli gratia) for example
IDV	Individualism
i.e.	(id est) that is
KBV	Knowledge-based view
LV	Latent variable
MAS	Masculinity
WOM	Word of mouth
n.a.	Not applicable
n.s.	Not significant
NWOM	Negative word of mouth
SEM	Structural equation model
SET	Social exchange theory
SR	Sales representatives
PWOM	Positive word of mouth
PDI	Power distance index
RBV	Resource-based view
RM	Relationship marketing
RQ	Reputation quotient
UAI	Uncertainty avoidance index

Formula Symbols

η	Vector of the dependent (endogenous) latent variables
ζ	The unexplained variance
ξ	Vector of an exogenous latent variable
R^2	Variance explained
Q^2	Stone–Geissers cross-validated R^2
f^2	Effect size
γ_i	Coefficient capturing effect of indicator x_i
z	Test value
VAF	Variance inflation factor
r_i	Regression coefficient

List of Figures

List of Tables

Chapter 1
Definition of Research Problem

> In today's world, where ideas are increasingly displacing the physical in the production of economic value, competition for reputation becomes a significant driving force, propelling our economy forward. (Alan Greenspan 1999).

This quotation of Alan Greenspan (1999) summarizes the importance today of corporate reputation (CR). This work is about creating global corporate reputations – using reputation transfer to enter new markets more easily – and focuses on special impact factors on both reputation and reputation transfer in the B-to-B context.

1.1 Introduction

Researchers recognize organizational reputation as a valuable intangible asset that contributes to organizational performance. However, limited attention has been paid to the extent to which CR encompasses different stakeholders' perceptions that may have differential effects on the positive economic outcomes associated with the possession of a favorable reputation (Rindova et al. 2005). Thus, CR has been the focus of much academic research (e.g., Deephouse, 2000; Lewellyn 2002; Longsdon and Wood 2002; Eberl 2006; Helm 2007; Bromley 2002; Fombrun et al. 2000; Walsh and Wiedmann 2004; Fombrun and Shanley 1990; Hall 1992). It captures a combination of social and economic contributions that a firm makes to its various stakeholders (Helm 2007; Bromley 2002). Reputation provides a company with sustainable competitive advantages (Barney 1996) because it influences stakeholders' economic choices vis-à-vis the organization (Deephouse 2000).

In 1997, Doney and Cannon called for more research that investigates the role of national culture on buyer-seller relationships in general. Prior cross-cultural studies in marketing have focused on various issues: advertising (Alden et al. 1993), product development (Nakata and Sivakumar 1996), fairness (Kumar et al. 1995), organizational culture (Deshpandé et al. 2000), innovativeness (Steenkamp et al. 1999) and customer benefits (Homburg et al. 2005). Nevertheless, cross-national

C. Falkenreck, *Reputation Transfer to Enter New B-to-B Markets*,
Contributions to Management Science,
DOI 10.1007/978-3-7908-2357-8_1, © Springer-Verlag Berlin Heidelberg 2010

differences in B-to-B marketing management have largely been neglected (Homburg et al. 2005), especially in the field of corporate reputation research (Gardberg 2006; Walsh and Wiedmann 2004). Although there are many studies of relationship marketing, they are mostly based on national data sets (Homburg et al. 2005).

Surprisingly, the factors "reputation" and "national culture" are discussed separately in recent research: Walsh and Beatty (2007) investigate the impact of customer-based CR on service firms' performance, while Hewett et al. (2006) evaluate the influence of national culture and industrial buyer-seller relationship in the US and Latin America and Griffith et al. (2006) investigate culture's influence on relationship and knowledge resources between the US and Japan. Very few empirical studies apply the America-based measurement concept "Reputation Quotient" (RQ) of Fombrun et al. (2000) outside the US (Gardberg 2006; Walsh and Wiedmann 2004; Aperia et al. 2004) – the aim was not to learn about cultural differences, but to test RQ measures internationally. Moreover, the studies concerned with reputation management and related fields of image transfer, as well as brand extensions, make up a continuum of the basic entity under consideration (Bromley 2002).

According to Fombrun (1996), a company's reputation is determined by four main elements: its values, actions it takes, open-minded and honest communication, and general company image. Völckner and Sattler (2006) as well as Doney and Cannon (1997) define a company's reputation as the extent to which firms and people in the industry believe a company is honest and concerned about its customers. Unfortunately, what is defined as "honest and concerned" varies significantly across cultures and, therefore, leads to different perceptions of CR on the one hand and different possibilities of reputation transfer on the other.

It is also true that a company can have a negative CR (Bromley 2002). What about a definition of CR if at least a certain stakeholder group believes a company is "devious" and "unconcerned"? Whether all types of stakeholders base their perceptions of CR on the same fundamental set of dimensions or on specific expectations, is still discussed controversially (Bromley 2002; Fombrun et al. 2000; Gatewood et al. 1993), leading to a variety of research questions such as:

- Do companies have one reputation or many? (Fombrun and Shanley 1990; Bromley 2002).
- Reputation for whom or for what purpose? (Lewellyn 2002).
- Do stakeholder groups use different criteria to evaluate a company's reputation? (Meffert and Bierwirth 2002; Helm 2007).
- If the criteria to evaluate CR are different, is there also a difference between CR in the context of B-to-B and B-to-C, and what about a cross-cultural impact on CR?

Popular measurement approaches of the "most visible companies" (Fortune 500-index) or so-called "reputation rankings of most admired companies" can hardly be applied to the "most invisible companies" in the field of Business-to-Business (B-to-B) relationships, companies just known by their own limited range of products, employees, competitors, suppliers and customers. Fortune magazine's *America's Most Admired Company* (AMAC) survey, as well as a similar study by Britain's *Sunday Times*, use determinants on CR like advertising or visibility in the media. Even charitable contribution (Fombrun 1996) is difficult to evaluate if applied to companies working in the field of B-to-B. The Harris-Fombrun Reputation Quotient (RQ), the Financial Times/Price WaterhouseCooper *World's Most Respected Companies*, the Hill and Knowlton/ Economist Intelligence Unit *Corporate Reputation Watch* are all focused on decisive determinants of reputation for companies working in the B-to-C context. How can these millions of perceptions be captured and measured or managed?

Today, companies need to differentiate themselves from their competitors, as products are more and more interchangeable. An overarching reputation in this context is a strategic tool for managing a company's external presence in global markets. To manage these corporate reputations – as they can vary from country to country, from stakeholder to stakeholder, or from decade to decade – they must be measurable (Fombrun 1996; Fombrun and Gardberg 2002; Helm 2007). Unfortunately, neither researchers nor practitioners have yet found a cross-nationally valid instrument to measure reputation (Fombrun and Wiedmann 2001; Fombrun and Gardberg 2002).

Corporate reputation radiates a strong company appeal-it helps companies to obtain good employees, makes customer acquisition easier, increases customer loyalty, can be implemented as a competitive performance factor and is helpful for the procurement of capital (e.g., Wiedmann and Buxel 2005; Helm 2007; Dowling 2001; Little and Little 2000; Eberl and Schwaiger 2005). The literature on reputation in general has been growing in recent years (e.g., Fombrun et al. 2000; Fombrun and van Riel 1997; Dunbar and Schwalbach 2000; MacMillan et al. 2005), although it is still restricted to the B-to-B context.

Interest in CR is growing while the globalization of companies is entering a new phase. Compared with one of the new "global players", the Chinese computer company, Lenovo, its major competitors, IBM, DELL and Hewlett-Packard, may feel old-fashioned and conservative: Lenovo has no headquarters, venues for meetings of its senior managers rotate among its bases around the world, and its development teams consist of people in several centers around the world, often working together virtually (Bishop 2008). When it became a global brand in 2005, the company located its marketing department in Bangalore and made huge efforts to integrate the different cultures within the company to divert from its image as a "Chinese company". IBM, instead of selling its PC business to Lenovo, could have used its valuable reputation to position against such newcomers. In times of sharp increases in the number of new companies in emerging markets, there is no weapon more effective than this inimitable resource of corporate reputation as one of the "best known American companies" (Fortune 500).

The study is located in the context of relationship marketing, which comprises the new institutional economic approach, the network approach and the behavioral approach (Kotler and Keller 2006).

- The new institutional economic approach uses modern economic theories to explain the development and breakdown of relationships like transaction cost theory and agency theory.

- The network approach focuses on the interactive character of relationships in the field of B-to-B marketing and takes an inter-organizational perspective.
- The behavioral perspective of relationships refers to relational constructs like trust and satisfaction, the conceptualization and economic evaluation of customer commitment.

Referring to the commitment-trust theory of Morgan and Hunt (1994), as well as to more recent resource-based and knowledge-based views, the concept of corporate reputation in this work is part of the behavioral perspective of relationships. The framework of the commitment-trust theory integrates elements of relationship marketing as a strategic option (Morgan and Hunt 1994). As customer commitment does not necessarily lead to customer loyalty (Fullerton 2003), relationship marketing needs to incorporate further activities (Homburg and Krohmer 2006).

Although widely outlined, the concept of CR today still seems to lack an agreed theoretical basis, and this limits practical applications (Bromley 2002) and the comparison of hypotheses results. With reference to the B-to-B context, little is known about the cross-cultural impact factors on CR: The use of direct marketing media, word-of-mouth communication (WOM), the perceived innovativeness of a company and the importance of trust. Therefore, in this study the author investigates two dimensions that reflect:

- how an organization is perceived in the minds of stakeholders from different countries (corporate reputation) and what influences this perception.
- the extent to which an organization is perceived by its customers as being able to produce a new product range (reputation transfer on pharmaceuticals) which differs significantly from the core products (medical devices).

A structural model of the suggested impact factors on reputation is developed and tested using data from Australia, Finland, Germany, Russia and Spain in the empirical context of organizational buyers.

1.2 Structure of Work

Marketing in the B-to-B context is very different from marketing in the B-to-C context (e.g., Backhaus and Voeth 2007). Are all the above perceptions of reputation in all contexts of equal importance? Can we expect the reputation of a B-to-B company to be influenced and generated by the same factors as in the context B-to-C? Is it really feasible and adequate to have one single measurement construct of corporate reputation, if there are so many different stakeholder groups in different contexts? In order to address the research questions, this work is structured in seven parts: theoretical (Chaps. 1–3), empirical (Chaps. 4–6) and "learning" (Chap. 7). This work introduces and tests a structural model that aims to extend the commitment-trust theory framework (Morgan and Hunt 1994) with respect to a company's reputation and comprises national culture as a determining variable for both reputation and reputation transfer.

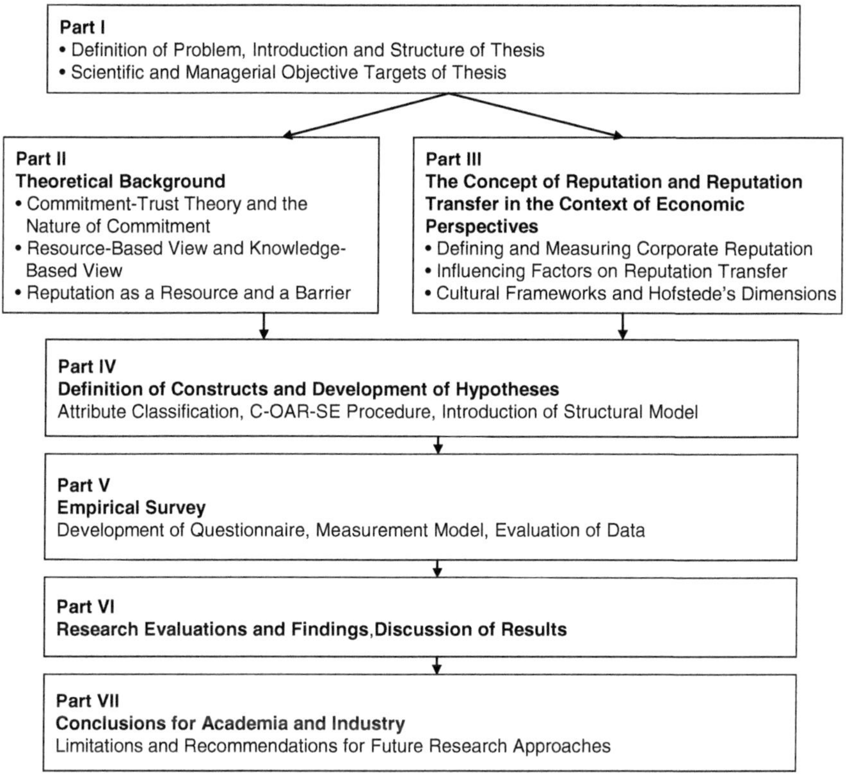

Fig. 1.1 Structure of work

Figure 1.1 presents the structure of this work. First, the theoretical part is introduced: In part I, the aim, the structure and the targets of this study are described. Part II explains the theoretical background and focuses on commitment, trust, and the resource-based and knowledge-based views. Reputation as a barrier and as an intangible resource is also outlined in part II. Part III completes the theoretical section by introducing the concepts of CR and reputation transfer as well as different cultural frameworks. Special attention is also focused on the relevance of direct marketing media to build CR.

The first three chapters of this work are the basis for generating the hypotheses, the constructs and the structural model. Part III discusses the current state of research in the fields of corporate reputation, reputation transfer, branding and culture and examines the definitional landscape of these keywords. Concepts of measuring corporate reputation are also presented and evaluated in this part. Different concepts for quantifying culture are introduced, and the cultural impact on organizational buying behavior is discussed.

Part IV defines the constructs, introduces the hypotheses and finally presents the structural model. The research design of this study is a multi-stage one, and essentially follows the C-OAR-SE procedure suggested by Rossiter (2002).

Therefore, one main objective of part IV is to discuss formative versus reflective measurement models as well as single-item indicators (Bergkvist and Rossiter 2007). As the research data are split not only into five country data sets, but also into three stakeholder groups, the Bonferroni-Holm's procedure is included in this chapter.

In part V, the empirical part of the thesis draws on an application example of selling medical equipment and pharmaceuticals to hospitals. A telephone survey based on a standardized questionnaire provides data from Australia, Finland, Germany, Spain, and Russia. This cross-cultural empirical example focuses on the stakeholder group of customers, divides them by purchasers, pharmacists, users and countries and discusses differences and similarities in the perception of CR. In part VI, research findings are presented and discussed, and scientific and managerial implications are outlined. Part VII draws general conclusions on the importance of CR and trust, subsumes the most interesting findings of this study, outlines limitations and gives recommendations for future research approaches.

1.3 Objective Targets of Thesis

Reputation is one of the rare subjects that can be put through different analytical frames to produce research that is exciting, path breaking, of interest to academics and practitioners, and incomplete (Mahon 2002). As research into reputation as such is at a nascent stage (Money and Hillenbrand 2006; Helm 2007), the construct of reputation is described first in a holistic context, and impact factors on corporate reputation in a cultural context are monitored. In contrast, factors influenced by CR are also discussed. The second objective is to develop hypotheses, perform empirical market research and discuss results to describe and analyze the relationship between the constructs corporate reputation and reputation transfer.

- Its impact on other constructs, embedded in the national culture of buyers
- The impact factors of other constructs on CR and reputation transfer in the B-to-B context

Therefore, the data set is not only evaluated country specifically (national culture), but also by stakeholder groups (B-to-B context) to compare potential different impact factors on CR and reputation transfer.

1.3.1 Scientific Objectives

In recent publications, CR has been interpreted as a stakeholder-related construct (Helm 2007). While some authors state that – according to stakeholder group affiliation – a specific set of criteria is relevant to accurately evaluate the reputation of a firm, others call for comparability of data and favor standardized measures.

Theoretical foundations of CR, as well as the empirical examination of the impact of reputation on stakeholders' buying decision, has remained scarce (Eberl 2006), this is especially true in the B-to-B context.

A framework is proposed delineating four stages through which reputation transfer research contributes to marketing science: theory development, acquisition of meaningful data, analysis of the data to test the theory, evaluation and learning. Thus, the scientific objective of this work is focused on:

- Developing a conceptual framework focused on impact factors on reputation and reputation transfer
- Discussing the differences in the importance of relationship quality, WOM communication and personal and media-enabled direct marketing media
- Presenting influencing factors on purchase decision involvement
- Challenging the overall need of a perceived fit of the new product category for reputation transfer
- Discussing differences in customers' opinions of CR
- Evaluating the chance to successfully transfer a company's reputation to a new product range

The aim is to understand the following:

- A cross-culturally valid construct of reputation applicable in a B-to-B setting, based exclusively on relationship and knowledge resources
- The cross-cultural importance of trust and CR
- Impact factors on reputation and reputation transfer in the B-to-B context, which are influenced by national culture
- Impact factors on reputation and reputation transfer, which are not influenced by national culture

The connectivity between CR, reputation transfer and related constructs is discussed: relationship quality, perceived innovativeness, WOM, personal and media-enabled direct marketing media, purchase decision involvement and the perceived fit of the new product range to the existing product portfolio.

1.3.2 Managerial Objectives

It is frequently assumed that CR has a positive effect on a variety of business-relevant economic and pre-economic variables (Groenland 2002; Davies et al. 2002; Walsh and Wiedmann 2004; Griffith et al. 2006). If a company transacts in international settings, the management of CR is confronted with the additional challenge of cultural differences. Learning about the impact factors on CR and reputation transfer in different cultures may lead to more focused communication strategies toward customers (or stakeholder groups) in different cultures.

The structural model introduced in this study outlines the impact of relationship quality, personal and media-enabled direct marketing media, purchase decision involvement, WOM, perceived fit and perceived innovativeness on reputation and reputation transfer in five different countries and three different stakeholder groups. Thus, the managerial objectives of this work are focused on:

- Providing advice for the use of different direct marketing media across countries and stakeholder groups
- Discussing the impact of WOM on reputation by also evaluating its influencing factors
- Outlining the impact factors on CR across countries and stakeholder groups
- Discussing the importance of reputation versus trust in different business relationships
- providing advice for impact factors on reputation transfer to find out if there are cultures or certain stakeholder groups where reputation transfer offers an easy-entry into new markets

Significant differences between the countries and stakeholder groups are discussed. Countries are identified where a positive reputation is more important than the trust in a supplier or its representatives. Conditions which either support or inhibit the transference of reputation are evaluated.

Following the findings of Hofstede (1983), nationality is important to management for at least three reasons:

- Nations are political units, rooted in history. This also influences the forms of government, legal and education systems, labor and employer association structures.
- Nationality or regionality has a symbolic value to citizens; they derive facets of their identity from it.
- Nationality is important for psychological reasons. Our thinking is partly conditioned by national culture factors.

Cultural programs are difficult to change; culture itself is quite stable and changes only slowly. The findings of this study support the results of Hofstede's (1983) work, claiming that the assumption that management is the same or is becoming the same around the world is not tenable in the light of differences in national cultures.

Chapter 2
Theoretical Framework

In 1968, Bartels proposed that a general theory of marketing should include seven subtheories: (1) theory of social initiative, (2) theory of economic market separation, (3) theory of market roles, expectations, and interactions, (4) theory of flows and systems, (5) theory of behavior constraints, (6) theory of social change and marketing evolution, and (7) theory of social control of marketing. This illustrates how extensive the fields of application in marketing theory are.

Since the 1960s, several marketing theories related to the above subtheories have been developed (Hunt 2002). The strategic area of relationship marketing was first defined by Berry (1983, p. 25) as "attracting, maintaining and [...] enhancing customer relationships". Thus, relationship marketing refers to activities directed toward establishing, developing, maintaining, and retaining successful relations (Berry and Parasuraman 1991; Morgan and Hunt 1994). Hunt (2002) also made it clear that a company's efficiency and effectiveness are always enhanced by establishing relationships with all potential stakeholders. Nevertheless, Gummesson (1995, p. 15) observes that "not all relationships are important to all companies all the time". For this reason, a fundamental thesis of relationship marketing strategy is to identify, develop and nurture a suitable relationship portfolio (Hunt, 2002).

A theory used in relationship marketing since the 1970s is social exchange theory (SET), based on works of Homans (1958, 1961, 1974), Blau (1960, 1964) and Thibaut and Kelley (1959). SET is widely viewed as one of the most influential conceptual paradigms in organizational behavior (Cropanzano and Mitchell 2005; Friman et al. 2002). As exchange ideology is also said to influence individuals' sensitivity to organizational politics, job satisfaction and commitment, SET is used to evaluate buyer-seller relationships (Witzel 2006). The following table differentiates SET from the theory of commitment and trust proposed by Morgan and Hunt (1994). The latter theory is also outlined and referred to in more detail in the following chapter.

SET suggests that there are as many as six different resources influencing interpersonal attachments: love, status, information, money, goods and services. Although most of these are not fully appreciated by organizational scientists, SET is

C. Falkenreck, *Reputation Transfer to Enter New B-to-B Markets*,
Contributions to Management Science,
DOI 10.1007/978-3-7908-2357-8_2, © Springer-Verlag Berlin Heidelberg 2010

said to have "the potential to provide a unitary framework for much of organizational behavior" (Cropanzano and Mitchell 2005, p. 875). This theory is based on certain rules of exchange, although it remains unclear which exchange rules apply to each resource. Reciprocity or repayment in kind is one of these exchange rules (Blau 1964) (Table 2.1).

Major objections to or problems with SET are quoted as follows (Miller 2001):

- SET reduces human interaction to a rational process that arises from economic theory.
- The theory assumes that the ultimate goals of a relationship are intimacy and reciprocity. These are not the "ultimate" relationship goals.
- SET proposes that relationships have a linear structure. In reality, relationships do not develop this way.
- SET is based on an individualist mindset, which may limit its application in and description of collectivist cultures.

The author supports Gummesson's observation that SET does not take into consideration that not all relationships are important to a buyer or seller all the time. This also impacts relationship portfolio investments and might influence the development of relationship commitment of suppliers and customers in equal measure.

In the light of the exchange orientation of relationships, in which trust and commitment are developed, the analytical approach of information economy does not seem appropriate. A theory focused on the explanation of mental processes relevant to the development of relationship commitment and trust is therefore regarded as more suitable: "To be an effective *competitor* (in the global economy) requires one to be a trusted *cooperator* (in some networks)" (Morgan and Hunt 1994, p. 20).

Table 2.1 Social exchange theory vs. commitment trust theory

Social exchange theory	Theory of commitment and trust
SET is a social, psychological and sociological perspective	This theory highlights the psychological and behavioral perspective
Social behavior is an exchange of goods, material goods but also non-material ones, such as symbols of approval or prestige	Relationship marketing refers to activities directed toward establishing, developing and maintaining successful relations
SET explains social change and stability as a process of negotiated exchanges between parties	This theory explains the formation of long-term relationships through the key mediating variables of commitment and trust
SET is mainly applied in the field of marital satisfaction and the quality of family life	This theory posits that relationship marketing requires commitment and trust
SET has roots in economics, psychology and sociology	This theory has roots in psychology and behavioral marketing
SET is tied to rational choice theory and structuralism, and features many of their main assumptions	This theory is tied to marketing theory
Whether or not commitment and trust emmerge between the exchanging partners is a function of the perceived costs or the rewards one expects at a later date from the relationship exchange	Commitment and trust are viewed as key mediating variables of successful relationships

There has been growing interest in possible additional factors contributing to a long-term prosperous exchange between business associates (e.g. Friman et al. 2000). For this reason, some studies (e.g. Eberl 2006) also evaluate the impact of CR on buying behavior based on stimulus-object-response (S-O-R) theory. This theory is based on stimulus-response theory, a theoretical model of behavioral psychology. S-O-R theory tries to explain buying behavior and enhances stimulus-response theory by integrating cognitive and affective (emotions, motives, attitudes) psychological processes. This theory is primarily focused on general buying behavior; the important antecedents of commitment and trust related to buying processes in the healthcare business are not explicitly discussed.

Game Theory – the science of studying agent behavior in a multi-agent environment (Aumann 1987) – is also a frequently used theoretical framework to explain reputational issues (Helm 2007). These "solution concepts" are usually based on what is required by norms of rationality. Today, game theory is a unified field theory for the rational side of social science, where "social" is interpreted broadly to include human as well as non-human players, such as computers (Aumann 1987). These models presume either no rationality or bounded rationality on the part of players. Weigelt and Camerer (1988, p. 443) point out that "in game theory the reputation of a player is the perception others have of the player's values... which determine his/her choice of strategies".

In this study, the theory of commitment and trust (Morgan and Hunt 1994) is used to analyze international B-to-B relations in the medical sector, as this theory postulates a number of psychological factors that may be important. Trust and shared values form the basis of buyer-seller relationships (Friman et al. 2002), especially in a competitive marketplace. Morgan and Hunt (1994) and Wilson (1994) suggest that commitment and trust are central constructs in marketing relationships as they positively influence cooperative behaviors.

Further important relationship factors are discussed in the theories of the resource-based view (RBV) and the knowledge-based view (KBV). These theories, discussed in the following chapters, conceptualize a company's relationship resources as consisting of commitment and trust (e.g. Johnson and Selnes 2004; Morgan and Hunt 1994) and knowledge resources (e.g. Grant 1996; Morgan et al. 2003).

2.1 Commitment-Trust Theory and the Nature of Commitment

Morgan and Hunt, as well as several other researchers (e.g. Ganesan 1994; Moorman et al. 1993; Keller and Stolper 2006) claim that B-to-B relationships require commitment and trust. Their results imply that commitment and trust are key mediating variables to understanding the relationship development process between buyers and sellers. According to the theory of Morgan and Hunt (1994), customer commitment to the vendor has been found to mediate the effects of a number of variables such as quality, shared values, communication and trust on a number of consumer behavioral intentions, including customer retention, advocacy, and acquiescence. Trust serves as a governance mechanism that limits opportunistic activities as well as a facilitating mechanism for developing commitment (Morgan and Hunt 1994). Commitment includes the desire to continue the relationship and work to ensure its continuance (Morgan and Hunt 1994; Moorman et al. 1993) in what is described as the long-term orientation of a party toward a partner (Morgan and Hunt 1994).

As business partners interact with one another on a regular basis, trust may develop (Friman et al. 2002). Trust is defined as one party's confidence in its partner's reliability and integrity (Morgan and Hunt 1994). According to the literature, the construct of trust is an important element of long-term buyer-seller relationships in a business environment (Griffith et al. 2006; Anderson and Narus 1990; Dwyer et al. 1987). Trust, the willingness to rely on an exchange partner in whom one has confidence, is viewed as an important feeling: because of its ability to moderate risk in the buying process (Morgan and Hunt 1994). Trust captures the company's belief that another company will perform actions that result in positive outcomes for the company, as well as not take unexpected actions that could result in negative outcomes (Anderson and Narus 1990). A trusted supplier reduces behavioral uncertainty of the buyer by reducing risk, search costs (such as opportunity or disincentive costs) and expenses (Ganesan 1994; Windsperger 1994) as well as opportunistic activities (Morgan and Hunt 1994). In the same vein, Moorman et al. (1992) claim that information provided by a trusted party is used more and provides greater value to the recipient.

Commitment is defined as a desire to maintain a relationship (Morgan and Hunt 1994; Moorman et al. 1992) or resistance to change the supplier (Pritchard et al. 1999). Commitment in the B-to-B context is closely related to loyalty (Abdul-Muhmin 2005; Homburg and Krohmer 2006). Organizational commitment is specified as "the relative strength of an individual's identification with and involvement in a particular organization" (Mowday et al. 1979, p. 226). Managers and researchers have paid considerable attention to organizational commitment, which has been shown to be a predictor of important organizational outcomes such as turnover, absenteeism, and tardiness (see also Brown and Peterson 1993; Ko et al. 1997).

Thus, relationship marketing literature has recognized that customer commitment is a complex multidimensional construct that includes at least an affective, continuance and normative component (Gruen et al. 2000; Gilliand and Bello 2002; Meyer et al. 2002). The first component, affective commitment, is based on liking, loving and identification (Allen and Meyer 1990; Albert et al. 2008). Customers acquire an emotional attachment to their partner in a consumption relationship and start to like, or even love, the brands or service providers they deal with (Albert et al. 2008; Fullerton 2003; Meyer et al. 2002). For this reason, friendship and trust are closely related to affective commitment (Price and Arnould 1999; Doney and Cannon 1997).

Continuance commitment refers to dependence and switching costs (Allen and Meyer 1990) and was developed as a means of explaining the extent to which employees feel bound to an organization (Fullerton 2003). Anderson and Weitz (1992) established that parties become committed when one party takes specific actions that will bind it to another party. These actions include contract or service agreements that limit free choice for the duration of the contract (Anderson and Weitz 1992). In 1990, Allen and Meyer suggested a third, distinctive component of commitment, normative commitment. This reflects a perceived obligation to remain in the organization, related to the propensity to leave of Morgan and Hunt (1994).

A single relationship can be based on either affective, continuance or normative commitment, all three forms of commitment or none of the forms of commitment (Meyer et al. 2002). Findings of Fullerton (2003, p. 343) also state that "the effects of affective commitment in a relationship must be viewed in the light of the degree to which continuance commitment is also present in the relationship". Taking into consideration affective, continuance, and normative components of commitment can lead to deeper understanding of customer relationship management (Meyer et al. 2002; Fullerton 2003).

Nevertheless, marketing science still offers no answers on how many dimensions or components are involved in relationship commitment (Witzel 2006; Albert et al. 2008), if and how the components differ between B-to-B and B-to-C-and how commitment and trust in a company influence its CR (Fombrun et al. 2000).

2.2 Resource-Based and Knowledge-Based View

Business strategy theorists have questioned the external-only focus of the industry-based theory advocated by Porter (1980, 1985), although this theory has contributed successfully to business strategy (Hunt and Lambe 2000; Jacobson and Aaker 1985). In contrast, the resource-based theory focuses on internal factors to explain business strategy (Hunt and Lambe 2000). The company, not the industry, is the appropriate unit of analysis for understanding performance in the theory of the resource-based view, industry structure does not determine company behavior. As CR is viewed as an intangible internal asset of a company, this chapter focuses on the basic items of the RBV and the theory of the KBV.

Penrose (1959) makes it clear that a company is more than an administrative unit; it is also a collection of productive resources. A company develops competitive advantages by expanding its unique knowledge and capabilities, and by knowing the specific product and market context in which this knowledge creates value. Resources, representing what can be done by the company and the competitive environment, representing what should be done to compete effectively in satisfying customer needs, are both essential in the strategy-development process (Priem and Butler 2001). According the RBV model of Peteraf (1993), four conditions underlie sustained competitive advantage, all of which must be met. These include superior resources (heterogeneity within an industry), ex post limits to competition, imperfect resource mobility, and ex ante limits to competition. Two factors which limit ex post competition are imperfect imitability and imperfect substitutability. As an example, Peteraf (1993) mentioned non-tradable assets that develop and accumulate in the company. Resources are imperfectly mobile if they cannot be traded.

Hunt and Morgan (1995) define resources as any tangible or intangible entity available to a company that enables it to produce a market offering efficiently and effectively and which has value for some market segments. Resources shall be hard to imitate and can be financial, physical, legal, human, organizational, informational or relational; their characteristics are heterogenic and only restrictedly mobile (Hunt and Morgan 1997; Hunt 2000; Barney 1996). Based on the work of Penrose (1959); Wernerfelt (1984); and Barney (1991), the RBV theory suggests that there can be heterogeneity or company-level differences among companies that allow some of them to sustain competitive advantage. Most scholars argue that it is mainly intangible resources that explain performance heterogeneity (Wernerfelt 1984; Peteraf 1993; Penrose 1959).

The key points of the RBV are listed in the VRIN criteria (Barney 1991; Peteraf 1993):

- **V**aluable – the resource must be used in a value-creating setting.
- **R**are – to be of value, a resource must be rare.
- **I**nimitable – if a valuable resource is controlled by only one company, it could be a source of competitive advantage as competitors are not able to imitate the strategic asset perfectly.
- **N**on-substitutable – if competitors are able to counter the company's value-creating strategy with a substitute, prices decrease.

The condition that resources need to be rare to be a possible source of sustainable competitive advantage is unnecessary (Hoopes et al. 2003), because within the implications of the other VRIN criteria, any resource that follows from the previous characteristics is inherently rare. Within the framework of the RBV, the chain is as strong as its weakest link and dependent on the resource displaying each of the four characteristics in order to be a possible source of sustainable competitive advantage (Barney 1991). Priem and Butler (2001) controversially claim that the VRIN characteristics of resources are necessary, but not sufficient to give them a sustainable competitive advantage.

Extending the literature on RBV, researchers have argued that the RBV of idiosyncratic interorganizational linkage can be a source of relational rents and competitive advantage (Dyer and Singh 1998; Griffith and Harvey 2001). In addition, researchers claim that both relationships (Johnson and Selnes 2004; Morgan and Hunt 1994) and knowledge (Grant 1996; Morgan et al. 2003) are key strategic resources, as they can provide a company with a unique resource barrier position in the marketplace. The greatest limitation of the RBV is that it only partially explains how companies develop strategies that allow them to exploit their individual resources. During the last two decades, extensions of the RBV have been developed to fill this gap in business strategy.

The dynamic capabilities view of the firm is one extension of the resource-based perspective. It refers to how capabilities evolve and how organizations deal with environmental turbulence (Helfat et al. 2007). The term "dynamic" differentiates one capability (e.g. the operational ability to develop new products) from another form of ability (e.g. the ability to reform the way the organization develops new products) (Zahra et al. 2006). As resources in the context of the dynamic capabilities view, the RBV and the KBV are developed to enhance customer value. These strategic management approaches can also help advance the subordinated direct marketing approaches of a company.

During the 1990s, a number of ideas and streams of research converged to produce what is described as "the knowledge-based view of the firm" (Grant 2002). Some researchers argue that the KBV is a natural development of resource-based thinking where the concept of resources is extended to include intangible assets and, specifically, knowledge-based resources (Grant 1996; Decarolis and Deeds 1999). These researchers identify four major streams of research on knowledge: sourcing, internal transfer, external transfer, and integration of knowledge. Other researchers consider the KBV as a useful extension of organizational learning to strategy and organization theory, an extension that is capable of informing research and providing new insights into organizational functioning (Kogut and Zander 1992, 1996). In the light of this, others argue that knowledge should be treated as a process of ongoing social construction and not as a resource (Spender 1996). Finally, some researchers believe that a theory of strategy must be a theory of the firm, if it is to be a theory of strategy at all (e.g. Conner and Prahalad 1996).

Eisenhardt and Santos (2001) claim that Penrose's seminal work on the growth of the firm (1959) is an important starting point for understanding organizational learning. Penrose describes how learning processes create new knowledge and form the basis of the growth of organizations through the recombination of existing resources: Companies are able to grow competitive imitation only by continuously recombining their knowledge and applying it to new market opportunities. In a pharmaceutical industry study, Henderson and Cockburn (1994) used knowledge sourcing arguments to explain research productivity. The findings are consistent with other studies that link external knowledge sourcing with innovation and performance (Powell et al. 1996). External linkages help managers become aware of the content and location of new technical knowledge. In dynamic environments, searching for, identifying, accessing, and sharing new knowledge are important activities to achieving innovative performance (Eisenhardt and Santos 2001).

Knowledge can also be transferred across a company's boundaries through alliances and acquisitions (Lane and Lubatkin 1998). External knowledge transfer is affected by the relationship between the sender and the recipient. According to Eisenhardt and Santos (2001), knowledge-based thinking may yet become a theory of strategy of an organization, as there is already a consistent body of empirical results capable of informing theory-building and managerial practice. These findings point to a knowledge-based theory.

Some streams of research include the resource or capability analysis of a company (Barney 1991; Prahalad and Hamel 1990). Extending this to the inter-organizational level, the KBV argues that individual and common knowledge bases of inter-organizational partners are developed by the sharing of information comprising local, social knowledge together with an understanding of the partner organization to allow for the development of competitive advantages of the inter-organizational relationship (Grant 1996; Morgan et al. 2003). The sharing of information accelerates problem resolution because of an increased amount of information in the relationship. This input then leads to the generation of new knowledge (Griffith et al. 2006).

- Knowledge is the important productive resource in terms of market value and the primary source of Ricardian rents (Grant 1996).
- Different types of knowledge vary in their transferability (Nonaka 1990).
- Knowledge is subject to economies of scale and scope. Its initial creation is more costly than its subsequent replication.
- Knowledge is created by human beings, and to be efficient in knowledge creation and storage, individuals need to specialize (Simon 1991).
- Producing goods or services requires the application of many types of knowledge (Kogut and Zander 1992).

According to Grant (2002), the key contribution of the knowledge-based approach is in offering understanding of the process in which knowledge inputs are converted into goods and services and the role of the company in this process. As illustrated in Fig. 2.1, and according to the exant literature (e.g. Morgan and Hunt 1994; Griffith et al. 2006) relationship resources consist of trust and commitment.

When a company has confidence in its partner's willingness to forgo opportunistic activities, it is more willing to commit to the relationship and pursue long-term, common goals (Morgan and Hunt 1994). In line with Grant (2002), the author conceptualizes "knowledge resource" as the sharing of generalized information about the company and its products. The term "problem resolution" explains the sharing of information to assist a partner, when unexpected problems arise that could disrupt the exchange relationship (Griffith et al. 2006). The view is that problem resolution and information sharing both contribute to the enhancement of trust.

If a company develops trust in and commitment to its partners, it is more willing to invest in a long-term relationship (Morgan and Hunt 1994). As a result, a

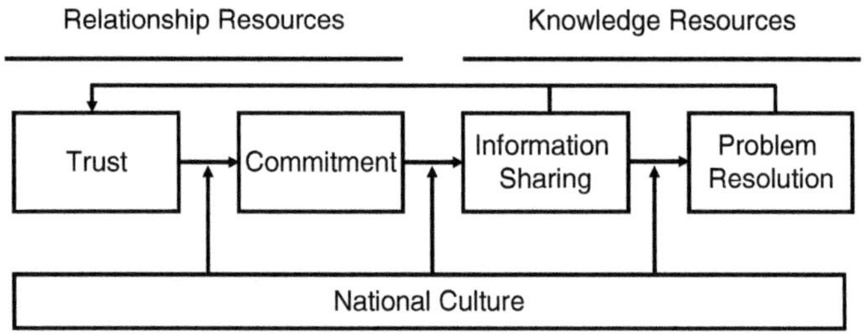

Fig. 2.1 National culture's influence on resources, based on Griffith et al. (2006)

resource is created that is valuable and unique to the inter-organizational partners, imperfectly imitable, and without a strategically equivalent substitute (Griffith et al. 2006).

The focus on specific customer needs and a general customer-friendly company setting will naturally lead to integrated, personalized direct marketing approaches. The goal is heterogeneity in marketing activities among companies that are conducive to sustaining competitive advantages by building relationship equity (Krafft et al. 2007). The development of new knowledge through information sharing contributes positively to the further enhancement of trust and improves the effectiveness of a relationship.

Research indicates that relationship and knowledge resources, as well as their linkage to trust and commitment, may vary under different national cultures (Griffith et al. 2006; Doney et al. 1998; Bhagat et al. 2002).

2.3 Reputation as a Resource, an Intangible Asset and a Barrier

In today's markets, marketers are faced with environmental turbulence stemming from technological advances, changes in consumer demand, and new regulations (Helfat et al. 2007). These developments can affect organizational performance and also cause competitive advantage to erode or even become redundant. The RBV approach characterizes companies as heterogeneous bundles of resources and rent seekers, aiming their strategies at obtaining superior performance in the form of Ricardian rents (Wernerfelt 1984; Hunt and Morgan 1995: Grant 1996). A company's sustainable competitive advantage and superior performance are then determined by the possession of valuable, rare and imperfectly imitable resources (e.g. Barney 1991; Srivastava et al. 2001). From this point of view, positive abnormal returns are economic rents for unique and specialized resource combinations, rather than market power.

Barney (1996, p. 45) describes socially complex resources as those "that enable an organization to conceive, choose, and implement strategies because of the values, beliefs, symbols, and interpersonal relationships possessed by individuals or groups in a firm". Examples also include organizational culture, trust and reputation among customers. In the resource-based view of the firm, CR is considered an extremely important resource (Schweizer and Wijnberg 1999) as it has been shown to be a determinant of corporate performance (Aaker 1989; Herbig and Milewicz 1993).

The RBV unites two approaches: on the one hand, strategic advantages of companies are traced back to the fact that companies dispose of strategically valuable resources. On the other hand, it is also necessary for a company to exploit its resource advantages in a more efficient and effective manner than its competitors. Interestingly, in 1991, Barney lists some examples of social complex resources:

- organizational culture
- trust
- reputation among customers
- managerial teamwork

Competitive intangible assets lead to competitive advantage. According to Fombrun et al. (2000) and Eberl (2006), trust and commitment are determinants of corporate reputation. As discussed within the theories of RBV and KBV, relationship and knowledge resources constitute a company's intangible assets, which are identifiable as non-monetary assets that cannot be seen, touched or physically measured.

Kaplan and Norton (2004) suggest splitting intangible assets into legal and competitive intangibles (see Fig. 2.2). According to Hall (1992), intangible resources which are assets, and which enjoy legal protection, are: intellectual property rights, contracts, copyrights and trade secrets. Following Kaplan and Norton (2004), competitive intangibles are: human capital (the skills, training and knowledge of employees), information capital (systems, databases and networks), and organization capital (company culture, leadership, alignment and teamwork). An organization is aligned when all employees have a commonality of purpose, a shared vision, and an understanding of how their work can support the overall company strategy (Kaplan and Norton 2004).

The author proposes to extend the definition of Kaplan and Norton (2004) regarding organization capital by focusing on the feature of CR. CR is an intangible asset that may lead to a company's competitive advantage (Barney 1991; Roberts and Dowling 2002; Zabala et al. 2005).

Hall (1992) argues that the analysis of a company's intangible resources should play a major role in a company's strategic management process. Certain resources

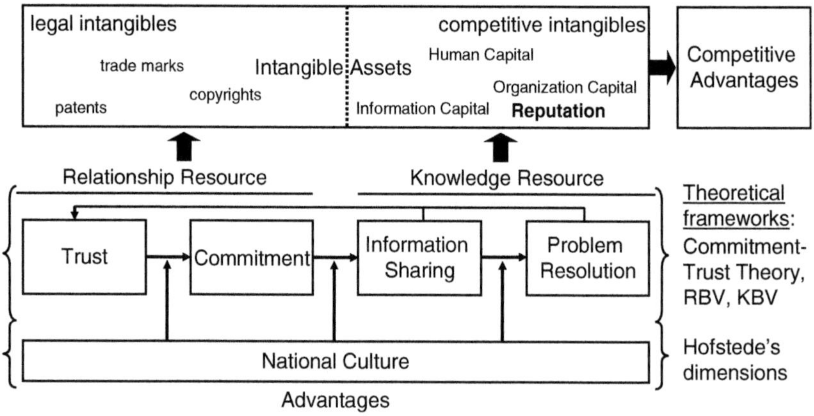

Fig. 2.2 Theoretical framework, formation of intangible assets and competitive advantages

like company reputation are built up over time and a competitor may not be able to perfectly imitate it (Santala and Parvinen 2007, p.172), so that they work like market barriers. Researchers found that a strong CR increases customers' confidence in products and services, avertising claims and in the buying decision (Fombrun and van Riel 1997; Lafferty and Goldsmith 1999).

The competitive landscape changes too much, too often, and too unpredictably for a company to forge a permanently sustainable advantage. The value of a good reputation is still given insufficient appreciation by investors (Vergin and Qoronfleh 1998) and other stakeholders. CR, as an intangible resource which is valuable, inimitable, and sustainable, can be regarded as a competitive advantage and also as a barrier to competitors. From this perspective, Griffith et al. (2006) claim that relationship resources, such as trust and commitment, and knowledge resources, characterized by information sharing in inter-organizational exchanges, for example, are key strategic resources because they provide a company with a unique resource barrier position in the marketplace.

Chapter 3
Perspectives on Corporate Reputation and Reputation Transfer

Research on reputation refers to the perceptions of a company by its stakeholders, how a company may manage these perceptions, and the effect these perceptions have on the company and its performance (Carter and Deephouse 1999). This chapter focuses on specific definitions of CR and argues the feasibility and sense (or non-sense) of a standardized construct of reputation. Different types of CR measures and the relevance of direct marketing to build CR in a B-to-B context are discussed. The author introduces the method of reputation transfer, before building a bridge between reputation, reputation transfer and different concepts of culture.

CR can be broadly defined as a set of collectively held beliefs about a company's ability to satisfy the interests of its various stakeholders. Bromley (1993) points out that the word reputation has a variety of meanings. Recent studies on corporate reputation have emphasized the plurality of perceptions and representations around a company, referring to "corporate reputation" as a multifaceted rather than a monolithic concept (Dowling 2001; Helm 2007). According to Balmer (1998), the word reputation is derived from the Latin word "reputance" which means "to recon". In German, reputation is a synonym of esteem and renown (Schwaiger 2004). Yet, although the interest in the concept of CR has constantly grown within the last two decades, a precise and commonly agreed upon definition is lacking. Empirical research exploring the drivers of reputation among specific categories of stakeholders, however, is still scarce (Gabbioneta et al. 2007). While the consequences of good reputation have been broadly investigated, research on the formation of judgment among different stakeholders is less abundant. Fombrun and Shanley (1990) observe how stakeholders evaluate companies based on a number of marketing and accounting signals indicating performance, institutional signals indicating conformity to social norms and strategy signals indicating strategic postures. A replication of this research on a different national sample essentially confirmed Fombrun and Shanley's findings (Brammer and Pavelin 2006). In 2004, building on Fombrun and Rindova's (1998) work, Sjovall and Talk draw on cognitive attribution theory in order to develop an interpretation of the formation of observers' impressions about companies. Their findings led to the result that stakeholders tend to pay attention to actions that are

C. Falkenreck, *Reputation Transfer to Enter New B-to-B Markets*,
Contributions to Management Science,
DOI 10.1007/978-3-7908-2357-8_3,

perceived as important to their interests and values. Stakeholders, then, tend to make inferences about corporate dispositions (their trustworthiness, reliability, social responsibility, etc.) based on observed actions that are interpreted as reflections of the former and/or situational constraints. While Sjovall and Talk's framework increases our knowledge of the mechanisms that underlie the formation of individual evaluation, virtually nothing is known cross-culturally about the relationship between CR and reputation transfer in different stakeholder groups. To find out about the main subject of this work, CR and reputation transfer, the evaluation of different definitions and measures of CR is essential.

In recent publications, CR has generally been interpreted as a stakeholder-related construct (e.g., Helm 2007; Eberl 2006; Carter and Deephouse 1999). Stakeholder literature refers to methods that organizations can use to assess and deal with external and internal groups on a given issue (Mahon and Wartick 2003). Stakeholder theory recognizes that various stakeholders – important groups that affect and are affected by a company, such as customers, suppliers or employees – may have different expectations of a company. Freeman's (1984) exposition of stakeholder theory directed managerial attention to the variety of individuals and groups that influenced, and were influenced by, a company. Stakeholder theory recognizes that different stakeholders may have different expectations of a company (Freeman 1984; Donaldson and Preston 1995). In line with this theory, Bromley (2002, p. 36) claims that commercial and industrial companies "have as many reputations as there are districts in social groups". These conflicting expectations lead to the development of multiple reputations as perceived by these groups (Carter and Deephouse 1999). Regarding stakeholder groups of suppliers and customers, it is not always possible to satisfy every stakeholder and have a favorable perception of a company's reputation from each. Inconsistent perceptions of a company's reputation may be held by different stakeholders (Zinkhan et al. 2001; Dowling 2001; Carter and Deephouse 1999). As for smaller or not widely known companies, in contrast, corporate reputations depend on the relatively homogeneous social networks of communication (Bromley 2002). This fact is also appropriate to the CR of widely unknown B-to-B companies.

Thus, empirical evidence on stakeholders' perception of CR is weak (Eberl 2006; Helm 2007) and even weaker in cross-cultural contexts (Gardberg 2006; Walsh and Wiedmann 2004). Following the literature, CR can be categorized in (Table 3.1) as follows:

Rowley (1997) incorporated a network perspective in stakeholder theory by recognizing that the company and its stakeholders are embedded in a set of relationships with different actors. This may be one reason why a company's reputation matures and develops over time. In line with Walsh and Beatty (2007) and MacMillan et al. (2005), CR implies:

- That different stakeholder groups may hold different views of the same company's reputation based on their own needs, economic, social, and personal background (Fombrun 1996; Zinkhan et al. 2001)
- And is enhanced in this study by the empirical investigation on the impact of a different cultural background on CR

Table 3.1 Categorization of reputation. Enhancement based on Fombrun and van Riel (1997)

Discipline	Categorization of reputation
Accountancy	Intangible asset (e.g., Barney 1991; Hall 1992; Grant 2002; Gabbioneta et al. 2007).
Economics	Sustainable competitive advantage (e.g., Deephouse 2000; Eberl 2006; Roberts and Dowling 2002; Zabala et al. 2005)
Marketing	Viewed from a customer's or end-user's perspective, concentrated on the development process of reputation (e.g., Fombrun et al. 2000; Williams et al. 2005; Helm 2007; Eberl 2006)
Organizational behavior	The perception of the organization held by an organization's internal stakeholders
Sociology	Aggregate assessment of a company's performance relative to expectations and norms in an institutional context
Strategy	Viewed as asset and mobility barrier (e.g., Griffith et al. 2006)

The definition of Fombrun et al. (2000, p. 243) of CR as "a collective assessment of a company's ability to provide valued outcome to a representative group of stakeholders" is not overall suitable, as it is focused on the positive and valued outcomes (Bromley 2002). As CR is also influenced by cultural and ethical evaluations, a further definition must also permit the attribution of negative or undesirable characteristics.

The subsequent sections focus on the definitions of CR and reputation transfer in economic science, where the emphasis is placed on the B-to-B context and a stakeholder-related definition of CR. Different clusters of meanings highlight the analysis of the concepts of reputation and reputation transfer. In detail, the next chapters will:

- Introduce the concept of CR within the context of relationship marketing
- Give an overview of actual definitions of CR
- Review different measurement concepts of CR
- Introduce the concept of reputation transfer
- Review actual cultural frameworks
- Investigate the impact of Hofstede's cultural values on stakeholders' attitudes toward the development of trust, use of media, innovations and relationships in the countries included in this research work

Past research indicates how good reputation draws customers to a company's products and enhances repeat purchases, improves a company's ability to recruit top people, and makes it a better candidate for favorable treatment by the media (Fombrun 1996; Fombrun and van Riel 2004). The aim of this work is to extend our knowledge of the method of reputation transfer by investigating the drivers of corporate reputation among a specific group of stakeholders: organizational buyers.

3.1 Perspectives of Relationship Marketing

Since being recognized as a separate field of inquiry over 80 years ago, marketing has made enormous strides in terms of becoming a scholarly discipline. The definition of marketing has evolved and changed throughout the last decades. To Kotler and Keller (2006, p. 6), marketing is "a societal and managerial process by which individuals and groups obtain what they need and want through creating, offering and exchanging products and services...". This chapter gives a short overview of two different theoretical approaches of relationship marketing (RM) and defines the outline of the research context of this study.

Today, marketing practice is related to the retention of customers and the management of relationships, also extending beyond the buyer-seller dyad to include partners through the value chain (Day and Montgomery 1999; Webster 1992; Morgan and Hunt 1994). RM has substantially influenced marketing theory and has become an important issue in this field (e.g., Palmatier et al. 2006). Several studies in both business-to-consumer (B-to-C) and B-to-B contexts suggest that there is considerable customer heterogeneity in relationship behavior. The belief that RM investments build more trusting customer relationships (Morgan and Hunt 1994) and improve financial performance has led to massive spending on RM programs (Palmatier et al. 2008). The RM concept was defined by Berry (1983, p. 25) as "attracting, maintaining and (...) enhancing customer relationships." Morgan and Hunt (1994, p. 22) define RM as "all marketing activities directed toward establishing, developing, and maintaining successful relational exchanges." Stone, Woodcock and Wilson (1996, p. 675) refer to the goals and benefits: "Relationship marketing is the use of a wide range of marketing, sales, communication, service and customer care approaches to

- Identify a company's individual customers
- Create relationships between the company and its customers that stretches over many transactions
- Manage that relationship to the benefit of the customers and the company."

In the context of industrial marketing, Jackson (1985, p. 2) describes RM as "marketing oriented toward strong, lasting relationships with individual accounts." Doyle and Roth (1992, p. 59) indicate that "the goal of relationship selling is to earn the position of preferred supplier by developing trust in key accounts over time." There is wide agreement that the concept of RM is different from traditional or transactional approaches to managing exchanges. Given the contextual character of marketing knowledge (Sheth and Sisodia 1999), there is no "general theory" of RM. Their concept of RM is built on three distinct, interrelated, theoretical approaches:

- The *behavioral perspective* of relationships refers to relational constructs like trust and satisfaction, and the conceptualization and economic evaluation of customer retention (e.g., Morgan and Hunt 1994).

- The *network approach* focuses on the interactive character of relationships in the field of B-to-B marketing and takes an interorganizational perspective (i.e., Håkansson and Snehota 2006) with reference to the development of intercompany relationships.
- The *new institutional economic approach* uses modern economic theories to explain the development and breakdown of relationships like transaction cost theory (e.g., North 1990) and agency theory (scholars in the field of marketing and organizational behavior include, among others, Basu et al. 1985; Eisenhardt 1985). RM in this context is seen as a question of matching particular relationship dimensions to the situation, with the overall goal of minimizing the costs of structuring and managing a given relationship.

According to the findings of Coviello et al. (2002), a more pluralistic conceptualization of marketing is required. They evaluated four aspects of marketing, classified by exchange and managerial dimensions:

- Transaction Marketing refers to economic transactions: The impersonal managerial focus is set on products or brands and formality in exchange.
- Database Marketing is based on information and economic transaction; the personalized managerial focus is set on products, brands or customers in a target market.
- Interaction Marketing is related to the interactive relationships between a buyer and seller; the interpersonal managerial focus is based on commitment, trust and cooperation.
- Network Marketing is a connected relationship between companies in which contact may vary from distant to close; the managerial focus is related to connected relationships between companies in a network.

According to Coviello et al. (2002, p. 42), the broad concept of RM is "redefined to reflect three separate constructs: database, interaction and network marketing." Their findings also support the assumption that B-to-B and service marketing are different from consumer and goods marketing. In 2002, database and network marketing were implemented and used with companies to a lesser degree. Nevertheless, since then, the network economy has been constantly growing.

Located in the field of direct marketing, this study is focused on organizational relationships, concentrating on the enlargement of the commitment-trust theory as well as the resource-based and knowledge-based views and conceptualizing customer retention. Understanding the nuances of the behavioral perspective of relationships in comparison to interaction marketing, instead of trying to find new clusters, may lead to a new strategic view of the goals of relationship marketing. In the author's opinion, a state-of-the-art approach in relationship marketing comprises personalized database marketing, which includes knowledge about the cross-cultural use of direct marketing media in certain stakeholder groups, as well as interaction marketing.

3.1.1 Organizational Buying Behavior and the Impact of Reputation

As already discussed, this work has its emphasis in RM in the B-to-B context and is closely related to the stakeholder group of organizational buyers. This subsection gives a short overview of the characteristics of organizational buying behavior and highlights the possible impact of CR.

Although in Western-type countries, the turnover in investment and industrial goods is four times as high as the turnover in consumer goods industries (Federal Statistical Office). The companies involved in this business are hardly ever known to the public.

As an example, let us think about two of the world's best-known companies: In the industrialized world, nearly everybody knows Coca-Cola and McDonald's, but who knows anything about companies supplying Coca-Cola with the colorants or McDonald's with the packing materials? Thus, the reputation of these B-to-B companies also plays an important role with regard to risk reduction of purchasing decision, customer relationship management and marketing strategies (Dowling 2001).

Purchasing decisions are not only made by individuals, but also by organizations. Raw materials, product components or machine equipment, spare parts, services, or commodities are internationally purchased by smaller or larger buying organizations (Webster and Wind 1972). A group of employees responsible for purchasing products for an organization is the "buying center".

If products today are more or less comparable, how can buying organizations differentiate between them? Perceived or cognitive differentiation is "the ability of individuals to perceive differences in the features of a stimulus object and to make fine distinctions between that object and others" (Zinkham and Munderrisoglu 1985). Customers must be aware and subjectively convinced of a certain advantage of a brand, a product or a service (Webster and Wind 1972). A supplier does not necessarily have to produce high-tech products, as long as this attribute is valuable and useful to its customers and their perception of this attribute related to this brand or product is dominant. A certain degree of formalism and individualism, as well as multi-organizational decision making, long-term relationships and a high degree of dynamic interactions between deciders, buyers and sellers determine the derived demand of organizations (Webster and Wind 1972; Kleinaltenkamp 2000).

As Håkansson and Snehota (1989, p. 187) note, when it comes to B-to-B, "no business is an island", referring to the interdependency of most B-to-B markets, in which business relationships of one sort or another are inevitable. The pioneer work of Naudé and Holland (1996) led to the development and application of relationship theory in the B-to-B sector, which refers to marketing concepts associated with long-term relationships. Håkansson and Snehota (2000) focus marketing research in the B-to-B setting on four cornerstones:

- Relationships exist between buyers and sellers.
- Business relationships are connected by networks.

- A relationship is a combination that includes elements of both market and hierarchy.
- Relationships are confrontational and therefore innovative.

To explain the differences between industrial marketing and B-to-B marketing, Fig. 3.1 shows the different steps involved in the markets for industrial goods, consumer goods and goods sold and purchased in B-to-B markets. Manufacturers can sell their goods directly to buying organizations through sales representatives or to wholesalers. The main difference between industrial marketing and B-to-B marketing is that the focus is not only on professional buyers. It is essential that the users of the goods are also included in the direct marketing approach of a company.

In the literature, industrial marketing, industrial goods marketing and investment goods marketing are often used synonymously (Backhaus and Voeth 2007; Ahlert et al. 2003). These types of marketing are exclusively concentrated on the marketing of goods and services which are not intended to be sold to wholesalers. On the other hand, B-to-B marketing also includes marketing activities to wholesalers, retailers and buying organizations (Webster and Wind 1972).

B-to-B relationships are characterized by an exchange between two or more parties (Backhaus and Voeth 2007). Research has identified several factors that enhance marketing and management in business relationships: commitment and trust, shared values and open and honest communication (Webster and Wind 1972). RM in international B-to-B relationships is more complicated to maintain because of language barriers and cultural differences (Friman et al. 2002).

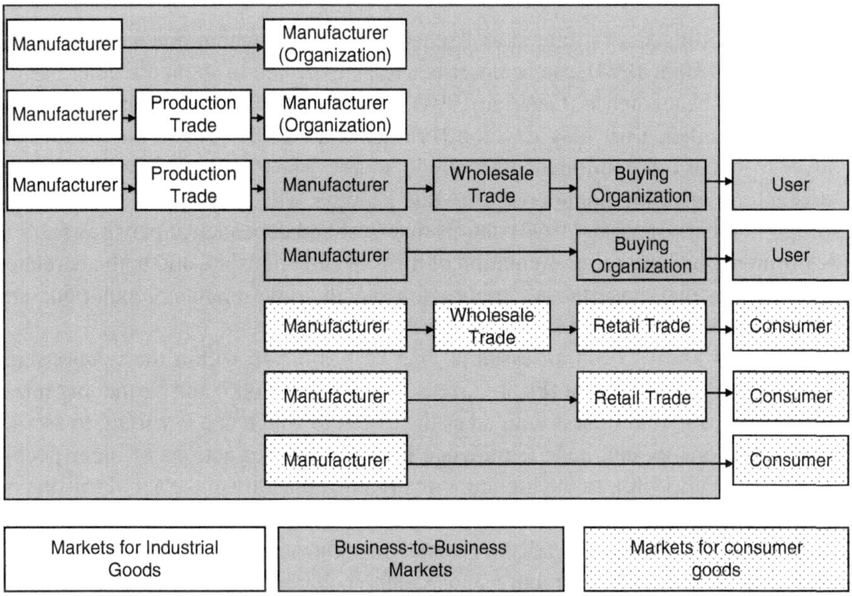

Fig. 3.1 Differences between B-to-B and B-to-C markets, Enlargement based on Backhaus/Voeth (2007) and Plinke (1999)

The buying decision-making process of an organization is characterized by the involvement of multiple individuals. Buying decision rules or standards may be applicable, and purchases occur as a result of derived demand (Backhaus and Voeth 2007). Differences in organizational transactions can be focused on the decision-making units (users, influencers, deciders, gatekeepers like secretaries, and buyers). For business companies, the buying objective is usually to increase profits by reducing costs or increasing revenues. Organizations often employ people who are professional purchasing agents and who are specialists at finding what their employer needs. Taking into consideration this special customer relationship, is it nevertheless possible to use CR as a competitive advantage and reputation transfer as a tool for an easier market entry?

Trust and commitment in B-to-B relationships are important, although the basic conditions between organizational buyers and suppliers are characterized by buying decision rules and derived demand: A positive reputation of the supplier and a trustful relationship between buyer and seller are ideal conditions for an easier market entry of new products.

Critical to a long-term buyer-seller relationship is a good understanding between partner companies. Friman et al. (2002) discuss the importance of knowledge and stress that acceptance of one another's organizational cultures is crucial to successful business relationships.

3.1.2 Commitment and Trust in Organizational Buying Behavior

Trust, the willingness to rely on an exchange partner in whom one has confidence (Morgan and Hunt 1994), can be described as an expectation about the other party's honesty and benevolence (Ganesan 1994). As business partners repeatedly interact with one another, trust may develop (Friman et al. 2002). This trust permits the buyer to make a commitment to a single source whose prior behavior has been satisfactory, with the confidence that this supplier will continue to perform in a similar manner. Ganesan (1994) claims that trust and dependence play key roles in determining the long-term orientation of firms in a relationship, and both are related to environmental uncertainty, transaction-specific investments, reputation, and satisfaction in a buyer-seller relationship.

Trust has always been an essential part of healthcare within the relationships between staff, management (Firth-Cozens 2004; Witzel 2006) and partner organizations. Organizational trust is defined as the extent to which one is willing to ascribe good intentions to, and have confidence in, the word and actions of other people (Cook and Wall 1980). In the literature on organizational trust, the act of trusting on the part of managers is almost never considered (Firth-Cozens 2004). Customer satisfaction and customer loyalty are seen to be influencing factors of organizational buying decisions (e.g., Homburg and Krohmer 2006). Satisfaction may develop through personal experience or, less directly, through opinion and the experience of peers, related to the perceived standard of delivery or product quality, and may also depend on the duration of the relationship (Swaminathan and Reddy 2000).

The development of purchasers' commitment refers to the motivation to stay with a supplier: a strong belief in and acceptance of the organization's goals and values, a willingness to exert considerable effort on behalf of the organization and a strong desire to remain in the relationship with the supplier (Porter et al. 1974; Moorman et al. 1992; Friman et al. 2002). Nevertheless, especially purchasers in organizational markets often face switching costs resulting from the fact that they have made a commitment to a certain technology product (i.e., all syringe pumps used in one hospital are bought from one supplier), or a certain buying organization (which may purchase products for more than 100 hospitals).

Organizational commitment, unlike satisfaction, is a relatively stable attitude. In various industry settings, a non-opportunistic and flexible nature of customer orientation has been found helpful to develop customer trust and commitment and thereby generate a competitive advantage for the supplier (Farrelly and Quester 2003; Saparito et al. 2004; Williams 1998). To reduce supply chain costs, hospitals no longer negotiate their contracts with their suppliers; instead, designated buying organizations are in charge. This may lead to the development of calculative commitment between buyers and suppliers. With regard to organizational buying behavior, calculative or continuance commitment can be caused, for example, by signing long-term purchasing contracts between numerous hospitals and buying organizations. In this connection, de Ruyter, Moorman and Lemmink (2001) propose to define commitment as a calculative act in which costs and benefits are examined.

It can be distinguish between two types of commitment: affective commitment expresses the extent to which customers like to maintain their relationship with their supplier, whereas calculative commitment refers to a company's motivation to continue the relationship because it can not easily replace its current supplier (Allen and Meyer 1990).

3.2 Defining Corporate Reputation in B-to-B Relationships

Although interest in the concept of CR is constantly growing, a precise and commonly agreed upon definition is still lacking (Barnett et al. 2006; Helm 2007). In addition, limited attention has been paid to the extent to which reputation encompasses various stakeholders' perceptions that may have different effects on the positive economic outcome associated with the possession of a favorable reputation (Eberl 2006; Helm 2007).

Reputation is viewed mainly as a valuable, intangible asset that provides a company with competitive advantages (Barney 1991; Roberts and Dowling 2002; Zabala et al. 2005), unless it is a positive reputation. CR influences stakeholders' economic choices (Fombrun 1996; Deephouse 2000; Rindova et al. 2005; Barnett et al. 2006). More than 10 years ago, Fombrun and van Riel (1997) identified several distinct views of reputation, including economics, strategic, marketing, organizational, and accounting, each with its own traditions of defining the concept and conducting research.

To ask people about a company's reputation in the B-to-C context is simple: Awareness and visibility of a company's reputation in this context is often associated with a positive reputation (Gardberg 2001, 2006). The more a company is known and visible, the better people are able to judge its reputation, based on past and planned actions the company has taken. Fombrun (1996, p. 72) defines CR as: "A corporate reputation is a perceptual representation of a company's past action and future prospect that describes the firm's overall appeal to all of its key constituents when compared with other leading rivals." Under this definition of CR, only affective reactions are integrated and cognitive components are excluded (Schwaiger 2004). According to Gray and Balmer (1998), CR is a valuation of a company's attributes, performed by the stakeholders, which almost excludes affective components.

In the context of B-to-B relationships, CR is considered as a general, spanning information substitute (Homburg and Krohmer 2006), evaluated by interested stakeholder groups. A good or bad reputation of an organization is determined by the signals that it gives out about its nature (van Riel 1995):

- It influences stakeholders' economic choices (Benjamin and Podolny 1999; Deephouse 2000) and may have a positive impact on a company's financial performance (Fombrun and Shanley 1990; Podolny 1993; Roberts and Dowling 2002).
- It is defined as a collective representation of a company's past behavior and outcomes that depict its ability to render valued results to multiple stakeholders in the future (Fombrun and Rindova 1998).
- It can be viewed as one of a set of organizational constructs, just like identity, image and learning, which are parallel, individual, level constructs (Gardberg 2006; Bromley 2000; Whetten and Mackey 2002).
- Positive CR makes it easier to charge premium prices by signaling product quality (Klein and Leffler 1981; Fombrun 1996), attracting better job applicants (Stigler 1962) and facilitating access to capital markets (Beatty and Ritter 1986).
- A favorable reputation can generate higher returns for companies by building mobility barriers against industry rivals (Caves and Porter 1977).

All the above-listed benefits are provided through CR by signaling information about past and future activities (Fombrun 1996). According to Lewis (2001, p. 31), CR "is the product, at any particular moment, of a fermenting mix of behavior, communication and expectations". At a strategic level, reputation is often viewed as a key, intangible asset of a company that helps to create value (Zabala et al. 2005; Roberts and Dowling, 2002) and explains certain facets of the performance of the company. Intangible assets are often associated with share price, and market assets such as customer loyalty are often linked to cash flow. Both concepts lead to value creation (MacMillan et al. 2004).

According to Dowling (2001), for companies in the risk management business such as pharmaceuticals and medical devices, CR is doubly important, as these companies have to rely on the trust of their customers. Wiedmann and Prauschke (2005) define CR as an overall stakeholder relationship variable and claim that the concept of CR can be either a market asset or a mediator or moderator between internal, intangible assets and market assets. Therefore, CR, as a determinant of corporate success, is a market asset.

To the author's best knowledge, no attention at all has been paid to differences in influencing factors on reputation in the B-to-B context compared with the B-to-C context. This may be one reason why, even today, there is a problem of defining the concept of CR (Barnett et al. 2006). According to the literature, even precisely distinguishing CR from corporate identity and corporate image seems to be difficult (e.g., Barnett et al. 2006; Helm 2007).

3.2.1 Reputation, Corporate Identity and Image

Following Fombrun and van Riel (1997), CR is often labeled "brand image" and focuses on the nature of information processing.

The role of corporate image and reputation has been studied in terms of its conceptualization, antecedents, and consequences (see reviews by Biehal and Sheinin, 2007). Empirical studies confirm the power of a corporate brand and the relationship between corporate branding and corporate reputation (e.g., Argenti and Druckenmiller, 2004). Balmer (1998, p. 963) postulates that "the key to acquiring a favorable image and reputation is the management of an organization's identity [. . .]." Reviewing the literature, the most fundamental barrier to the creation of one definition is the confusion concerning the concepts of identity, image and reputation (e.g., Barnett et al. 2006; Eberl, 2006; Helm, 2007; MacMillan et al.; 2004; Money and Hillenbrand, 2006).

Subsequent studies have measured the benefits of well-managed corporate identity, and have thus concentrated on the concepts of corporate image and reputation. In 1960, Bristol (p. 13) defined corporate image the way Fombrun defines corporate reputation today: "It is in all essentials, merely the picture which your organizsation has created in the mind of your various publics." Bevis (cited by Bernstein 1984, p. 125) defined corporate image as ". . . the net result of interactions of all the experiences, impressions, beliefs, feelings and knowledge that people have about a company." Fombrun and van Riel (1997) sought to subsume image and identity with reputation, as image and identity, from their perspective, are the basic components of reputation. According to Dowling (2001), corporate image (CI) refers to stakeholders' overall evaluation of the qualities associated with the company, and the emotional reaction those qualities produce. Dowling also links a company's image to its perceived ability to meet the needs of the stakeholders.

The term image is defined as the subjective attitude and impression a person has with regard to a certain object, in that the image is able to replace the missing information about a product if the brand is known. (Kroeber-Riel and Weinberg 2003, Mayer and Mayer 1987). For this reason, image plays an important role in the behavior and the decision process of the customer. The following image functions are part of this decision process (e.g., Kroeber-Riel and Weinberg 1996; Mayer and Mayer 1987):

- knowledge function
- ego defensive function
- value expression function
- adjustive function

Burmann, Schaefer and Maloney (2008) also discuss the impact of the industry image, not only on the perception of potential investors but also on other relevant stakeholders of corporate brand management.

The following Fig. 3.2 outlines the different approaches to defining CI and CR separately. Unfortunately, even measurement concepts of CI do not differentiate the wording correctly. Presenting measurement concepts of CI, van Riel, Stroeker and Maathuis (1998) claim that a "good reputation" is an influencing factor of CI. Falkenreck and Wagner (2008) extend the cluster of defining CR of Schwaiger (2004), Eberl (2006) and McMillan et al. (2005) by not only referring to relationship drivers like commitment, trust and knowledge resources: Their findings additionally highlight and confirm the impact of national culture on CR.

Similarly to Foreman and Whetten (1994), van Riel (1995) claims a possible multiplicity of organizational identity. He developed a method to access organizational identities that focused on the design of a branding strategy and distinguished four identity strategies depending on the degree of endorsement that the business

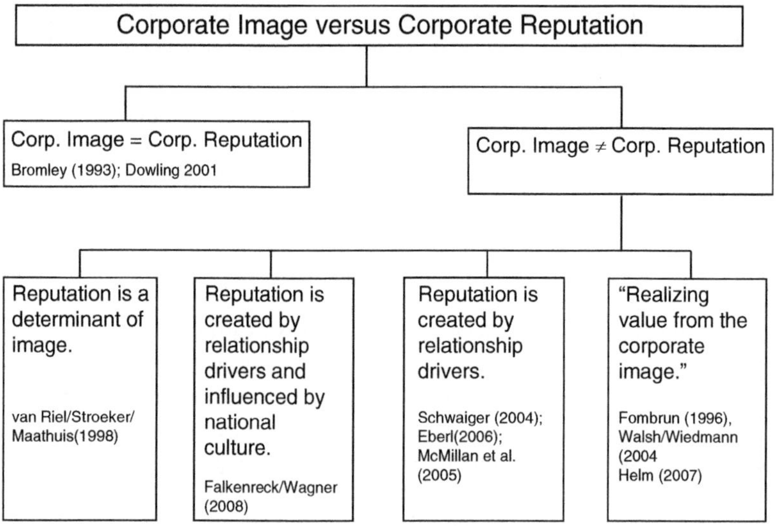

Fig. 3.2 Different clusters of definitions of image and reputation

unit label uses. These range from "low degree of parent visibility", and "low identification with parent brand" to "high parent visibility", and "high identification with corporate brand level". According to van Riel (1995), the last approach requires a strict coordination of communication strategy to show the strength of the group, whereas a low degree of parent brand visibility leads to greater autonomy at the business unit level.

The next Fig. 3.3 the author summarizes the link between corporate identity, image, culture, buying behavior and CR in B-to-B settings: In line with Bruhn (2004), corporate identity and corporate image of the company and its products are interactive. In addition, this study claims that corporate identity is also influenced by the culture of the parent company and the culture of its international stakeholders. Through direct marketing media, or WOM, the image of a company or its products influences organizational buying behavior.

Corporate image generates CR, and CR determines how a company is perceived by its stakeholder groups.In the context of Fig. 3.3, the author defines CR as

- The "net" affective or emotional reaction of stakeholders in the B-to-B context.
- CR-influencing features in this context are exclusively linked to relationship drivers and
- Are influenced by the national culture of the different stakeholder groups.

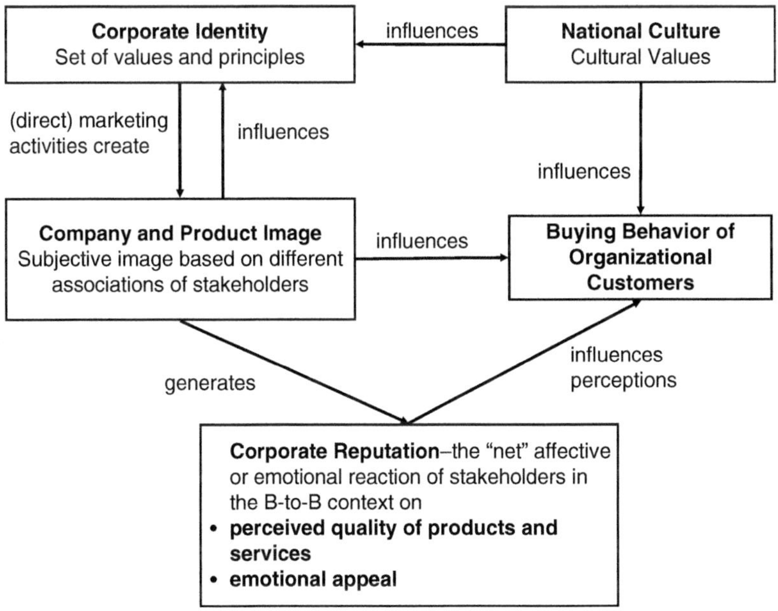

Fig. 3.3 Linking identity, image, culture, buying behavior and reputation

3.2.2 Reputation vs. Brand Identity, Brand Imagery and Brand Equity

According to Aaker (1991, p. 7), a "brand is a distinguishing name and/or symbol (such as a logo, trademark, or package design) intended to identify the goods or services of either one seller or a group of sellers, and to differentiate those goods or services from those of competitors." Powerful brands create meaningful images in the minds of consumers (Keller, 2003), with brand image and reputation enhancing differentiation, and this could have a positive influence on buying behavior (Gordon et al. 1983; McEnally and de Chernatony 1999). While the power of branding is widely accepted in consumer markets, knowledge of the nature and importance of branding in industrial markets is limited (Kuhn and Alpert 2004). Rosenbroijer (2001) claimed that in the sales-dominated nature of the industrial marketing environment, it is important that brands have no place in the B-to-B context. Others are of the opinion that brands are nevertheless valuable in such an environment (e.g., Gordon et al. 1993; Low and Blois 2002; McDowell Mudabi et al. 1997). Fournier (1998) argues that brand realtionships have many of the characteristics of human interpersonal relationships, including commitment or attachment. According to Aaker (1991), while deciding between industrial purchase alternatives, the decisive factor can be influenced by what a brand means to the buyer. Thus, a company's reputation can also be a decisive factor with regard to industrial purchase alternatives.

Brand equity is the effect that brand knowledge has on consumer response to the marketing of a brand (Keller 2003). This effect can only occur when the brand is known and when the customer possesses favorable, strong and unique brand associations. This can be triggered through the initial choice of the brand identity (brand name and logo) and through the integration of brand identities into the supporting marketing program.

The idea of branding has been increasingly extended from products to corporations. Keller (2003, p. 83) defines brand imagery as referring "to a more intangible aspect of the brand", how people think about a brand in abstract terms, rather than what the brand actually does. Imagery associations can be formed directly (own experience and contact with the brand) or indirectly (e.g., communicated through advertising or by word of mouth). In a B-to-B setting, user imagery can be related to the size or type of organization. User imagery may also be focused on the perceptions of a group as a whole (Keller 2003). A number of different types of associations related to either performance or imagery may be linked to a brand (Keller 2003). Regardless of whether the corporate branding is focused on the corporation itself, it derives from an alignment between strategy and communication (Forman and Argenti 2005).

Brand associations make up the brand image. Keller (2003, p. 87) argues that to "create brand equity, it is important that the brand has some strong, favorable and unique brand associations." Brand awareness refers to linking brand elements, the brand name, logo, packaging, product jingles and slogans, to the brand associations in the memory of the user. According to Keller and Sood (2003), brand elements make up the brand identity; therefore, they are important to enhance brand awareness and facilitate the formation of brand associations. In the B-to-B context, studies now show that brand awareness plays a less important role than suggested by Keller (2003). In their study, Kuhn and Alpert (2004) tried to transfer Keller's model for building brands empirically to the B-to-B context. Their findings do not support some of Keller's brand equity building factors. In their Australian B-to-B study, organizational buyers care less about product slogans or brand names, but more about the company itself and its products. Caring about the company itself means caring for its reputation (Fombrun 1996).

Although often unavailable in the consumer market, the sales force is a major brand-building tool in the B-to-B setting (Gordon et al. 1993). Purchase choice can therefore also depend on the company's people. The study of Kuhn and Alpert (2004) confirmed that Australian customers identified with manufacturer brands and spoke about relationships with company representatives rather than products. Respondents of their study mentioned their positive relationships with company representatives, but in no way expressed a sense of community or engagement. Brand resonance and brand feelings also do not seem to be evident among the organizational buyers surveyed. Keller's (2003) brand building block model lacks relevance in the B-to-B market investigated in Kuhn and Alpert's study. In discussing their experiences, respondents referred to the product functionality and tangible product information as reasons for purchasing. This outlines the difficulties of transferring the theoretical brand building process unchanged from B-to-C to B-to B contexts. The purchase decisions in the study of Kuhn and Alpert (2004) were involved in tender processes, and are therefore comparable to the setting of the study underlying this work. According to Argenti and Druckenmiller (2004), branding and reputation are closely linked, if they refer to corporations.

Careful management of a corporate brand can enhance reputation by guiding a company's actions (Forman and Agenti 2005). Bergstrom, Blumenthal and Crothers (2002, p. 133) claim that a "brand is the sum total of all perceived functional and emotional aspects of a product or service [...]." Brands can be sold, balanced or trademarked. Most marketing literature deals with the endorsement of one brand by another brand in the same product category (image transfer by line extensions, e.g., Aaker and Keller 1990; Park et al. 1991), products complementing one another or linking organizational associations to product associations (Keller 2003). Reputations are the product of relationships between organizations and the general public (Dozier 1993), influenced by internal and external elements. Leading companies understand that a strong reputation is not built overnight. It is an ongoing process that involves rigorous measurement and tracking as well as creative strategies for engaging with stakeholders (Fombrun 2008).

As Fig. 3.4 shows, a strong link between brand performance and CR is essential, since the brand is the promise and the reputation is the external evaluation of whether or not the company is delivering on this promise (Fombrun 2008). Just as branding is closely related to CR, so is corporate communication (CC). Fombrun and Rindova (1998) point out that communication benefits do not only result from the frequency of communications: As communications make a company more transparent, stakeholders know more about the company's operations and goals.

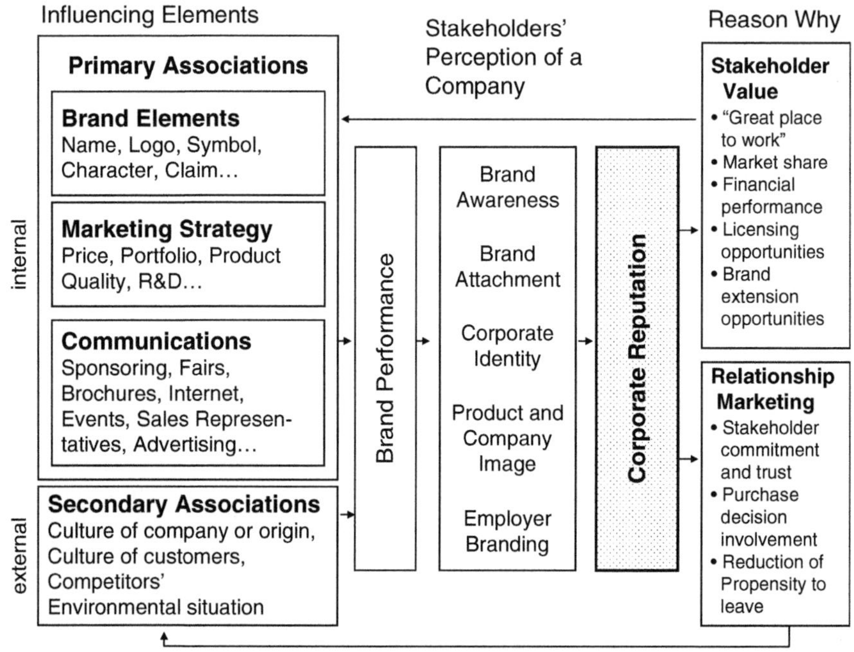

Fig. 3.4 Linking influencing elements of stakeholders perception

3.3 A Standard Construct of Reputation–Useful and Appropriate?

As Larkin (2003, p. 5) pointed out, "The biggest hurdle in making the case for building, maintaining and managing reputation is how to measure it effectively." A large body of academic literature is concerned with the conceptualization and measurement of CR. This chapter offers an overview of this issue.

The abstract construct of reputation is difficult to measure in a mathematical way. Thus, it is difficult to define conceptualization and measurement of CR (Sandig 1962; Money and Hillenbrand 2006; Eberl 2006; Helm 2007). Due to the increasing awareness of the value of the concept to both practitioners and scholars (MacMillan et al. 2005; Fombrun and van Riel 2004; Bromley 2002), more measurement concepts of CR have emerged. Recent reputation studies (Fombrun and Shanley 1990; Cordeiro and Schwalbach 2000; Wartick 2002; MacMillan et al. 2005) and formative versus reflective measurement concepts (Eberl 2006; Helm 2006, 2007) provide some insights into the relationship between stakeholder-specific activities and the problem of measuring corporate reputation.

On the one hand, due to the variety of measurement concepts and definitions of CR, researchers (e.g., Money and Hillenbrand 2006; Helm 2007) assert that companies do not know what reputation measures they should use in which circumstances and what aim and value the different models offer. On the other hand, Bennett and Kottasz (2000), as well as Waddock (2003), claim that the need for a valid measurement concept of CR is just applied pressure of the practitioner world. How useful are CR measurement concepts, if they can not be used by practitioners to answer strategic questions?

Is it possible to standardize measurement of CR even if there is not a precise and commonly agreed upon definition (Barnett et al. 2006)? Some authors supporting the perceptual view of reputation doubt that the diverse reputations of a firm are comparable. Dowling (1988, p. 28) states that investigations of reputation call for an adaptive approach: "It is necessary to customize this set of factors (and attributes) used to describe a company (...). The role of people and their norms and values will determine which types of factors should be selected". He concludes that a measurement model for reputation needs to be adapted to each stakeholder group. Unfortunately, this makes it impossible to compare the results.

Other research approaches show that financial performance, which is often analyzed within the context of CR (Deephouse 2000, does not have a decisive impact on reputation at all (Helm 2007). As suggested by Gatewood et al. (1993), inconsistent perceptions across stakeholder groups might be attributed to different correlates of reputation, whereas consistent perceptions indicate that reputation is a general construct. In the first case, reputational analysis needs to be limited to specific roles of a firm: reputations such as a firm's reputation as a supplier, as an investment choice, or as an employer.

Studies describing organizational identity are primarily based on input from organizational members. Most studies examine the identity of the organization as a whole (Bernstein 1986; Atamer and Calori 1993; Foreman and Whetten 1994, Gioia and Thomas 1996), whereas others consider that an organization has multiple identities or reputations (Helm 2007; Dowling 2001; van Riel 1995; Gustafson and Reger 1999). Regarding research work on CR, authors normally focus on one to three stakeholder groups in one country. For example, Helm (2007) and Eberl (2006) concentrate on customers, shareholders and employees in a German B-to-C setting. Both researchers use different constructs of CR.

Bernstein (1986), together with a focus group of top managers concluded that organizational identity is influenced by the following dimensions: value for money, technical innovation, service, social responsibility, reliability, imagination, quality and integrity.

The following sub-chapters focus on actual measurement concepts of CR. As an introduction to the various concepts, the first type of CR measurement is presented: league tables outline the score of the "most visible" or "most admired" companies. On a more strategic level, the reputation models of Fombrun et al. (2000, Sect. 3.3.2), Gardberg (2006, Sect. 3.3.3) as well as Walsh and Wiedmann (2004, Sect. 3.3.3) provide information on the use of a "Reputation Quotient" (RQ). The RQ model suggests to understand the beliefs of individuals as well as stakeholders regarding an organization's reputation impact on their attitudes in terms of the emotional appeal that people feel toward a business (Money and Hillenbrand 2006).

A different approach on the measurement of CR is provided by MacMillan et al. (2005) and Eberl (2005). Details on the relationship-driven measurement approaches can be found in Sect. 3.3.4.

3.3.1 League Tables

In 2007, the Reputation Institute identified and examined 183 public lists that provide ratings and rankings of companies in 38 countries (Fombrun 2007). Sixty-one of the lists provide a rating and/or ranking of a set of companies (most of which, also 61, were located in the US), based on an overall measure of reputation. Only two lists focus exclusively on providing ratings based on perceived quality of products or services of the rated companies. The main criteria used to rate companies in these internationally publicized reputation lists are the following (Fombrun 2007): overall reputation, workplace, citizenship, performance, leadership, innovation, governance, and products.

The first and best-known league tables of reputation for industrial and commercial companies are those published annually in the US business magazine, Fortune (Bromley 2002). League tables have existed since 1983 and are based on large data samples from executives, directors and, among others, securities analysts, who rate a selection of companies on various attributes relevant to corporate success.

The often-cited rankings in Fortune, Management Today and the Financial Times emphasize reputation criteria such as being well-known, respected and having high or low levels of financial performance or innovativeness. The most enduring and visible reputation survey in the market is probably Fortune's annual list of "America's Most Admired Companies". Similar ratings can be found in the Financial Times, Asian Business and the Manager Magazin. Since 1987, the latter has conducted surveys to measure CR. In 2000, the authorized agent performed a random CATI survey of about 2,500 executives, who were asked to rate the top 100 German companies according to the following criteria: quality of management, innovativeness, ability to communicate, environmental responsibility, financial and economic stability, product quality, value for money, employee orientation, growth rates, attractiveness to executives, and internationalization. However, the calculation of the "overall reputation index" is not explained.

Social rating agencies such as the Council on Economic Priorities (CEP) and investment funds such as Kinder, Lydenberg and Domini (KLD) also rate companies on various aspects of social performance and contribute to the current proliferation of reputational ratings (Fombrun 1998).

Stakeholders can be influenced by these lists and the visibility conferred upon them by the media. How are companies selected for inclusion in these lists? According to Fombrun (2007), none of the 183 lists are comprehensive, as various filters are applied by the rating agents, which also influence which companies are included in the lists. The "top of the mind awareness of corporate brands" (van Riel 2002, p. 368) generally refers to visibility of the company in the media, stock quotation, size (referring to turnover or number of employees), long-establishedness and company activities of general interest (Fombrun and van Riel 2004). Some rankings include all types of companies, whereas others examine only the largest companies or focus on a certain type of industry. Among others, Gatewood et al. (1993) claim that using Fortune criteria to measure reputation is not appropriate for all stakeholder groups. They especially focus on job applicants' perception of corporate reputation, which does not seem to be correctly captured by the set of criteria. The authors conclude that any perception is a function of the information that is available to an individual at a given time. This would also not make it possible to standardize a reliable measurement model of corporate reputation.

The traditional league table approach to assessing and comparing CR faces a number of problems associated with defining and measuring reputation:

- Bromley (1993) criticizes the eight categories of Fortune magazine as being inconcise.
- A survey may not sample the stakeholder groups best informed about the company (Bromley 2002).
- The particular attributes on which respondents are asked to rate a number of selected companies vary from one survey to another (Kay 1993).

This leads to the fact that not even the results on the same company coming from different league tables are comparable. None of the above-mentioned rankings can be considered as an objective measure of CR–and particularly not in the B-to-B context.

3.3.2 The Reputation Quotient

In the definition of Fombrun and Gardberg (2003, see also Fombrun 1996, Fombrun and Rindova 1998; Fombrun and van Riel 1997), CR is a collective representation of a company's past actions and results that describes the company's ability to deliver valued outcomes to various stakeholders.

To develop a cross-national instrument to measure reputation, in 1999 the Reputation Institute created an index called Reputation Quotient (RQ) that summarized people's perceptions of companies based on twenty attributes (Fombrun and Gardberg 2002). Researchers agree that a stakeholder-specific approach can be delicate (Sobol et al. 1992; Fryxell and Wang 1994; Rindova et al. 2005) because one stakeholder group can hardly reflect the "overall perception of a firm by its stakeholders", i.e., CR (defined by Fombrun and Rindova 2000, p. 78).[1]

[1]For recent stakeholder-specific studies, see, e.g., Wright and Fill (2001), Helm (2007), and Rindova et al. (2005). For a cross-stakeholder approach, see, e.g., Ravasi and Fombrun (2004), Rabe (2005), and Carter and Deephouse (1999).

Figure 3.5 lists the various components influencing corporate reputation. As van Riel and Fombrun (2002) explained, the six components were designed for using the RQ with any stakeholder group. So far, the collected RQs only focus on the general public (Wartick 2002), and apply mostly to "most visible" and generally known B-to-C companies. Nevertheless, Fombrun and Wiedmann (2001) assume that there are no great differences between the perception of individuals belonging to different stakeholder groups. Different perceptions between stakeholders with regard to B-to-C or B-to-B contexts are not discussed at all. Thus, with the RQ measurement concept in mind, Groenland (2002, p. 308) concludes that "a rigorous conceptual definition still lacks in this study" and that "the validity of the construct remains unclear."

The literature has already discussed that the RQ dimensions "vision and leadership" and "financial performance" might be more important to investors than to customers (Gabbioneta et al. 2007; Fombrun and Wiedmann 2001; Reynolds et al. 1994; Caruana, 1997). Moreover, some dimensions are difficult to measure across cultures (Gardberg 2006; Walsh and Wiedmann 2004). Nevertheless, there are several empirical studies which try to measure corporate reputation based on the above components (e.g., Helm, 2007; Gardberg 2006; Walsh and Wiedmann 2004).

To construct a global database, the 20 attributes on the left side of Fig. 3.5 were grouped into six conceptual categories: Emotional Appeal, Vision and Leadership, Products and Services, Workplace Environment, Social Responsibility, and Financial Performance (Fombrun et al. 2000). This "balanced instrument for measuring reputation" was developed by reviewing the items contained in the eight most visible measures of corporate reputation, including Fortune's Most Admired Companies, Far Eastern Economic Review and Financial Times (Fombrun et al. 2000).

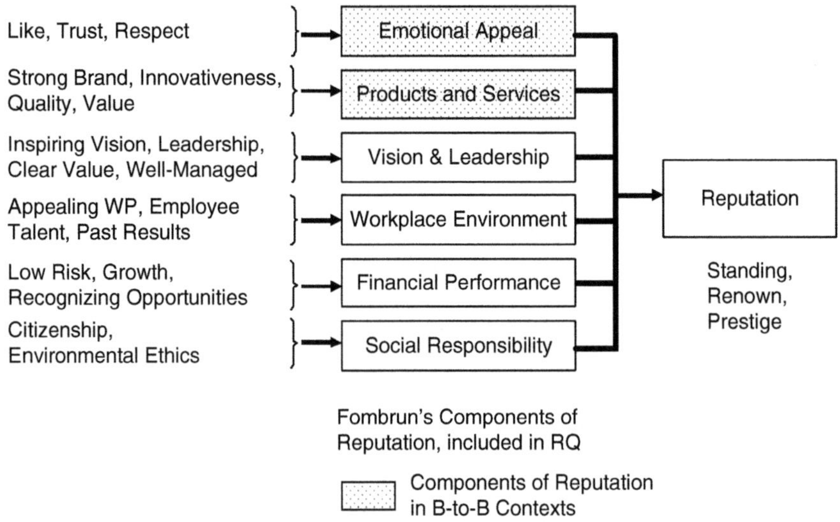

Fig. 3.5 Different components forming corporate reputations based on Fombrun et al. 2000

Table 3.2 Items and components of the reputation quotient

Emotional appeal
• I have a good feeling about this company
• I admire and respect the company
• I trust this company
Products and services
• Stands behind its products and services
• Develops innovative products and services
• Offers high-quality products and services
• Offers products and services that are good value for money
Vision and leadership
• Has excellent leadership
• Has a clear vision for its future
• Recognizes and takes advantages of market opportunities
Workplace environment
• Is well-managed
• Looks like a good company to work for
• Looks like a company that would have good employees
Financial performance
• Has a strong record of profitability
• Looks like a low-risk investment
• Is better than its competitors
• Looks like a company with strong prospects for future growth.
Social responsibility
• This company supports good causes
• Is an environmentally responsible company
• Maintains high standards in the way it treats people

From these publications, 27 items were listed and reviewed by their research partner, Harris Interactive. This company added five items, so that the item list contained a total of 32 items (Fombrun et al. 2000) (Table 3.2).

Results show that constructs referring to the components "vision and leadership", "social responsibility" and "workplace environment" reveal more missing values than "emotional appeal" and "products and services" (Fombrun and Gardberg 2002). Possibly, with reference to organizational buyers, these so-called "general reputation drivers" (Genasi 2001; Fombrun 2001) are of no interest to these stakeholder groups, assuming they are able to judge it. The author therefore suggests that important components of CR in the B-to-B context are barely related to vision and leadership, workplace environment, financial performance or social responsibility, as B-to-B companies are simply not "most visible", and only little is known about these companies. On the other hand, "emotional appeal" as well as "products and services" have a strong impact on a B-to-B company's CR, even in the eyes of buying organizations.

Companies doing well in these annual RQ surveys were B-to-C companies like Johnson and Johnson, Lego, Ferrari and Microsoft. No details are published in the above papers regarding the measurement scales used, but before filling out the questionnaire, people were also asked to rank the importance of the single items determining the constructs.

Bromley (2002) notes that even though the name "Reputation Quotient" implies arithmetic attributes, Fombrun does not calculate an arithmetical quotient. According to Bromley (2002), calculating RQs or benchmarks for comparing CRs calls for a departure from the traditional league table method, but still depends on questionable assumptions about the legitimacy of psychometric assessment.

Using the dimensions of the RQ, Helm (2007) developed a formative construct of CR based on the following ten indicators: quality of products, value for money, environmental engagement, company's attitude toward employees, company growth, social responsibility and citizenship, financial performance, qualification of management, compliance with advertising promises. In addition, the constructs loyalty and own experiences were used to evaluate different stakeholders' perceptions of a company's reputation. This structural model was tested on three different stakeholder groups (shareholders, employees, and customers), and no significant differences were found regarding the company's reputation, which is located in the B-to-C setting.

The aim of the study of Helm (2007) was to create one valid construct of reputation to be used comprehensively on all stakeholder groups. However, taking into account the comments of Bromley (2002), that a survey may not sample the stakeholder groups best informed about the company, the reputation construct of Helm (2007) can not be used in the B-to-B context, as knowledge about, as well as the interest in, organizational suppliers varies significantly among the various stakeholder groups (Meffert and Bierwirth, 2002).

3.3.3 Measuring RQ in Different Cultures

Most empirical research work on CR has been conducted in the US, using US samples (Brown and Perry 1994; Fombrun and Shanley 1990; Fryxell and Wang 1994). Many of these studies were based on data from Fortune magazine's "America's Most Admired Companies", and were mostly related to CR features of B-to-C companies.

Recently, some authors have published papers using German (Dunbar and Schwalbach 2000) or Scandinavian (Aperia et al. 2004) data or conducted a qualitative analysis of CR on a cross-cultural basis (Gardberg 2006). Nevertheless, little empirical research has examined CR formation and implications in a cross-cultural or comparative context. The external validity, or generalize ability of existing empirical research related to CR in the B-to-B context is still lacking.

In 2000, the Reputation Institute initiated two empirical studies, nominations and focus groups, to explore cross-cultural validity issues. Companies examined in the course of these studies were the ones with "the most visible reputations in 12 European countries" (Gardberg 2006, p. 40). The target group of the survey comprised five focus groups averaging seven participants, with no direct customers of the companies included. The goal was to find out if CRs may or may not be functionally equivalent cross-culturally and to determine if the RQ (see Sect. 3.3.2) could serve as a cross-cultural measure of CRs. In this context, and in line with Singh (1995) and Brislin (1980), the following cross-cultural equivalences were investigated:

- Functional equivalence – the relationship the variable has with its antecedents or consequences (Singh 1995).
- Conceptual equivalence – this term refers to whether the variable is expressed in similar attitudes or behaviors across nations.
- Instrument equivalence – whether "the scale items, response categories and questionnaire stimuli [are] interpreted identically across nations", (Singh 1995, p. 605).
- Translation equivalence – translated items measure the identical concepts to the original items (Brislin 1980).

According to Gardberg (2006), some findings of the above study were:

- The participants' replies reflect corporate branding strategies or a visible division or brand rather than the corporate parent.
- Some consumers believed that a certain product was a separate entity.
- The Dutch and British focus groups suggested additional items that were neither elements of the RQ nor items in prior CR scales.
- The role of the CEO in reputation formation was in dispute in three of the five focus groups.

The literature on cross-national differences in expectations of appropriate leadership styles suggests that charismatic leadership is not universally appreciated (House et al. 1999; Lord and Maher 1991). According to Gaines-Ross (2000), David Larcker claimed that a 10% change in CEO reputation results in 24% change in a company's market capitalization, which seems to be relevant only in the US.

Visionary leadership of a company involves a relationship between an individual (leader) and one or more followers based on leader behaviors (Waldman et al. 2004) and is related to cultural values impacting on the decision-making process: e.g., perceptions of respect, strong admiration, distance, integrity or trust. It should therefore be noted that the importance of vision and leadership on CR is also influenced by cultural values. In line with Hofstede (2001, p. 232) it is argued that leadership is more important in individualist cultures: "managers from more individualist cultures tended to stress leadership and variety, whereas those from less individualist countries tended to stress conformity and oderliness."

Following the findings of Gardberg (2006), this cross-cultural research still supports the contention that constructs and instruments developed in the US context may require review before generalizing to other institutional environments (Rosenzweig, 1994; Boyacigiller and Adler 1991). "Developing a scale for measuring corporate reputation that is cross-culturally valid will facilitate rigorous research on a valuable intangible asset" (Gardberg 2006, p. 60).

Walsh and Wiedmann (2004) measured an extended RQ, based on a qualitative analysis of CR in Germany. Study results suggest that when using the RQ model in Germany, additional variables need to be added. Walsh and Wiedmann (2004) called for future researchers to measure stakeholders' experience as well as their involvement in the requested company. According to Walsh and Wiedmann (2004), measuring CR in Germany requires dimensions like sympathy, transparency, fairness, perceived customer orientation of the organization and stakeholder feelings of satisfaction and trust.

Using US RQ scales in CR measurement approaches in European countries, the studies of Gardberg (2006) and Walsh and Wiedmann (2004) have shown that this can not be carried out without changes or amendments in the RQ dimensions.

Interestingly, neither study argues that the differences found in CR measurement criteria between the US and Europe may be influenced or caused by cultural differences between the countries.

To the author's best knowledge, the link between a company's reputation and the national culture of buyers has not been investigated at all. Although the cultural dimension of individualism versus collectivism has been widely researched (e.g., Homburg et al. 2004; Waldman et al. 2004) and has also been linked to economic growth (Hofstede 1980, 2001, Waldman et al. 2004), up to now no empirical study crosslinked the different impact factors on reputation to the cultural backround of the country under consideration.

3.3.4 Relationship-Driven Measurement Approaches

In addition to the dominating RQ concept of Fombrun et al. (2000), there exist CR measurement approaches based on relationships drivers. In this work, the concepts of MacMillan et al. (2005) and Eberl (2006, based on the CR measurement concept of Schwaiger 2004) are introduced. Interestingly, both concepts do not measure CR directly, but use other constructs (sympathy, competence, trust, and commitment) to circumscribe it. Both concepts also try to enhance the theory of commitment and trust (Morgan and Hunt 1994).

Taking into consideration the remarks of Bromley (2002), the SPIRIT (Stakeholder Performance Indicator and Relationship Improvement Tool) approach of MacMillan et al. (2004) proposes a measure of the experiences that stakeholders have of a business. On a strategic level, the measurement criteria provide an insight into the asset-generating activities that an organization could perform or engage in to improve CR as an intangible asset. As a consequence, the SPRIT approach also follows the "visibility approach" of companies proposed by Fombrun et al. (2000). The main difference is that in the SPIRIT model of CR is located in the B-to-B context, and measures are exclusively based on the direct experiences of the stakeholders with the companies in question: a measure of stakeholders' experience of inside and outside influences of the company.

This includes experiences of what the media and pressure groups say about an organization, and is therefore focused on the constructs of loyalty and WOM. The measures can be used to assess an organization's ability to engage in asset-generating activities, such as investing in positive public relations (Money and Hillenbrand 2006).

No single construct of reputation exists in this approach. CR is measured indirectly by evaluating antecedents of commitment and trust, and ten other latent variables are included in the structural model for business relationship customers: other trust-related behaviors, compliance, loyalty, creative cooperation, material and non-material benefits, coercive power, termination costs, communication and past trust-related behavior (MacMillan et al. 2004).

The measurement concept of CR used in the study of Eberl (2006) is based on CR determinants of Schwaiger (2004). In line with the concept of MacMillan et al. (2005), no single construct of reputation is used. CR is measured by evaluating the following antecedents of competence and sympathy: quality, attractiveness, performance and responsibility (Eberl 2006). The construct of responsibility incorporates indicators like fairness, merited identity over time, credibility or corporate social responsibility. The construct of attractiveness is related to the findings of Fombrun and Shanley (1990) and refers to the stakeholders' perception based on a company's visibility in the media. As the study of Eberl (2006) is located in the B-to-C context, this can be regarded as appropriate. The goal of the study by Eberl (2006) was to develop a CR measurement concept that contains cognitive and affective components of CR. For this reason, the constructs "quality" and "performance" have also been included in the measurement concept.

3.3.5 *The Need for Valid and Cross-Culturally Practicable Measures of CR*

Bromley (2002) reviewed existing approaches to assessing and comparing CR such as league tables (e.g., Fortune), Fombrun's RQ, benchmarks and case study methods. With regard to the first three measurement concepts, Bromley (2002) questioned the legitimacy of the applied psychometric assessments. He had two further concerns:

- The first is his skepticism of overall scores of reputation such as the RQ of Fombrun et al. (2000) and the Fortune measures, which are derived from applying exactly the same model of reputation across different stakeholder groups and cross-culturally.

MacMillan et al. (2005) and Helm (2007) agree that this is seen as problematic, as different stakeholder groups are likely to vary regarding their values and beliefs (still without discussing cultural differences).

- Bromley's (2002) other criticism is related to reputation scores and rankings that are derived from the sum or average of scores on a number of sub-scales. Bromley recommended that there should be certain thresholds for an organization to have a good reputation including, for example, the achievement of a minimum score on product quality.

Judgment of CR is based on different issues that are important to different stakeholder groups (Bromley 2002; Wartick 2002).

The following Table 3.2 lists the measurement concepts evaluated in Sects. 3.3.2, 3.3.3 and 3.3.4. Two main actual approaches can be distinguished:

- measurement concepts based on Fortune's ranking and the dimensions of the RQ (Fombrun et al. 2000) and
- concepts, where impact factors on CR are created by relationship drivers like trust, sympathy, competence or commitment.

This study aims to extent the latter approach by cultural impact factors on CR. Nevertheless-contrary to the relationship drivers approaches of Eberl (2006), Schwaiger (2004) and MacMillan et al. (2004)-in this work one construct of reputation is used to investigate the impact factors on CR (Table 3.3).

In their book on market research, Lee and Lings (2007) point out that for the reliability of research data, it is essential to avoid asking respondents things they can not judge. As already discussed, studies have confirmed that Keller's (2003) brand influencing and building elements like brand feelings and slogans are of minor importance in B-to-B relationships. These companies are neither "most visible" nor "most admired", and are therefore hardly included in Fortune's rankings. The findings of Helm (2006) and Gardberg (2001) show that consumers usually have no detailed knowledge about the special characteristics of a company. Some stakeholders may have more profound knowledge of a firm's reputation than others (Helm, 2006). This may lead to a rather narrow view of reputational attributes, which therefore argues against the detailed formative construct of CR proposed by Helm (2007).

According to Helm (2006) and Schultz, Mouritsen and Gabrielsen (2001), respondents often use "intuition" when answering multi-faceted scales of reputation, and they are unable to discriminate between the criteria they are asked to quantify. Respondents can not remember company-specific undertakings, and everything gets lost in "a general impression of how the company performs" (Schulz et al. 2001, p. 37). No wonder Wartick (2002) called for more explanatory and predictive power while measuring reputation. No wonder Drolet and Morrison (2001) claim that even the second or third item contributes little to the information obtained from the first item.

Dutton and Dukerich (1991) examined how perceptions of identity guided individuals' interpretation of organizational features. In open-ended questions, all the respondents replied that organizational identity of a certain B-to-B company was related to a "professional organization with uniquely technical expertise", whereas only 44% connected this company's identity with "ethical, scandal-free, and altruistic", and 36% to "commitment to welfare of the region". Gestalt psychologists confirm that a holistic perception of the overall CR leads to a more intense mental effect than the summed perceptions of the single facets of CR.

While the ranking approaches are highly influenced by past financial performance data, Brown and Perry (1994) agree with Fombrun and Shanley (1990) that CR is also determined by non-economic criteria. In line with these statements, Dowling (2004) states that two major factors need to be considered while analyzing CR: a fact-oriented reputation referring to a company's financial and product

Table 3.3 Measurement concepts of corporate reputation: An overview

Strategic level	Asset generating activities	Intangible asset	Market asset/ performance/ barrier for competitors
Fombrun et al. (2000), Gardberg (2006) Walsh and Wiedmann (2004) measurement concept is based on the reputation quotient beliefs helm (2007)	Relying on visibility and uniqueness	Beliefs: based on Fortune's ranking: vision & leadership financial performance social responsibility products and services workplace environment attitude: Emotional appeal	Intention and behavior: Suggestion of a development of scales recommended for B-to-B, B-to-C
	Activities associated with the development of a monolithic reputation development of scales to measure reputation, loyalty and consumer experience	Beliefs: based on Fombrun's RQ Quality of products value for money social responsibility leadership work environment corporate citizenship financial performance qualification of management attitude: Loyalty	Intention and behavior: Development of loyalty, positive consumer experiences empirically tested in B-to-C context
MacMillan, Money, Downing, Hillenbrand (2005) concept is based on drivers in relationships Eberl (2006) Schwaiger (2004)	Outside influences of media and pressure group. Services, communications, shared values	SPIRIT approach attitude: reputation is created by trust and commitment, positive or negative emotions	Intentions: suggest scales to measure loyalty and word of mouth empirically tested in B-to-B
	Activities associated with the development of commitment	Beliefs: based on Schwaiger (2004). Reputation is created by competence and sympathy attitude: Commitment	Intention and behavior: Observe and understand what consumers want empirically tested in B-to-C

performance and an emotional reputation, based on a company's "personality" and social responsibility. According to Helm (2006), a measure of overall reputation performs rather well when integrated into a structural model that links reputational perceptions to attitudinal, intentional, and behavioral outcomes. The structural model on CR and reputation transfer introduced in this work deals with these criticisms by focusing on reputation in the particular stakeholder relationship of organizational customers. It does not seek to aggregate the scores from one stakeholder group with those from other stakeholder groups, nor does it use dimensions to quantify CR, which can not be judged by organizational customers.

Just like the SPIRIT approach proposed by MacMillan et al. (2004), the predictive power of the structural model used in this work derives from the overall pattern in each stakeholder relationship and in each of the five countries. It is the key aim of this work to achieve additional knowledge on the cross-cultural influencing factors on CR and on the possibility of transferring CR on new product ranges.

3.4 The Concept of Reputation Transfer

One of the main arguments of this study focuses on the transferability of reputation and on the question of how CR can be derived from reputations at other levels. The name of a company, as with any name, can carry and develop a complexity of associations pointing to particular reputational content (Schweizer and Wijnberg 1999). In addition, the company name can function as a reputation indicator of a group (Landon and Smith 1997). Understanding better how this transferability operates is of great importance, especially in the B-to-B context. The concept of transfer can be found in studies on "image transfer", "attitude transfer" or "affective transfer" (Ganassali and Didellon 1996; Gwinner 1997).

In this study, the transfer of reputation is also referred to as part of the knowledge resources of a company. The way a company "shares knowledge" with its customers by communicating details of new products or product ranges, is an essential part of relationship marketing (Grönroos 2000). Heider's (1958) Balance Theory refers to relations and attitudes that describe a theoretically relevant property of the knowledge structure. Heider (1958) argues that when two unlinked or weakly linked nodes (e.g., different product ranges of one company) share a first-order link (e.g., a company's reputation), the association between these two should strengthen.

As discussed before, a company's CR is built on signaling information about past and future activities (Fombrun 1996). Thus, following Heider's (1958) Balance Theory and the concept of CR, customers unconsciously transfer their attitude toward the company and its products on the new product (or product range) and, by doing so, facilitate the market entry of the new product. Facing some new or unexpected associations (e.g., a new product or product range), consumers tend to alter their perceptions in order to harmonize them (Heider 1958; Cornwell et al. 2005). A comparable process of "meanings transfer" takes place in the celebrity endorsement process. The mental associations the new product or product range receives by transferring the reputation of the parent company, generates a positive goodwill effect among customers that translate into attitude and behavior toward the new product. In line with Keller's (2001) impact factors on brand transfer processes, Gwinner (1997) argues that the image transfer process is influenced by moderating factors such as product involvement and the degree of similarity or fit between the new product and the parent image. In this context, the perceived fit is conceptualized as the extension's perceived similarity to the parent brand and refers to dimensions such as product category and attributes, e.g., image (Keller 2003; Park et al. 1991). Keller argues that the higher the perceived fit of the new product with the parent brand, the more positive customers evaluate the extension. From a marketing communications perspective, introducing a new product as a brand extension means that the introductory campaign can concentrate on the product itself without having to create brand awareness (Keller 2003). The literature on the abstract term image transfer uses this wording differently, and mostly refers to sponsorship activities (Chien, Cornwell and Stokes 2005; Gwinner 1997; Cliffe and Motion 2005). Image transfer defined by Bruhn (2005) refers to the possibility of transferring the positive image of the sponsored person to the advertising company or related product.

To study the ways of transferring reputation also refers to external trust in a certain company (Schweizer and Wijnberg 1999), but the nature of this relationship is not immediately clear due to the lack of precise definitions of either concept. Related to the marketing context, Doney and Cannon (1997) define trust as the perceived trustworthiness and credibility of a target. In most relevant studies, the definition of reputation in some way includes the concept of credibility (Fombrun 1996; Ganesan 1994; Doney and Cannon 1997); a favorable reputation is seen as the prerequisite for the attribution of credibility or trustworthiness to a company. In this context, trust is also closely related to the way a company communicates (Schweizer and Wijnberg 1999), including assumptions about the trustworthiness of the media used.

Thus, trust can play different roles in the reputation building process, depending on the mode or media of information transmission. According to Schweizer and Wijnberg (1999), three different modes of how information about a particular entity is acquired can be distinguished:

- A stakeholder can acquire firsthand experience by direct interaction with a company. Reputation, in the eyes of this particular actor, is then influenced by gathering and evaluating company-specific information.
- Information on a specific company may be acquired in an indirect mode through an agent acting as a "reputation maker". Trust in this company can then develop based on secondhand information.
- A stakeholder can acquire information about a company by deriving and transferring it from other related entities or levels to the company.

The next subsection outlines the differences between reputation transfer and brand transfer, and also focuses on the chances and risks of these concepts.

3.4.1 *Reputation Transfer vs. Brand Transfer: Chances and Risks*

Introducing new products is both risky and expensive, especially without the help of an established brand. For many companies, brand extensions are part of their marketing strategies, a way to complete their product portfolio and also to meet their customers' needs (Keller 2003; Sjödin 2007). Companies try to capitalize on brands that already draw favorable attention from customers (Aaker and Keller 1990; Blichfeldt 2005). Keller (2003) identifies three choices a company can make when introducing a new product:

1. It can develop a new brand for this new product.
2. It can apply it to one of the existing brands.
3. It can use a combination of a new brand with an existing brand.

Approaches 2 and 3 describe a brand extension, when a company uses an established brand name to introduce a new product (see Fig 3.6). In the case where the parent brand is used to introduce a new product that targets a new market segment within an existing product category, a line extension has been made (Keller 2003; Kaufmann et al. 2006). A category extension is defined by the fact that the parent brand is used to enter a different product category from that currently served by the parent brand. Literature reviews by Czellar (2003), Grimes, Diamantopoulos and Smith (2002), as well as Hem et al. (2003), confirm that most research has been

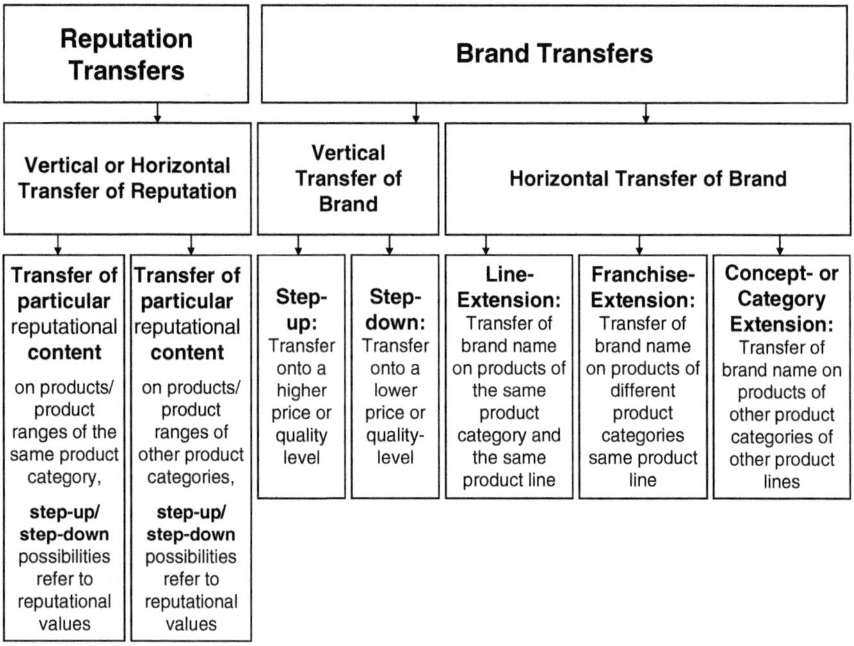

Fig. 3.6 Typs of reputation- or brand transfers

carried out on understanding the factors that determine whether customers form positive or negative attitudes toward products that are introduced through brand extensions. The conclusion of these authors is that brand extensions from well-liked brands are accepted by the customers if the new product "fits" to the existing parent brand. On the other hand, the risk of dilution or damage to the perceptual equity of the brand has been discussed (Keller and Sood 2003). A well accepted strategy to enter new markets is to take advantage of an existing brand's equity and launch brand extensions into related product categories (Aaker 1991). Thus, marketers are concerned about the negative impact that brand extensions may have on the parent brand (Schwager 2004; Keller 2003). Nevertheless, the empirical evidence on this issue is mixed. Loken and John (1993) claim that unsuccessful extensions can dilute a brand by diminishing the attribute-specific beliefs that are associated with it. Other studies find that brand equity is not diluted by unsuccessful extensions (John et al. 1998; Keller and Aaker 1992), and may even be enhanced if high-quality products are added to the brand portfolio (Dacin and Smith 1994). The concept of brand transfer needs to be separated into vertical and horizontal transfers, whereas the concept of reputation transfer unites both types of transfer, but is closely related to CR itself. A vertical step-up or step-down reputation transfer onto a lower or higher price or quality level may only be successful if this fits to the company's reputation and is closely related to its values and identity.

According to Keller (2003), typically 80–90% of new products are line extensions. With regard to the empirical study introduced in this work, the medical devices company is carrying out a category extension into pharmaceuticals. Tauber (1981) identifies seven general strategies for establishing a category or franchise extension:

1. Introducing the same product in a different form (chewing gums and chewy candy).
2. Introducing products that contain the brand's distinctive taste, ingredient, or component (a certain cake is available as a cookie).
3. Introducing companion products for the brand (Levi's jeans and sweat shirts).
4. Introducing products relevant to the customer franchise of the brand (motorcycles and bicycles).
5. Introducing products that capitalize on the firm's perceived expertise (new research products within the product range).
6. Introducing products that reflect the brand's distinctive benefit, attribute, or feature (new types of Rolex watches).
7. Introducing products that capitalize on the distinctive image or prestige of the brand (like Porsche selling not only cars, but also sunglasses, shoes and suitcases).

In this work, and in line with Helm (2007), Schweizer and Wijnberg (2004), the last strategy on the list is identified not as a brand – or franchise extension – but as a transfer of a brand's reputation: If this new product is advertised using the image or prestige of the parent brand, the reputation of a brand is transferred (see Sect. 3.4.2) (Fig. 3.6).

Table 3.4 Chances and risks of brand extension. Based on Aaker (2003)

Risks	Chances
– Parent brand is not strong enough for brand extension (weak transfer of image) – Image of parent brand does not fit to the brand extension – Only weak synergy effects regarding Marketing mix activities – Brand erosion – Negative spill-over effects on parent brand – Spill-over problem: Image problems of one product are transferred on other products – Neglecting marketing activities of the parent brand may lead to chances for competitors	– Customers transfer the positive image on a new product ("goodwill" transfer) – Advancement of publicity and trust – Synergy effects regarding marketing mix activities – Exploitation of new target groups – Enhancement of brand competence – Revitalization and consolidation of parent brand – Positive spill-over effects on the parent brand

Keller (2003) claims that the main advantage of a well-known and well-liked brand is that customers form expectations over time concerning a brand's performance. These expectations may be transferred, in part, also to the extension product, and may lead to an improvement of parent brand image, while at the same time, reducing the risk perceived by the customer.

"When a brand extension succeeds and is accepted as a member of the extension category, the number of elements that are unique and distinctive to the parent and extension categories decreases, and the number of elements that are common between them increases" (Kumar 2005, p. 184).

As listed in Table 3.4, previous research on the effects of brand extensions have focused on whether the failure, poor quality, or low typicality of an extension has an adverse effect on parent brand evaluations (Keller 2003; Kumar 2005). Quality perceptions and other positive associations are more easily transferred to the extension product when the similarity between the two categories is high (Cohen and Basu 1987).

3.4.2 Levels of Reputation and their Transferability

The ability of transferring the organization's positive reputation when introducing new products and services ensures its long-term success in evolving markets (Schweizer and Wijnberg 1999). Particularly in industrial markets, where function and importance of brands differ from those in consumer markets, the more general concept of transferring a company's reputation is appropriate. Important features referring to a successful transfer of reputation can be listed as follows:

- Concept-consistency perceptions of customers rely on the extension product's ability to accommodate the reputation concept of the parent brand. This requires the transfer of the values and identity of a company to new products and/or services and the related brands when entering new markets. Reputational content

of the corporate level of reputation may be derived from inside and outside a company's boundaries (Schweizer and Wijnberg, 1999).
- Findings (e.g., Doney and Cannon 1997; Zaheer et al. 1998) identify a positive relationship between the extent of external trust and reputation. This explains the transferability of reputational content between the individual and the corporate level. The level of individual reputation can be defined as including reputations of particular individuals who are employed by the company or who represent it, i.e., sales representatives.

As already discussed, previous studies on CR have investigated the multi-dimensionality of a company's reputation (e.g., Fombrun and Shanley 1990; Meffert and Bierwirth 2002). The transference of reputation between the individual product level and the corporate level can work both ways, either CR being perceived as a substitute for individual reputation, or vice versa (Schweizer and Wijnberg 1999). In this study, the focus is on transference from the corporation to the new product range.

With this transference pattern, the reputation of the company rubs off on the new product range; it is attributed with characteristics which are derived from the perception of the company. This mechanism has also been observed in a study where different reputations of companies forming an alliance had an impact on the level of trust between the representatives of the companies involved (Smith and Barclay 1997) and where CR generally impacted the trust in representatives of a certain company (Dasgupta 1988). To the author's best knowledge, and in contrast to brand extension literature, no theoretical framework has yet been established for the investigation of reputation transfer.

3.5 The Relevance of Direct Marketing Media to Build CR

When pursuing a relationship marketing strategy, the supplier has in mind the welfare of its customers. To generate relationship benefits, a customer needs to perceive value when consuming goods, services or information, and this can only be achieved if suppliers improve the quality of customer contacts. Therefore, a new or improved way of communicating with customers as well as the management of activities and handling of interactions is an essential part of relationship marketing (Grönroos 2000). The belief that the success of relationship marketing efforts is positively related to the amount and specificity of consumer information, however, raises questions about what media are used by the customers and if these media have an impact on a company's reputation. Saxton (1998) asserts that CR is the reflection of an organization over time as seen through the eyes of its stakeholders and expressed through their thoughts and words. Therefore, the company's responsibility is to shape those thoughts and words (Forman and Argenti 2005).

In an age of 24/7 media coverage, the Internet, and always-on communications, coupled with the growing interest in sentational news, companies and even entire industries have to face the influence of direct marketing media and WOM on reputation. Nevertheless, to the author's best knowledge, the connectivity between direct marketing media, reputation and reputation transfer has not yet been empirically investigated. This chapter highlights the importance of corporate communication and direct marketing media in building corporate reputation (CR) and introducing new product ranges.

Corporate communication (CC) can be defined as "an instrument by means of which all consciously used forms of internal and external communications are harmonized as effectively and efficiently as possible to create a favorable basis for relationships with the groups upon which the company is dependent" (van Riel 1995, p. 26). In general, the literature on CC focuses on the value of corporate communication to brand management and reputation management (Forman et al. 2005) as an important means of targeting or informing stakeholders (Wiedmann and Prauschke 2006, Dentchev and Heene 2004).

Corporate image and CR are driven mostly by the need to offer good value to the stakeholders, corporate communication plays an important role in image formation (Dowling 2001): It can publicize an organization's strengths and successes and help position the ideal image of the company, the brand or the product.

Direct marketing is a special, individual aspect of classic marketing (Wagner and Parwoll forthcoming). It is the tool for informing and targeting customers, for example, and involves all sorts of marketing media meeting the requirements, expectations and interests of stakeholder groups (Mann 2004). Direct response marketing media focus on direct contact to target groups like customers and opinion leaders, among others (Krafft et al. 2007).

Direct marketing media can be used to reach all stakeholder groups, possibly with different messages: to influence the interpretations and perceptions of stakeholders, for example (Rindova and Fombrun 1998, Forman and Argenti 2005). Knowledge about what media customers use to be informed about new products and services is essential for companies to use these media efficiently for reputation building. Bruhn (2003) distinguishes three types of direct marketing:

- Passive direct marketing, used specifically to introduce new products, is characterized by only a small degree of individualization (mailings, mail packages including brochures, etc.). Generally, the consumer is given no possibility for response.
- Response-oriented direct marketing offers the possibility to react (see-and-write-card, electronic newsletters, mailings, Internet sites with integrated possibility to react, and online hotlines). Regarding electronic newsletters, the degree of individualization may vary, and the kind of information sent can be selected and requested by the addressee (Mann, 2004). However, the way to react is determined by the sender, which restricts individual communication.
- Interaction-oriented direct marketing is individually designed. Face-to-face communication, telephone calls, meetings during fairs, Internet relay chats, and via virtual communities. Both communication partners need to act flexibly to avoid an ineffective or sudden end.

Studies by Wiedmann (2004) and Dowling (2001) confirm that a company's communication policy influences public CR. Also, Fombrun and Rindova (1998, p. 210) note that "communications that make a firm transparent enable stakeholders to appreciate the firm's operations better, and so facilitate ascribing to a better reputation".

3.6 Defining and Quantifying Culture

This section aims to propose a definition of culture and highlight its impact on buying behavior in organizations. It also gives a short overview of different cultural approaches and focuses especially on Hofstede's cultural values. The last subsection highlights the cultural particularities of the countries involved in this survey.

Increasingly, international markets create not only opportunities but also challenges for companies in B-to-B markets (Homburg et. al. 2005). More open and integrated markets make it more complex to understand customer needs and to what extent culture affects relationships. Culture, which supports openness of communication and involvement in decision making and sharing of information, will also encourage and reward trustworthy behavior (Firth-Cozens 2004) and relationships.

Thus, when its customers are located in various countries, companies must be responsive to local cultures (Bower 2005). Corporate culture influences managers' perceptions and motivations (Barney 1991), corporate identity affects how managers both interpret and react to environmental circumstances (Dutton and Dukerich 1991). Shared cultural values and a strong sense of identity therefore guide managers, not only in defining what their companies stand for, but also in justifying their strategies for interacting with key stakeholders (Porac and Thomas 1990).

How to define culture? Taylor provides one of the earliest definitions of culture: "...the complex whole which includes knowledge, belief, art, morals and custom and any other capabilities acquired by a man as a member of society." (1871, in McCort and Malhotra 1993, p. 97). Kroeber and Kluckhohn argue that "Culture consists of patterns, explicit and implicit, of and for behavior acquired and transmitted by symbols, constituting the distinctive achievement of human groups, including their embodiments in artifacts. The essential core of culture consists of traditional (i.e., historically derived and selected) ideas and especially their attached values. Cultural systems may, on the one hand, be considered as products of action, and on the other, as conditioning elements of further action." (Kroeber and Kluckhohn 1952, in Brislin et al. 1973, p. 4).

In the literature, national culture is defined as the values, beliefs and assumptions learned in early childhood that distinguish one group of people from another (Beck and Moore 1985; Hofstede 1991). This definition corresponds to Hofstede's (1991) notion of national culture as software of the mind and with Jaeger's (1986, p. 179) "common theories of behavior or mental programs that are shared". National culture is embedded in everyday life. In this work, "national culture" is defined in line with Hofstede (2001) as the homogeneity of characteristics that separates one human group from another, provides a society's characteristic profile with respect to norms, values, and institutions, and affords an understanding of how societies manage exchanges.

There is empirical evidence that national cultures vary and that a variety of management practices, including strategic decision making (Schneider and DeMeyer 1991; deMooij and Hofstede 2002; Homburg et al. 2005) and leadership style (Dorfman and Howell 1988) are influenced by cultural impacts. These studies indicate that different cultures are likely to interpret and respond to the same strategic issue in different ways. Strategic issues are external and internal events, conditions or trends of an organization which affect the company's performance (Schneider and DeMeyer 1991). However, the impact of culture often tends to be neglected in the investigation into different stakeholder attitudes (e.g., Gardberg 2002; Walsh and Wiedmann 2004).

Attempts to understand cultural systems traditionally focus on values (Burgess and Steenkamp 2006). Cultural value priorities affect behaviors that interest marketers by shaping and justifying individual, group, and organizational beliefs and goals. The cultural framing of vendors and customers impacts all types of businesses, and consequently also has an impact on the success of reputation transfer.

The culture of the national environment in which an organization operates affects the management process through the collective mental programming of its members and managers (Trompenaars and Hampden-Turner 1997). Culture, according to the above definition, is neither observed nor measured directly. Instead, indicators, grasping particular aspects of the knowledge reservoir, are considered. A quantification of culture according to this definition is essential to derive sound results which are superior to conceptual considerations and anecdotal evidence.

Although in relationship marketing literature, the concepts of trust, commitment and knowledge resources play an important role, researchers have yet to gain an understanding of the influence of national culture on theses key resources (Griffith et al. 2006; deMooij and Hofstede 2002). Researchers have explored the influence of national culture on specific relationships or knowledge constructs (e.g., Doney et al. 1998). Prior research has largely overlooked the influence of national cultures on the development of relationships between suppliers and buying organizations.

The failure to address national culture's influence on reputation building and the different uses of direct marketing media has resulted in limited theoretical and managerial insights into how culture influences a company's intangible resources. Moreover, much of the existing international business research on customer relationships consists of single-country studies (Griffith et al. 2006), and research work focused on CR has been mostly conducted in the US (Fombrun 2007).

The competitive advantages regarding relationship marketing derived from correctly adapted management practices come from the congruence between management practices and the characteristics of customers' national culture: better performance outcomes (Denison and Mishra 1995). Given the existing literature's limitations, this work makes its contribution by specifically addressing the following research questions:

- Does national culture influence the impact of a company's reputation on organizational buying decisions?
- Does national culture influence the possibility of transferring a company's reputation on new product ranges?

To answer these questions, Hofstede's (2001) multidimensional, national cultural framework is integrated in the survey to theorize differences in relationship resources (i.e., the influence of relationship quality on word of mouth, reputation and reputation transfer), and knowledge resources (i.e., the influence of perceived innovativeness on reputation) in intercultural B-to-B buyer-seller relationships. Given the theoretically meaningful national cultural distinction between Russia, Australia, Germany, Finland and Spain, and the continued importance of business relationships between a German-based company and companies in other countries, understanding how organizational buyers from other countries perceive a company's reputation has significant theoretical and managerial implications.

3.6.1 Cultural Frameworks–an Overview

A lot of different models of national culture can be found in the literature assuming that societies vary along specific cultural dimensions. Kluckhohn and Strodtbeck (1961) classified cultures in terms of value orientation. Dimensions included in their framework were: the nature of people, a person's relation to nature and to others, time and space orientation, and doing versus being.

The Rokeach Value Survey (RVS) is a survey instrument introduced by Rokeach (1969) to operationalize the value concept. The RVS is characterized by two different kinds of values: instrumental values apply to many different countries and are socially desirable, while terminal values refer to idealized end states of existence or lifestyles. Clearly, the value of being broadminded is the antagonism of being dogmatic in the sense of Rokeach (1973).

The latest studies based on the Rokeach Value Survey are related to ethical questions (Marques 2009; Sheppard and Young 2007) or refer to gender differences (Kracher and Marble 2007; Stedham et al. 2007).

Hall (1976) separates cultures into high- and low-context and refers to the impact of context on how communication occurs within a culture. Triandis (1994) argues that cultures differ with regard to the information they gain from the environment. He classifies culture types in simple versus complex, individualist versus collectivist, and tight versus loose. During the 1990s, several studies were published based on Hall's cultural framework (e.g., Singelis and Brown 1995; Gudykunst et al. 1996).

Trompenaars and Hampden-Turner (1998) refer to universal problems that lead to corresponding cultural dimensions: Individualism versus communitarianism, universalism versus particularism, specific versus diffuse, affective versus neutral, achievement versus ascription, and so on. The basic assumption is that the culture of any country becomes salient in dealing with the following three main problems: employees' attitude toward their fellow men, time and the environment.

Most recent cultural studies based on the cultural dimensions of Trompenaars and Hampden-Turner (1998) refer to cultural effects on job satisfaction and organizational commitment (Lok and Crawford 2004) as well as on information technology usage behavior (Calhoun et al. 2002) or business ethics (Moon and Woolliams 2000).

The Schwartz Value Survey (1994) is based on an empirical study of over 60,000 individuals in 63 countries worldwide. In this approach, the responses are characterized by ten motivational values and seven cultural-level dimensions. Each of these dimensions is a composite index of a set of values which varies according to the culture.

Studies of other scholars based on the Schwartz Value Survey were mostly published in the 1990s and refer to managerial work values. More recent studies have been published by Schwartz himself (Schwartz and Boehnke 2004), evaluating the structure of human values.

Although each of the above cultural frameworks has certain advantages, this work focuses on four of the five dimensions identified by Hofstede (2001). Hofstede's model is generally accepted as the most comprehensive (Kogut and Singh 1988) and remains the dominant, most cited model of culture used in international business research (Kirkman, Lowe and Gibson 2006; Griffith et al. 2006; Homburg et al. 2005). Hofstede (2001) used a work-related context and originally applied his framework to human resources management. The framework is increasingly being used in business and marketing studies to compare cultures, to support hypotheses, and as a theoretical framework for comparing cultures even if the dimensions are measured with new or adopted instruments (e.g., Milner et al. 1993; Homburg et al. 2005; Griffith et al. 2006; Lu et al. 1999).

The work of Hofstede (2001) is most applicable to this study, because the norms and value approach underlying Hofstede's framework is directly related to the attitudinal and behavioral approach in the current study (see Doney et al. 1998). One major criticism of Hofstede's assessment of culture is that the scales assess national organizational culture, but since this application domain is selling products to hospitals, this feature is an advantage in this application. The organizational context has been identified as important for research examining individual responses concerning job-related attitudes (Rousseau 1978; Sutton and Rousseau 1979). As in Hofstede's original survey, organizational members are involved in this empirical research project (purchasers, pharmacists and product users like doctors and nurses). His conclusions regarding "cultures in organizations" are therefore applicable.

Generally, the model's validity, reliability, stability and usefulness have been confirmed over time (Hofstede 2001; Newburry and Yakova 2006). Four indices of culture were developed during the 1960s and 1970s based on surveys of IBM employees: power distance (PDI), uncertainty avoidance (UAI), individualism (IDV) and masculinity (MAS). As only Western countries were included in the survey, the fifth dimension, long-term orientation, which focuses on virtues leading to future rewards, versus short-term orientation, referring to virtues associated with the past and the present, has not been taken into account. The scores of this dimension do not vary significantly in Western cultures. The next chapter explains the different dimensions in more detail.

3.6.2 Hofstede's Cultural Dimensions

To quantify cultural differences in the relationship between key company resources and customers' attitude toward the company, Hofstede's (2001) multidimensional, national cultural framework is used in this work. According to the classic definition of Hofstede (2001, p. 9), culture is a "collective programming of the mind that distinguishes the members of one group or category of people from another". Hofstede (2001, p. 15) also clearly distinguishes between values and culture: "In studying 'values', we compare individuals, in studying 'culture', we compare societies."

Hofstede (2001) identified five dimensions along which countries can be classified: power distance index (PDI), individualism (IDV), uncertainty avoidance index (UAI), masculinity (MAS) and long-term orientation (LTO). He argues that a country can be positioned along these five dimensions to provide an overall summary of its cultural type. Hofstede's five dimensions are describes as follows:

PDI is the way that society addresses inequalities among people when they occur (Homburg et al. 2004). This dimension describes the extent to which the less powerful members of organizations and institutions (like the family) accept and expect that power is distributed unequally. This represents inequality (more versus less), but defined from below, not from above. According to Hofstede (2001, p. 29), PDI is related "to the different solutions to the basic problem of human inequality."

IDV refers to how people in a society perceive themselves in relation to others. Individualism versus collectivism refers to the degree to which individuals are integrated into primary groups (Hofstede 2001). The word "collectivism" in this sense has no political meaning: it refers to the group, not to the state. The level of individualism or collectivism in a society affects the organization's members' reasons for complying with organizational requirements. A meta-analysis by Bond and Smith (1996) indicates that collectivist cultures tend to show higher levels of conformity than individualistic cultures, whereas individualistic cultures place higher emphasis on individual initiative (Hofstede 2001). Thus, this cultural dimension is the most commonly used to study, compare and explain organizational behavior in B-to-B or B-to-C settings (e.g., Homburg et al. 2004).

Masculinity (MAS) versus femininity, refers to the distribution of emotional roles between the genders, which is another fundamental issue for any society to which a number of solutions are found. According to Hofstede (2001), masculinity is the degree to which a society exhibits assertive versus nurturing behavior. In the sense of Hofstede, masculinity and femininity refer to the dominant gender role patterns in the vast majority of traditional and modern societies. Hofstede's (1980) studies reveal that women's values differ less across societies than men's values. In cultures with high scores in MAS, the dominant value is success; masculine values reflect emphasis on work goals, assertiveness, and earnings (Hofstede and Associates 1998; Srite and Karahanna 2006). Status, performance, competitiveness, independence and achievement are also important in cultures with high scores in MAS, and role differentiation between males and females is large (de Mooij 1998). The dominant values in countries with low scores in MAS care for others and value quality of life, status is not so important. Role differentiation between males and females is small.

UAI measures the degree to which societies perceive themselves as threatened by uncertain, risky, ambiguous, or undefined situations (Homburg et al. 2004). According to Hofstede (2001, p. 29), UAI is related to the "level of stress in a society in the face of an unknown future." People in uncertainty avoiding countries are more emotional and motivated by inner nervous energy. The opposite type, uncertainty accepting cultures, are more tolerant of opinions which differ from their own, and they try to have as few rules as possible. It indicates to what extent a culture programs its members to feel either uncomfortable or comfortable in unstructured situations. Unstructured situations are novel, unknown, surprising, and unusual (Hofstede 1980). Uncertainty avoiding cultures try to minimize the possibility of such situations by strict laws and rules, safety and security measures, and on the philosophical and religious level by a belief in absolute truth: "There can only be one truth and we have it" (de Mooij 1998). In terms of information processing and persuasion, uncertainty-oriented individuals tend to process arguments and use few heuristic cues (Petty and Cacioppo 1981). On the other hand, certainty-oriented individuals engage in less systematic information processing and rely more on heuristic cues.

Above Table 3.5 outlines Hofstede's dimensions. Hofstede (2001) added a fifth dimension after conducting an additional international study with a survey instrument developed with Chinese employees and managers. This dimension, long-term orientation (LTO), based on Confucian dynamism, was applied to 23 countries. Hofstede's five dimensions can also be found to correlate with other country, cultural, and religious paradigms.

Four out of the five countries included in the survey are Western-type countries; according to Hofstede (2001), all five countries score similarly in LTO and are short-term oriented. For this reason, this dimension has been excluded from the evaluation of the survey.

Although Hofstede's (2001) dimensions provide a way to classify a country's culture, countries share similarities as well as differences across cultural dimensions. Selecting the countries included in the survey, one goal was to find five countries which differ significantly regarding the scores of Hofstede's dimensions.

In the field of RM, the existence of trust and commitment between the parties, as well as the intense exchange of information, are considered to be important for business relationships (Homburg and Krohmer 2006; Huff and Kelley 2003; Morgan and Hunt 1994). An important question is whether societal culture influences the tendency of individuals and organizations to trust (Huff and Kelley 2003).

Table 3.5 Hofstede's scores regarding the five countries included in the survey Based on http://www.geert-hofstede.com

Individualism (IDV) vs. collectivism	Masculinity (MAS) vs. femininity	Power distance (PDI)	Uncertaintyavoidance (UAI)
Australia: 93	Germany: 72	Russia: 93	Russia: 95
Germany: 73	Australia: 68	Spain: 50	Spain: 80
Finland: 68	Spain: 48	Australia: 32	Germany: 60
Spain: 53	Russia: 36	Germany: 30	Finland: 54
Russia: 39	Finland: 30	Finland: 28	Australia 48

Above Table 3.5 outlines Hofstede's dimensions. Hofstede (2001, p. 159) argues that trusting someone "implies some tolerance of ambiguity and a potential loss of control." Thus, he concludes that cultures scoring low in the dimension of uncertainty avoidance (UAI) tend to trust others more easily. Griffin (1975) suggests that the protection of one's reputation is a force for being trustworthy. In addition, Hofstede (2001) argues that preferential treatment of one customer over others is considered bad business practice and unethical in individualist societies. In collectivist societies, to treat one's friends better than others is natural and ethical, and sound business practice. Hofstede's (2001) findings on business practices imply that the importance and the impact of a positive reputation differ across cultures, although this topic is not explicitly discussed in his study. "Although supplier commitment is not a necessity in most B-to-B relationships, it benefits the customer by reducing uncertainty" (Homburg et al. 2005, p. 9). Uncertainty is more prevalent in cultures scoring high in UAI; according to Hofstede (2001), these countries show more fear of the unknown and more fear of tomorrow. "In collectivist societies, the personal relationship prevails over the task and over the company and should be established first" (Hofstede 2001, p. 239). In contrast, in individualist societies, the task and the company prevail over any personal relationships. Commitment influences the supplier evaluation process and serves as a choice criterion that qualifies one supplier over the others. Nevertheless, a supplier's commitment is not a qualifier during partner selection, because the enduring desire and effort to maintain a valued relationship is not a necessary condition for all B-to-B relationships. Homburg et al. (2004) claim this to be an additional "nice-to-have" feature.

3.6.3 Hofstede's Cultural Characteristics of Countries under Consideration

According to Hofstede (2001), organizations are symbolic entities working according to implicit models in the minds of their members. The crucial dimensions are power distance and uncertainty avoidance. Power distance has an impact on "who decides what, and uncertainty avoidance is involved in answering the question how one can ensure that what should be done will be done" (Hofstede 2001, p. 375). Therefore, national culture, in which an organization operates, affects the management process through the collective mental programming of its members and managers (Trompenaars and Hampden-Turner 1997).

This chapter highlights the cultural differences and characteristics of the five countries included in the survey. As the establishment of commitment is fundamental to a company's success in its operations (Morgan and Hunt 1994; Griffith et al. 2006), special attention is focused on differences in the underlying intercultural associations of relationship resources (i.e., the attitude toward trust and commitment, and relationship quality), knowledge resources (the importance of information sharing: WOM, use of media, perceived innovativeness of a company) and their linkage (i.e., the influence of relationship quality or innovativeness on WOM).

3.6.3.1 Australia

The Geert-Hofstede analysis for Australia reflects the high level of individuality. This refers to a preference for a loosely knit social framework in which people are supposed to take care of themselves and their families (Hofstede 1980). The Individualism (IDV) index for Australia is 93. This individuality is reinforced in Australian's daily lives and must be considered when traveling and doing business in their country. Privacy is considered the cultural norm and attempts at personal ingratiating may meet with rebuff. Although trust is more easily developed in lower UAI societies like Australia (Hofstede 2001), it is difficult for trust to transfer from one entity to another (Doney et al. 1998).

Given this cultural foundation, Australian companies are expected to attempt to minimize social interdependence in its interactions with others (Hofstede 2001; Triandis 1994). Companies "tend to focus on benefits to the individual" (Cutler et al. 1997, p. 43). People in highly individualistic cultures like Australia tend not to follow norms (Roth 1995). Although companies from this cultural type engage in relationships, they tend to restrain themselves from fully trusting their partners to minimize potential opportunistic behavior of others, to whom they are not strongly tied by cultural norms or group goals (Griffith et al. 2006). Although trust builds commitment, in strong individualistic societies, full commitment to its interorganizational partners is difficult to achieve (Hofstede 2001).

Australia, Finland and Germany are countries with small power distance (indices between 28 and 32), compared to the world average of 55. This is indicative of a greater equality and low hierarchy ranks across societal levels, including government and organizations. It reinforces a cooperative interaction across power levels and creates a more stable cultural environment.

3.6.3.2 Finland

The Geert-Hofstede analysis for Finland reflects extremely low levels in MAS (index of 30) and PDI. This is indicative of a very feminine country with low hierarchy levels. Finnish society, which is based on a strong need for technology (less traditional agriculture), fosters openness with information and welcomes innovations and changes. Decision structures are decentralized, managers are involved in relevant purchasing decisions (Hofstede 2001). As Finland also scores very low in UAI, the uncertainty inherent in life is easily accepted, and people have a trusting attitude toward others.

3.6.3.3 Germany

In this survey, Germany scores highest in MAS (72) and second lowest in PDI (30) compared to the other countries involved. Germany can be viewed as a very masculine society, which nevertheless has low hierarchy levels. Individualistic cultures, which tend to focus on individual benefits, typically value personal achievements (Hofstede 2001), and consumers expect greater supplier flexibility to meet their individualistic needs (Salter and Niswander 1995). Employees are expected to act as "economic men" and commitment to the organization is higher than in cultures scoring low in IDV. Individualistic societies tend to see advertising as a useful source of new product information and rely on the media. In these societies (Germany, Finland, and Australia), a larger share of public and private money is spent on healthcare.

According to Hofstede (2001), cultures scoring low in UAI are expected to show more confidence in the advertising industry, although these societies are more concerned with data and facts.

3.6.3.4 Russia

The Geert-Hofstede analysis for Russia indicates just estimated scores. Russia was not included directly in Hofstede's country survey. The analysis reflects the extremely high level in UAI (index of 95) and PDI, with an index of 93. Countries scoring high in UAI show low professionalism, high uniformity, high conservatism, high secrecy (Salter and Niswander 1995) and stronger interpersonal and interorganizational ties (Money et al. 1998). Authority is based on tradition, and as decision structures are centralized, managers rely on formal rules (Hofstede 2001). What is different, first of all, is that dangerous innovations can be successful simply if they are supported from upper hierarchy levels. Information is constrained by hierarchy. These cultures tend to focus more on problem solving and prevention as well as on control (Roth 1995).

In this study, Russia is the society scoring lowest in IDV (index value: 39). According to Hofstede (2001), this leads to relying on social networks for information rather than using the media as a useful source of new product information. Concerning the presentation of data and facts, feminine cultures are more interested in "the stories behind the facts" (Hofstede 2001, p. 311). DeMooij (1998, p. 71) claims that the skepticism of feminine cultures like Russia and Finland toward advertising stems from their markets having been "swamped by advertising reflecting US masculine values, thus advertising is not made for the local culture and is not liked." The masculine orientation of imported advertising from the US is a lesser problem for other masculine markets such as Australia and Germany.

3.6.3.5 Spain

The Geert-Hofstede analysis for Spain indicates that it is an average society in terms of the dimension of MAS, scoring high in UAI and above average in PDI. Low scores in IDV lead to low commitment of employees toward the organization. In business, personal relationships prevail over task and company. Members of Spanish society believe in collective decisions. Persons in low IDV societies tend not to believe in advertising or other direct marketing media, but in social networks for information. Innovations are less important, and fewer invention patents are granted within these societies. According to Hofstede's (2001) findings, in Spain and Russia less money is spent on healthcare.

Chapter 4
Development of Constructs and Related Hypotheses

The theoretical parts I–III of this work have paved the way to generate the constructs and develop the hypotheses for the explorative study, which is based on an empirical survey. Part IV is structured as follows: First, a short overview of the C-OAR-SE procedure (Rossiter 2002) is presented, followed by an introduction of formative versus reflective measurement models as well as moderating and mediating effects. The following sections outline the requirements of the Bonferroni-Holm's test and its execution and demonstrate the development of constructs and related hypotheses. Finally, the structural model of reputation and reputation transfer is introduced.

4.1 The C-OAR-SE Procedure for Scale Development

As the research design of this study is a multi-stage design and essentially follows the C-OAR-SE procedure suggested by Rossiter (2002), this chapter gives a short introduction of this method.

The C-OAR-SE procedure refers to a sixfold classification of measures, allowing for both reflective and formative perspectives as well as single- and multi-item scales (Diamantopoulos 2005). How to establish content validity is the main purpose of this method (Rossiter 2002, 2005): "construct definition, object classification, attribute classification, rater identification, scale formation, and enumeration and reporting". The C-OAR-SE procedure draws mainly on the works of Bollen and Lennox (1991), Edwards and Bagozzi (2000), and Fornell and Bookstein (1982), on attribute classification and posits that a new scale development procedure in marketing is needed (Rossiter 2002). In line with Jarvis et al. (2003), Rossiter (2002, 2005) argues that the traditional procedure, with its strict emphasis on factor analysis and internal consistency reliability has led to the delineation of conceptually necessary items and the

C. Falkenreck, *Reputation Transfer to Enter New B-to-B Markets*, Contributions to Management Science,
DOI 10.1007/978-3-7908-2357-8_4,

addition of unnecessary and conceptually inappropriate items just to obtain a high alpha value.

According to Rossiter (2002) the first step of the C-OAR-SE procedure for scale development requires that constructs be conceptually described in terms of the object and the attribute (dimension of judgment) and their components. Furthermore, the construct has to by specified by a certain rater entity. In applying C-OAR-SE, expert judges are used to ratify the classification of the object. Rossiter (2002) distinguishes between group raters (e.g., industrial buyers) and expert raters (in this study: sample of market managers). The object part can be classified as concrete singular or have multiple components (Rossiter 2002; Bergkvist and Rossiter 2007). The goal is that nearly every rater describes the object in an identical way.

Subsequently, the item parts of the object or construct are put together with the item parts of the attribute, including all the main components in a scale. Attribute classification decisions refer to the general construct definition of formative (formed) versus reflective (eliciting, see Sect. 4.2) or concrete (e.g., a single item construct). Rossiter (2002) recommends randomizing the order of the multiple-item scales while carrying out the survey, which has also been accounted for in the CATI survey of this study.

With reference to the enumeration rules, different objects and attribute types lead to variations: "Enumeration rules imply that indexes will receive absolute total scores and items for reflective attributes will receive averaged scores" (Rossiter 2002, p. 325). For indexes as well as reflective constructs, Rossiter (2002) recommends using a scale of 0–10, where 10 is the maximum score, rather than open-ended total scores. He also proposes a polarity of scales and scales having a common-sense meaning and adds that "no number of additional items, the standard way to increase reliability, would compensate for lack of validity" and produce a better score (Rossiter 2002, p. 328). To Rossiter (2002, p. 332), reliability measure should be regarded as no more than a precision of score estimate, and not as an "ersatz estimate of evidence of validity".

Unlike Diamantopoulos and Winklhofer (2001), Rossiter did not confine this treatment to formative measurement. He proposed a general procedure for developing marketing measures. For this reason, the C-OAR-SE approach is discussed controversially in the literature. Finn and Kayande (2004) suggest that while Rossiter's procedure refocuses on the conceptualization of constructs, it has the potential to create an important gap by advocating against empirical validation of constructs. Diamantopoulos (2005) identifies some potentially problematic areas under the various steps of C-OAR-SE and also questions the procedure's sole reliance on content validity. In this study, the following steps of C-OAR-SE procedure have been carried out:

Following the recommendations of Diamantopoulos and Winklhofer (2001) and Rossiter (2002, 2005), the next section outlines the different types of measurements related to a construct (Table 4.1).

Table 4.1 Applying the C-OAR-SE procedure

Steps of C-OAR-SE procedure	C-OAR-SE procedure applied in this study
Construct definition	Initial definitions of all constructs
Object classification Attribute classification	Interviews with two marketing research experts about the classification of objects and attributes. One object was defined as concrete singular. In addition, concrete, formative and eliciting attributes were found
Construct definition	Object and attribute classification was added to the definition of constructs
Rater identification	This step was omitted – no rater entity judged further on the object-on-attribute finalizations
Scale formation	Appropriate rating scales were discussed, and four-point Likert-scales as well as rankings from 1 to 5 were used
Enumeration	This step was omitted – no indexes or averages were used to report an estimate of the reliability

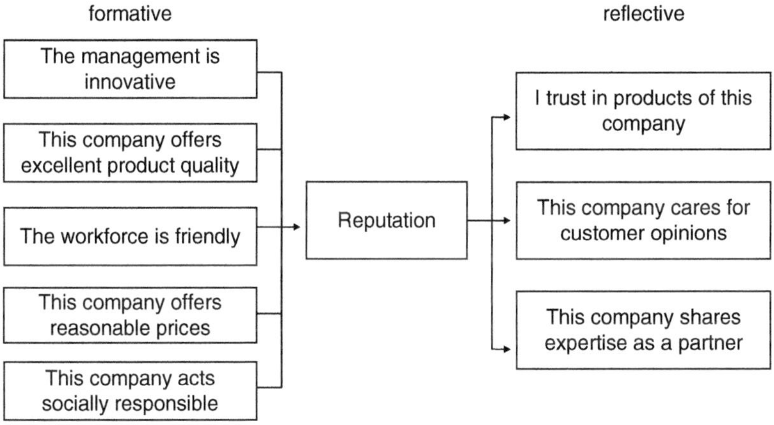

Fig. 4.1 Reputation: A formative or a reflective construct?

4.2 Formative Versus Reflective Measurement Models

A construct is a "conceptual term used to describe a phenomenon of theoretical interest" (Edwards and Bagozzi 2000, p. 156–157). Structural equation models include relationships among sets of latent constructs. The assessment of these variables has a long tradition in social science (Churchill 1979; Nunally 1978). Related measurement scales for such constructs are either formative or reflective in nature (e.g., Bollen and Lennox 1991; Diamantopoulos and Winklhofer 2001).

Figure 4.1 shows that the measurement of a construct it is solely dependent on the content: The formative indicators are viewed as an explanatory combination and are all referring to different components or fields of reputation. With reference to the reflective formation of construct, all indicators are related to a perceptual, subjective view of reputation.

Figure 4.1 indicates that the use of an incorrect measurement model undermines the content validity of constructs, misrepresents the structural relationship between them and also diminishes the usefulness of management theories (Coltman et al. 2008). With reflective (or effect) measurement models, causality flows from the latent construct to the indicator. When causality flows in the opposite direction – from the indicator to the construct, a formative (or causal) index is generated (Edwards and Bagozzi 2000; Diamantopoulos and Winklhofer 2001).

The following subsections describe the attribute classification of constructs in more detail and offer an overview of theoretical and empirical considerations in the literature.

4.2.1 *Reflective Measures*

"Most researchers in the social sciences assume that indicators are effect indicators. Cause indicators are neglected despite their appropriateness in many instances" (Bollen 1989, p. 65). The reflective measurement model is based on classic test theory (Lord and Novick 1968), whereas measures denote effects of an underlying latent construct (Bollen and Lennox 1991). Causality leads from the construct to the indicator, and according to the literature, these indicators are "reflective" (Fornell and Bookstein 1982), "effect" (Bollen and Lennox 1991) and "eclicting" (Rossiter 2002). Figure 4.1 indicates the latent variable ξ representing the common cause shared by all items x_i reflecting the construct (Diamantopolous et al. 2008) (Fig. 4.2).

Each item corresponds to a linear function of its underlying construct plus measurement error. If the measurement error $\delta_i = 0$, the reflective construct would represent a perfect correlation between the indicators (Eberl 2006). This also explains why reflective measurement models must have highly positive correlations of the indicators (Bollen 1984). A change in the reflective variable causes variation in all measures simultaneously (Diamantopolous et al. 2008).

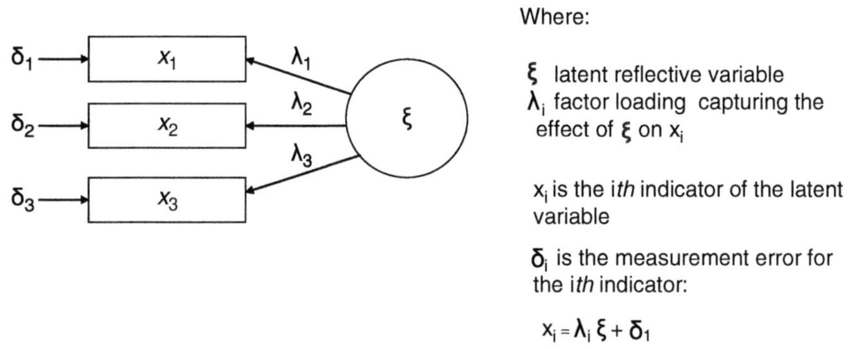

Fig. 4.2 Reflective measurement model
Source: Edwards and Bagozzi (2000)

4.2.2 Formative Measures

With few exceptions (e.g., Law and Wong 1999), formative measures have been a largely neglected topic within organizational research. Nearly all the work in the area of formative measurements has been published by researchers housed in sociology or psychology (e.g., Bollen and Lennox 1991), marketing (e.g., Diamantopoulos and Winklhofer 2001; Jarvis et al. 2003; Rossiter 2002) and strategy (Fornell et al. 1990).

Formative scales are used when a construct is viewed as an explanatory combination of its indicators (Fornell and Bookstein 1982; Fornell 1987). In the literature, these scales are also referred to as "cause" (Bollen and Lennox 1991) and "formed" (Rossiter 2002). The formative construct is defined as a total weighted score across all the items, where each item represents an independent dimension (Fig. 4.3).

Causality flows from the indicators to the construct (Edwards and Bagozzi 2000; Diamantopoulos and Winklhofer 2001). The disturbance or error term ζ is specified at the construct level and comprises all remaining causes of the construct, which are represented in the indicators and are not correlated to the latter. A good formative scale is one that completely exhausts the entire domain of the construct (Diamantopoulos, Riefler and Roth 2008).

Attribute classification of a construct is formative if the construct is viewed as an explanatory combination of its indicators (Fornell and Bookstein 1982: Fornell 1987). All indicators need to represent an independent dimension on its own (Diamantopoulos et al. 2008); for this reason, "omitting an indicator is omitting a part of the construct" (Bollen and Lennox 1991, p. 308).

A formative measurement model, in isolation, is underidentified and can therefore not be estimated (Bollen 1989); the established measures are only applicable for reflective scales. Indicators of formative constructs are therefore tested on multicollinearity to examine possible linear dependencies (see Fig. 4.4). In addition, the nomological validity is tested (Diamantopoulos 1999).

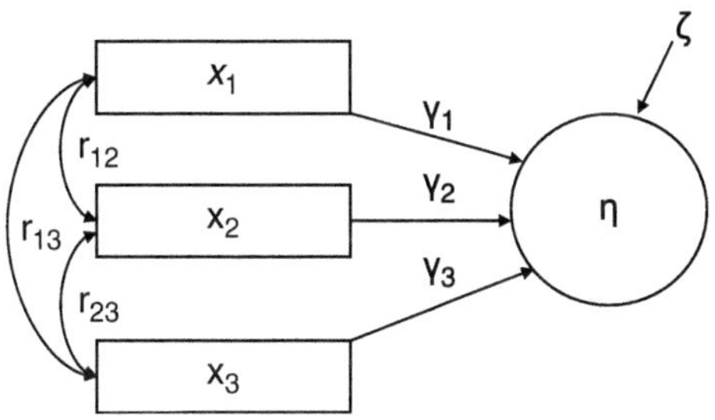

Where:

η latent formative variable

ζ disturbance term

x_i the *ith* indicator of the latent variable η

γ_i coefficient capturing effect of indicator x_i

r_{13} regression coefficients of η on x_3

Fig. 4.3 Formative measurement model
Source: Diamantopoulos et al. (2008)

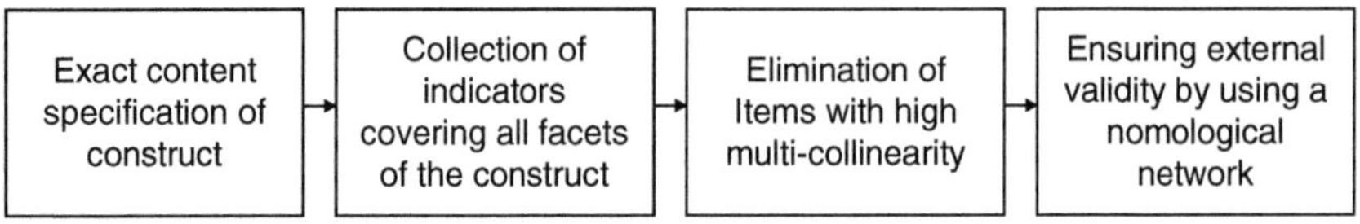

Fig. 4.4 Measure development of formative constructs, based on Diamantopoulos (1999)

4.2.3 Single Item Indicators

During the last few years, a discussion on the predictive validity of multiple-item versus single-item measures of the same construct has emerged. Increasingly, marketing academics advocate the use of multiple-item measures. Others, like Bergkvist and Rossiter (2007) argue that single-item measures are acceptable. According to Drolet and Morrison (2001), even the second or third item contributes little to the information obtained from the first item. In the case of very modest error term correlations between items, the incremental information from each additional item is extremely small. As the increasing information content of the reflective constructs is only marginal after the third indicator, in this survey all reflective constructs have been restricted to up to three items.

Rossiter (2002) proposed one theoretical argument for using a single-item measure rather than a multiple-item measure: If the object is concrete singular (it consists of one object that is uniformed imagined) and the attribute is concrete, too. In addition, Bergkvist and Rossiter (2007) argue that single items can be used if additional items run the risk of tapping into other predictive attributes, i.e., if the items are attempted synonyms of the original attribute. Moreover, if common methods bias in predictor and criterion, a single-item measure can be used.

4.2.4 Overview on Theoretical and Empirical Considerations

Latent variables are widely utilized by organizational researchers in studies of intra- and inter- organizational relationships (Diamantopoulos et al. 2008). As Jarvis, Mackenzie and Podsakoff (2003) observe, conceptual definitions of constructs are specified at a more abstract level, which sometimes includes multiple formative and/or reflective first- or second order dimensions (e.g., Diamantopoulos and Siguaw 2006; Diamantopolous et al. 2008). Diamantopoulos and Siguaw (2006) as well as Rossiter (2002), strongly recommend that the choice between formative and reflective models be driven fundamentally by theory. It should be based on the "auxiliary theory", specifying the "nature and direction of the relationship between constructs and measures" (Edwards and Bagozzi 2000, p. 156). When developing a multi-item organizational measure from a pool of items, the decision, whether the construct is formative or reflective, needs to be made. The only difference resulting from applying a formative versus reflective measurement approach relates to the causal priority between the construct and its indicators (Diamantopoulos and Siguaw 2006). It should be based on the "auxiliary theory" (Blalock 1968; Costner 1969), specifying "the nature and direction of the relationship between constructs and measures" (Edwards and Bagozzi 2000, p. 156).

The following tables show a review of the current literature on reflective and formative measurement models and refer to theoretical and empirical considerations. The theoretical implications refer to the nature and content of the constructs, whereas the empirical considerations are focused on correlations between the items and measurement errors.

Edwards and Bagozzi (2000) recommend the use of a combination of reflective and formative specifications in more complex measurement models. This has been taken into consideration with regard to the empirical survey: eleven constructs are included in the structural model – four constructs are reflective, four are formative, one is a single-item measure, and two other scales consist of international scales on e-readiness (EIU 2007) and culture (Hofstede 2001). The constructs and measurement models are presented in further detail in Sect. 4.5.

Tables 4.2 and 4.3 show the differences between empirical and theoretical considerations when deciding on multi-item measures of constructs and give an overview on the existing literature.

Table 4.2 Theoretical framework for assessing reflective and formative models

Consideration	Reflective model	Formative model	Relevant literature
Theoretical considerations			
1. Nature of construct	Latent construct exists • Latent construct exists independent of the measures used	Latent construct is formed • Latent construct is a combination of its indicators	Borsboom et al. (2003, 2004)
2. Direction of causality between items and latent construct	Causality from construct to item • Variation in the construct causes variation in the item measures • Variation in item measures does not cause variation in the construct	Causality from construct to item • Variation in the construct does not cause variation in the item measure • Variation in item measures causes variation in the construct	Edwards and Bagozzi (2000) Rossiter (2002) Jarvis et al. (2003) Diamantopoulos et al. (2008)
3. Characteristics of items used tomeasure the construct	Items are manifest by the construct • Items share a common theme • Items are interchangeable • Adding or dropping an item does not change the conceptual domain of the construct	Items define the construct • Items need not share a common theme • Items are not interchangeable • Adding or dropping an item may change the conceptual domain of the construct	Rossiter (2002) Jarvis et al. (2003) Diamantopoulos et al. (2008)

Source: complied from Coltman et al. (2008)

Table 4.3 Empirical framework for assessing reflective and formative models

Consideration	Reflective model	Formative model	Relevant literature
Empirical considerations			
1. Iteminter correlation	Items should have high positive intercorrelation • Empirical tests: assessing internal consistency and reliability by Cronbach's alpha, average variance extracted, and factor analysis	Items can have any pattern of intercorrelation but should not possess the same directional relationship • Latent construct is a combination of its indicators	Cronbach (1951) Churchill (1979) Diamantopoulos and Siguaw (2006) Diamantopolous et al., 2008
2. Item relationships with construct antecedents and consequences	Items have similar sign and significance of relationships with the antecedents/ consequences as the construct • Empirical tests: establishing content validity by theoretical considerations, assessing convergent and discriminant validity empirically	Items may not have similar significance of relationships with the antecedents/ consequences as the construct • Empirical tests: assessing nomological validity by structural linkage with another criterion variable	Bollen and Lennox (1991) Diamantopoulos and Winklhofer (2001) Diamantopoulos and Siguaw (2006)
3. Measurement error	Identifying the error term in item is possible • common factor analysis	Identifying the error term is not possible if the formative measurement model is estimated in isolation	Diamantopoulos (2006)

Source: Compiled from Coltman et al. (2008)

4.3 Moderating and Mediating Effects in Causal Models

In this section, we attempt to distinguish between the properties of moderator and mediator variables. First, a clear differentiation needs to be made between these two functions, which are often used interchangeably (Baron and Kenny 1986):

- The moderator function of third variables partitions a focal independent variable into subgroups that establish its domains of maximal effectiveness in regard to a given dependent variable.
- The mediator function of a third variable represents the generative mechanism through which the focal independent variable is able to influence the dependent variable of interest.

A moderator can be defined as a qualitative or quantitative variable that directly affects the direction and/or strength of the relation between a predictor variable and a dependent variable (Baron and Kenny 1986). Although they may influence

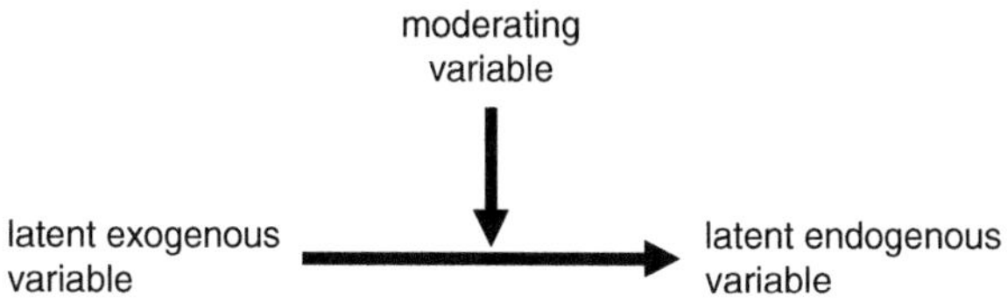

Fig. 4.5 Moderator model
Source: Eggert et al. (2005)

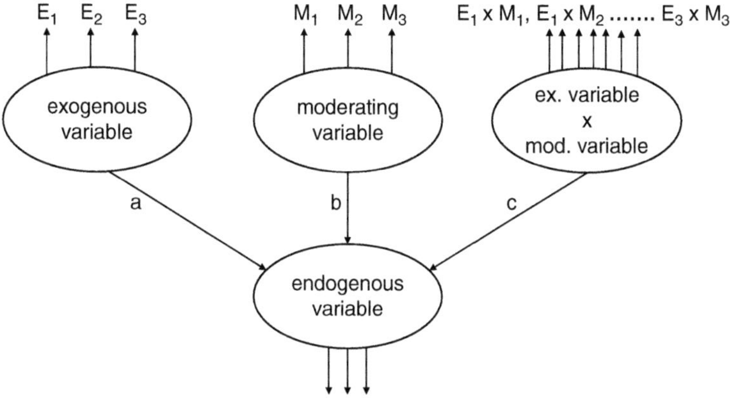

Fig. 4.6 Modeling moderating effects in PLS using reflective constructs
Source: Eggert et al. (2005)

complex formative and reflective effects, moderating effects are rarely examined in economic research (Homburg and Giering 2001).

The principle of a moderating effect is presented in Fig. 4.5. To analyze moderating effects using the PLS software, not only the relationship between exogenous and endogenous variable but also the direct impact of the moderating variable on the endogenous variable as well as the impact of an interacting variable is investigated (Eggert et al. 2005). Using a path diagram framework, the interacting variable is calculated as a product of the exogenous variable and the moderating variable. The essential properties of a moderating variable are summarized in Fig. 4.6: The impact of the predictor variable (path a), the impact of the moderating variable (path b) and the interaction or product of these two (path c). The moderating hypothesis is supported if, independently from the strength of the path coefficients a and b of the exogenous variable and the moderating variable, the interaction (path c) is significant (Baron and Kenny 1986).

Moderating effects specify when certain effects will hold, while mediating effects specify how or why such effects occur (Baron and Kenny 1986). A given variable functions as a mediator to the extent that it accounts for the relation between the predictor (exogenous) variable and the endogenous (criterion) variable.

Modeling moderating effects using SmartPLS is more comfortable than using covariance-based software such as LISREL, as these correlations may help to provide a more accurate estimation of the interaction effect.

Using reflective variables for exogenous and moderating variables, the original indicators need to be standardized (mean = 0, variance = 1) or centered (mean = 0) (Eggert, Fassott and Helm 2005) and then integrated in the structural model. Since formative indicators are not assumed to reflect the same underlying construct, the product indicators between two sets of formative indicators will not necessarily tap into the same underlying interaction effect. PLS calculates for the exogenous variable as well as for the moderating variable the standardized construct values on case level. The interacting effect is then calculated by one single indicator, generated by the multiplication of each construct value.

The strength of interaction effect f can be calculated by using the R-square values:

$$f^2 = \frac{R^2_{\text{incl. interacting variable}} - R^2_{\text{baisc model}}}{1 - R^2_{\text{basic model}}} \tag{4.1}$$

Even a small interaction effect can be meaningful under extreme moderating conditions if the resulting changes are meaningful (Chin et al. 2003). To illustrate mediation, the basic causal chain involved in mediation is depicted in Fig. 4.7. This model assumes a three-variable system, two causal paths feeding into the endogenous variable: The direct impact of the independent variable (path c) and the impact of the mediator (path b). Path a leads from the independent variable to the mediator (Baron and Kenny 1986).

The path from the dependent variable to the mediator is denoted as a, and its standard error is s_a. The path from the mediator to the dependant variable is b, and its standard error is s_b (Fig. 4.8).

$$z = \frac{a \cdot b}{\sqrt{b^2 \cdot s_a^2 + a^2 \cdot s_b^2}} \tag{4.2}$$

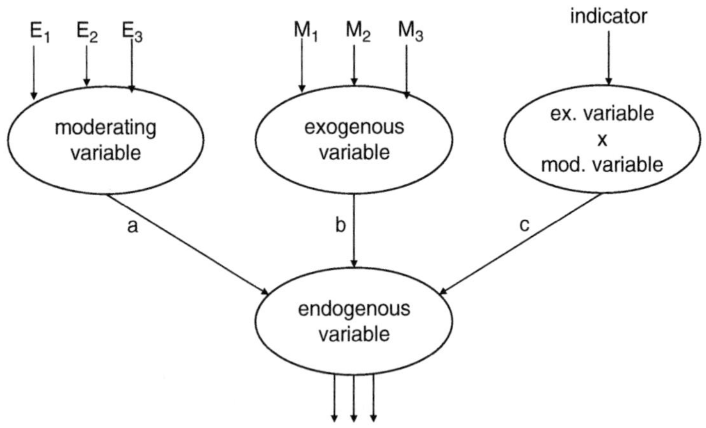

Fig. 4.7 Modeling moderating effects in PLS, using formative constructs
Source: Eggert et al. (2005) p. 113

Fig. 4.8 Mediator model, *Source*: Eggert et al. (2005)

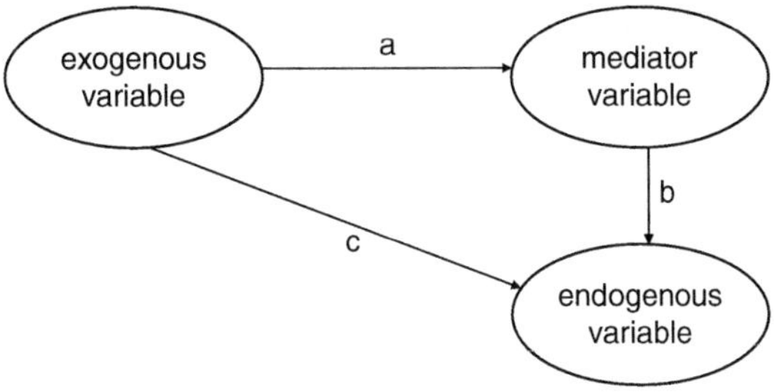

If the test value $z \geq 1.96$, it can be concluded on a significance level of $p < 0.05$, that there is no significant direct effect ($a \cdot b = 0$).

To calculate the strength of the mediating effect, the formula to calculate the variance accounted for is:

$$\text{VAF} = \frac{a \cdot b}{a \cdot b + c} \tag{4.3}$$

A VAF-value of 0.5 means that 50% of the effect of the exogenous variable on the endogenous variable is based on the mediator variable. Regarding behavioral intention, Fishbein and Ajzen (1975) assumed that the impact of both attitudes and normative factors on behavior is mediated through it.

4.4 Applying the Bonferroni-Holm's Procedure

Interpretation of results that include multiple statistical tests has been an issue of great concern for some time in the literature. The basic problem is that when multiple tests are undertaken, each at the same significance level (α), the probability of achieving at least one significant result is greater than that significance level (Zaykin et al. 2002; Hochberg 1988). In this study, multiple treatment comparisons are also carried out. The survey data set is split twice: in five different countries and, additionally, in three different stakeholder groups. Moreover, the data are evaluated threefold: results related to all countries, split into single country data and by stakeholder groups. For this reason, each participant in this survey may be included in three different data-evaluations.

This fact may result in an increased probability of rejecting a null hypothesis when it would be inappropriate to do so. The typical solution to this problem has been to lower the α values for the table (i.e. establish a table-wide significance level) and therefore reduce the probability of a spurious result. In this study, an enhancement of the sequential Bonferroni test – the Bonferroni-Holm's procedure – was used for multiple comparisons to retain a global risk of 5% by the adaptation of the decisional threshold to each comparison.

According to Moran (2003), the most common procedure has been the application of the sequential Bonferroni adjustment (Holm 1979; Miller 1981; Rice 1989). The application of this procedure was chosen because the modified Bonferroni procedure is less conservative than the sequential Bonferroni test (Hochberg 1988). Both procedures contrast the ordered p-values with the same set of critical values. Holm's procedure rejects a hypothesis only if its p-values and each of the smaller p-values are less than their corresponding critical-values (Holm 1979). Thus, it controls the family-wise error rate in the strong sense.

The problem of statistical data involving multiple statistical tests is the following: the more individual tests that fall below α, the lower the probability that they are all spurious (Hochberg 1988). It also illustrates the principle that several relatively high p-values can be a stronger indication of significance than one relatively low p-value. To address the problem of multiple statistical tests within this study, all path correlations significant in the countries or stakeholder groups on a $p = 0.05$ level were successfully tested based on the Bonferroni-Holm's procedure. The results are shown in the Annex.

4.5 Development of Constructs

A central concern in scientific research is external validity, or the extent to which a theorized or observed relationship among variables can be generalized to other settings (Rosenzweig 1994; Gardberg 2006).

Bernstein (1986) concluded that organizational identity is influenced by the following dimensions: value for money, technical innovation, service, social responsibility, reliability, imagination, quality and integrity. Can the relationship in question replicate with people of other cultures, in other countries of the world (Krathwohl 1985)? Following the literature on the development of one valid construct of CR, there have been frequent discussions about international generalization (MacMillan et al. 2005; Eberl 2006; Helm 2007). Particular attention has been paid to the methodological dilemmas of cross-cultural research (Negandhi 1983; Ronen 1986; Gardberg 2006; Walsh and Wiedmann 2004).

As the current work is based on a cross-cultural study concerning five different countries, the indicators of the construct "reputation", as well as its influencing factors, need to be suitable for all the countries included in the survey. The questionnaire took some of the RQ dimensions of Fombrun et al. (2000, see Sect. 3.3.2), but then, several others were added. While concentrating on cross-cultural CR in a B-to-B context, only the following RQ questions were chosen:
Emotional Appeal

- I trust this company

Products and Services

- develops innovative products and services
- offers high-quality products and services
- offers products and services that are good value for money

Stakeholder groups in a cross-cultural B-to-B context may not have any knowledge of some of the RQ dimensions. Moreover, the impact of financial performance on CR is controversially discussed (Dunbar and Schwalbach 2000; Roberts and Dowling 2002; McGuire et al. 1990).

In the light of the fact that Australian, Finnish and most of the German and Spanish organizational buyers only purchase goods based on tender businesses, their knowledge of "vision and leadership" approaches and their interest in the financial performance of their suppliers is extremely limited. In tender businesses, hardly any purchaser cares about the financial performance of future suppliers: If the company which has won the tender is not able to supply, the next one on the list will simply be chosen.

Regarding CR and the dimension of the workplace environment, for organizational buyers, the only personal contacts, if any, are the sales representatives of the suppliers, so general judgments of the workplace environment can hardly be made, as visits of these sales representatives take place exclusively in the offices of organizational purchasers. The visibility of sponsoring activities is low, and they are not usually communicated directly to all stakeholders. Consequently, it is difficult for organizational buyers to evaluate the social responsibility of a company in the B-to-B context. In the light of the recommendations of Gardberg (2006); Walsh and Wiedmann (2004); Berens and van Riel (2004); Helm (2007), as well as Lee and Lings (2007) discussed earlier, the following dimensions were excluded from the empirical research of this work: vision and leadership, workplace environment, financial performance and social responsibility.As the above stakeholder-specific concept of CR indicates, the importance of certain dimensions varies according to stakeholder group: To employees, the workplace environment is most important. Customers are focused most on product and service quality. The workplace environment of the suppliers' employees is of minor importance, as long as this dimension is not discussed negatively in the media (which then already influences the CR factor of social responsibility). Regarding the impact factors on B-to-C consumer specific reputation is concerned, one connection between consumers and social responsibility is added by the author, as literature shows that social responsible behaviour of companies does also impact CR (Fombrun et al. 2000; Walsh and Wiedmann 2004).

Helm (2006) argues that from a managerial standpoint, the conceptual disadvantages of using one identical measure of reputation for all stakeholder groups are possibly outweighed by the opportunity to compare stakeholder groups' perceptions. With regard to Fig. 4.9 and the various dimensions of reputation, the author doubts that one single measure of reputation will help to work toward one consistent reputation. The author casts doubts on the fact that "a consistent reputation" (Helm 2006) exists at all – although this is an understandable managerial goal. Helm (2007) tried to solve this problem of a multi-faceted view of reputation by developing a formative construct of CR consisting of nine completely different indicators related to all dimensions of CR. This completely disregards the fact

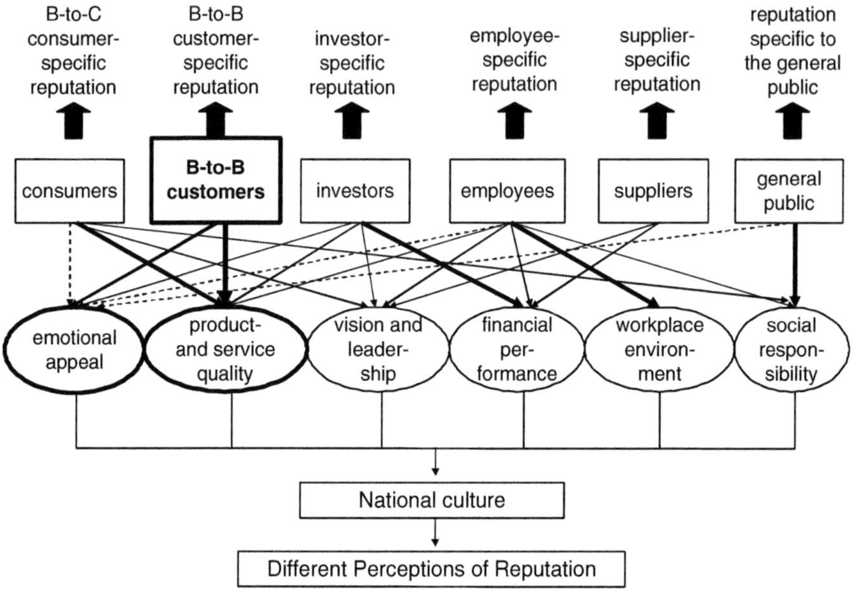

Fig. 4.9 Stakeholder-specific concepts of corporate reputation, modified from Meffert and Bierwirth (2002); Helm (2006)

- That certain dimensions of CR are unimportant to specific stakeholder groups, and
- That most stakeholder groups are neither in a position to judge nor interested in some of the dimensions

This work focuses on the B-to-B setting of organizational customers. In contrast to customers in the B-to-C context, organizational customers are exclusively focused on product and service quality. In both B-to-B and B-to-C contexts, the emotional appeal of a company has an impact on CR. Thus, this work proposes only to include these two dimensions in the survey. In line with the study of MacMillan et al. (2005), all 250 survey participants had practical experience in a medical device manufacturing company. For this reason, as suggested by Walsh and Wiedmann (2004); Berens and van Riel (2004), and Bernstein (1986), constructs such as innovativeness, relationship quality, purchase decision involvement and WOM have been included:

Relationship Quality

- I am satisfied with this company
- This company offers value for money
- This company takes my concerns and request seriously

Reputation

- I trust in products of this company
- This company cares for customers' opinions
- This company shares expertise as a partner

Purchase Decision Involvement

- Even if competitors offer the same features as company X, I would prefer to buy the products of company X
- I regularly check the outcome of my purchasing decisions
- I don't care which brand I buy (reverse coding)

Innovativeness

- This company is known for innovative products
- This company is known for leading products

Word of Mouth

- I would recommend the medical devices of this company
- I would recommend the pharmaceutical products of this company

To find out about the influencing factors of the transferability of reputation, statements on the use of certain direct marketing media, reputation transfer, and perceived fit have also been included. The following chapters first give an overview of the classification of the above constructs. Second, the derivation of each construct integrated in the structural model is presented. Finally, the complete structural model is introduced.

4.5.1 Overview of Measurement and Formation of Constructs

To find out about the impact factors on corporate reputation and reputation transfer in the B-to-B context, the ability of organizational customers to perceive the fit of a new product to the existing product range, the perceived innovativeness of a certain company as well as the quality perception of brand or products are included in the range of constructs. Scholarly work has also examined brand attributes such as quality and advertising and their effects on the success of the introduction of new brands or products (e.g., Grewal et al. 1998; Smith and Park 1992). The impact of these factors on reputation transfer has not yet been examined. The following tables give a short overview of the constructs used, their types of measurement and the questions related to each construct. Details on the classification of each construct can be found in the following chapters (Table 4.4).

The next table introduces the latent variables used with formative constructs together with the related indicators.

In addition, as discussed in Sect. 4.2.3 and listed below, three single-item indicators are used (Table 4.5).

Now that the manifest variables are presented in an overview, the constructs used in the structural model are presented in detail (Table 4.6).

Table 4.4 List of manifest variables used with reflective constructs

Latent variable, reflective construct	Questions defining the constructs/manifest variables
Reputation,4-point-Likert scale	Do you agree or disagree with the following statements on company X? • This company cares for customers' opinions • This company shares expertise as a partner • I trust in the products of this company
Reputation transfer,4-point-likert scale	Company X also supplies injectable drugs to more than 80 countries. Knowing that, what is your opinion on purchasing these injectable drugs? • You would purchase them because you trust in the prod. of company X You would expect the same high product quality standard as with other products of company X
Word of mouth,4-point-likert scale	To what extent would you recom. medical devices/ products of company X? To what extent would you recom. the pharmaceutical products / of comp. X?
Perceivedinnovativeness 4-point-likert scale	Do you agree or disagree with the following statements on company X? • Company X is a leading company • Company X is an innovative company

Table 4.5 List of manifest variables used with formative constructs

Latent variableformativeconstructs	Questions defining the constructs/manifest variables
Media-enabled direct marketing media	Which sources do you use to be informed about products? • Brochures • Internet • Mailings
Personal direct marketing media	Which sources do you use to be informed about products • Symposia • Fairs • Visits of sales representatives
Relationship quality	• This company offers value for money • I am satisfied working with this company • This company takes my concerns and requests seriously
Purchase decision involvement	If you think of the products you are purchasing/involved in the purchase process – to what extent do you agree with the following statements? • I do not care at all which brand I buy • I regularly check the outcome of my purchasing decision • Even if competitors offer the same features as company X, I would prefer to buy the products of company X

Table 4.6 List of manifest variables used with single Item constructs

Latent Variablessingle item construct	Questions or scores defining the constructs/manifest variables
E-readiness	E-readiness scores of the five countries involved in the survey
Perceived fit	I think that injectable drugs fit to the product range of company X
Culture	Hofstede's score of the five countries involved in the survey

4.5.2 Corporate Reputation

Even in the economics literature, the term "reputation" is used differently in different contexts. A survey on the diverse perceptions is given by Fombrun (2001). CR is regarded as the result of a corporate branding in the area of marketing, as a kind of goodwill in accounting and as the manifestation of a corporate identity in the field of organization theory. Fombrun and Shanley (1990) argue that the public construe a company's reputation on the basis of information about its relative position in an organizational field. The public do so by using market and accounting signals indicating performance, institutional signals indicating conformity to social norms, and strategy signals indicating strategic position. The difficulty arises when one tries to work out how to measure the less visible B-to-B companies, where neither conformity to social norms nor strategic positions are visible.

Current research on CR suffers from the fact that available studies are not based on identical conceptualizations and formation of the reputation construct. Furthermore, most of the constructs on CR refer to the B-to-C context. Without conceptualization and measurement, strategies to develop a company's reputation remain nebulous (Helm 2006). Generally, the proliferation of different measurement methods of CR has raised the question of whether or not a standard construct of CR is useful and appropriate (e.g., Helm 2007; Schwaiger 2004).

CR in this context is interpreted as a perceptual phenomenon that can be measured by gathering information from observers. As theorized in sects. 2.2 and 2.3, unique key firm resources like CR may lead to competitive advantages (Fombrun 1996; Gardberg 2001). According to behavioral theories, all the positive behavioral effects are triggered by perceptions and attitudes. CR needs to be interpreted as a perceptual, subjective construct, when taken as an explanation for stakeholders' behavior, and this calls for a poll- or survey-based measurement approach (Helm 2006).

The combination of affective and cognitive components leads to the conceptualization of CR as an attitudinal construct (Eberl 2006; Schwaiger 2004; Kroeber-Riel and Weinberg 2003). Thus, evaluating CR not only appraises subjective perceptions of a company's attributes, but allows an intrinsic disposition toward these attributes (Schwaiger 2004). This notion can also be found in US publications, although they do not differentiate explicitly between the terms "corporate image" and CR (Bromley 1993, see also Sect. 3.2.1) While conducting a cross-cultural study using the RQ dimensions of Fombrun et al. (2000), Gardberg (2006) noted that, although very often measured in the US, the dimension of CEO leadership does not seem to be an appropriate measure of CR in some European countries. In a buyer-seller relationship, Ganesan (1994) claims that trust plays a key role in determining the long-term orientation of firms in a relationship, and that this factor is closely related to reputation.

Trust is the key coordinating mechanism in community form (Adler 2002); it can be engendered by direct interpersonal contact, for example, or by reputation through a network of other trusted parties (Coleman 1990). Being an essential part of the healthcare business, organizational trust is also fragile, and easily broken by disconfirming acts (Firth-Cozens 2004).Values and norms can generate trustworthy behavior that leads to commitment (Morgan and Hunt 1994). Transferring knowledge from beyond the company's boundaries is an important strategy for organizations to add depth and breadth to their knowledge-based capabilities (Simon 1991). Sharing knowledge with customers and suppliers impacts positively on a company's reputation.

A study of Friman et al. (2002) indicates that sharing information and communicating in a proper way seem to enhance commitment and trust. In the literature, customer orientation, as well as trust, is considered as a determinant of CR. In their studies on CR, Fombrun et al. (2000), MacMillan et al. (2005), Helm (2007) and Eberl (2006) included questions referring to the evaluation on external trust and customer orientation (i.e., This company makes an effort to fulfill customers' needs, I trust in this company).

Commitment in B-to-B relationships refers to the partners enduring desire and effort to maintain a valued relationship (Moorman et al. 1992). According to Morgan and Hunt (1994), commitment to a relationship decreases the propensity to end a relationship and increases the willingness to invest in a relationship.

In line with above Fig. 4.10, the construct of CR is based on the theory of commitment and trust (Morgan and Hunt 1994) as well as the RBV and the KBV. Using the following indicators, the multi-item indicator of "reputation" is measured on a four-point Likert-scale:

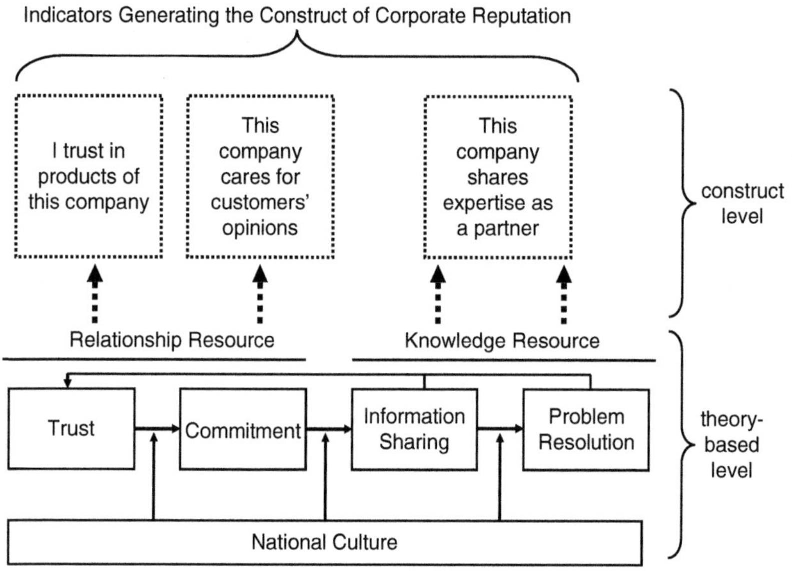

Fig. 4.10 Development of the construct "reputation" based on implications of Griffith et al. (2006)

- I trust in the products of this company (Fombrun et al. 2000; Schwalbach 2002; de Ruyter et al. 2001).
- This company cares for customers' opinions (akin to studies of Helm 2007; Schwalbach 2002; Eberl 2006).
- This company shares expertise as a partner (akin to studies of Friman et al. 2002).

In line with Jarvis et al. (2003), Diamantopoulos and Siguaw (2006), and Rossiter (2002), the attitudinal construct of reputation is viewed as a reflective latent variable:

- Each of the three items shares a common core, which is related to the construct of reputation: trust, caring, sharing of expertise.
- The above indicators characterize a set of distinct causes which are interchangeable. Dropping an indicator from this measurement model does not alter the meaning of the construct (see also Jarvis et al. 2003 and Rossiter 2002).
- Direction of causality is from the construct to this measure (e.g., Diamantopoulos and Siguaw 2006; Jarvis et al. 2003).

4.5.3 Perceived Innovativeness

According to Wieseke et al. (2008), marketing innovations are crucial to continuing company success. In a survey conducted with 1,221 managers, 79% agreed with the statement: "For the long-term success of our company, innovations are more important than cost reductions" (Witt and Witt 2008). It can also be taken as proof of the impact of innovativeness on CR, that the Fortune magazine, as well as the German Manager Magazin, have included "innovativeness" as an influencing factor in their CR measurement approaches.

Innovativeness forms the basis of a company's success. It helps companies to access resources, improve products and services, develop linkages and gain competitive advantage (Wieseke et al. 2008). Innovations refer to creating new resources or combining existing resources in new ways to develop and commercialize new products, move into new markets, and/or services, and acquire new customers (Swedberg 2000).

In the literature, there are reputational surveys including innovativeness (e.g., Fombrun et al. 2000; Eberl 2006), although some do not include it in their measurement approaches (e.g., Helm 2007). Within the B-to-B context and in line with Fombrun et al. (2000) and Eberl (2006), the construct of "perceived innovativeness" is included in this survey. Fombrun et al. (2000) included the following questions in their RQ-questionnaire: This company develops innovative products and services, This company offers high-quality products and services.

Using the following indicators, the multi-item indicator of "perceived innovativeness" is measured on a four-point Likert-scale:

- Company X is known for innovative products
- Company X is known for leading products

In line with the classification criteria of Diamantopoulos and Siguaw (2006) and the criteria evaluations described in Sect.´4.2.1 and according to Jarvis et al. (2003), the attitudinal construct of reputation is viewed as a reflective latent variable.

4.5.4 Perceived Fit

Given that brand names are a firm's most important assets, a substantial part of a brand's value is derived from its contribution to the launch of new products. Perceived similarity, also called perceived fit, is characterized by "the number of shared associations" between parent brand and extension product (Czellar 2003, p. 103). Most prominently, Aaker and Keller (1990) argue that a greater similarity between the parent and extension category should be conducive to successful brand extensions.

However, the results of Smith and Park's study (1992) do not support this claim. Despite the empirical counter examples (e.g., Porsche or Yamaha), most marketing scholars believe in the folklore of the necessity of the pre-condition of product-related, or at least category-related, fit for the successful transfer of a company's reputation, a concept already included in modern marketing textbooks (e.g., Keller 2003). One of the rare exceptions is the study by Klink and Smith (2001), who claim that brands may also be extended to perceptually distant categories. The latter endeavor – sometimes referred to as concept extension – highlights the importance of investigating the valuation of companies' reputations in a more general way in order to have a clear view of reputation transfer.

Prior research suggests that the transfer of a company's reputations is constrained by the degree of perceived fit between the established and the new product categories, as well as the perceived brand strength. As with many other marketing research results, all theory development, as well as empirical evidence in this research domain, is almost exclusively restricted to Western-type markets (Falkenreck and Wagner forthcomming).

According to Aaker and Keller (1990), perceived fit is determined and defined mainly by the transferability – the proof of competence of the brand for the new product.

Park et al. (1991) claim that fit can be divided in two dimensions: product fit (product-feature similarity perception) and brand fit (concept-consistency perception). The current work is focused on the concept-consistency perception of the customers.

Bergkvist and Rossiter (2007) evaluated single-item measures and concluded that one empirical-based argument for the use of a single item can be made for measures, in which the multiple items representing the construct are synonymous attributes (see Sect. 4.2.3). The remaining attribute then needs to have a single object and a concrete attribute. Following the arguments of Bergkvist and Rossiter (2007), the question related to this single-item indicator to evaluate the general fit of brand extension to the existing product range was measured on a four-point Likert-scale and asked as follows:

- I think the new product range fits to the rest of the company's product range.

4.5.5 Purchase Decision Involvement

To find out why customers choose certain brands, it its important for the marketers to understand the complex decision process a customer goes through (Dholakia 2001). Many psychological factors affect the consumer's decision when purchasing a product, and some of these factors are also valid in the B-to-B context.

The examination of consumer involvement is well established in the marketing literature (Mittal 1989; Petty and Cacioppo 1981; Helgenson et al. 1984; von Wangenheim 2003; Dholakia 2001), although cross cultural examination of the influence purchase decision involvement has on CR is virtually non-existent.

Among numerous definitions of involvement in the consumer literature, the most commonly used definition is the one that includes the element of "personal relevance with a product, purchase or advertising" (Petty and Cacioppo 1981; Zaichkowsky 1984, 1985). Studies show that involvement strongly influences the consumer decision-making process (e.g., Krugman 1965; Gensch and Javalgi 1987; Helgenson et al. 1984). Nevertheless, high involvement in products can rarely be found, as consumers are usually concerned about a very small number of goods they are planning to purchase (Richins and Block 1991). Furthermore, in the B-to-B context, the impact of involvement is controversially discussed and does not seem to play an important role in influencing consumer behavior (von Wangenheim 2003; Giering 2000). As a result, inconsistency in the conceptualizations and operationalizations of involvement across studies has produced conflicting results concerning the exact nature and intensity of the influence of involvement.

Houston and Rothschild (1978) tried to develop a comprehensive definition of involvement, and distinguish three types: product, purchase and response involvement. As different organizational user groups are involved in this study, it focuses exclusively on the impact of purchase decision involvement on CR and reputation transfer in a cross-cultural context.

Some researchers support the notion that differentiation is an antecedent of (purchase) involvement (Batra and Ray 1985). Others point out their questioning of whether differentiation is an antecedent, a component or a consequence of involvement (Zaichkowsky 1984; Zaichkowsky 1985). The multiple conceptualizations of involvement generate confusion in the relationship between involvement and perceived differentiation. Perceived or cognitive differentiation is "the ability of individuals to perceive differences in the features of a stimulus object and to make fine distinctions between that object and others" (Zinkham and Munderrisoglu 1985).

Not only the definition, but also the measurement of involvement has long been a controversial topic for researchers. There are many different involvement-driven models in advertising, such as the elaboration likelihood model (Petty and Cacioppo 1981, 1983, 1986), the attitude-toward-the-ad model (Lutz 1985; Shimp 1982), and the integrated information response model (Smith and Swinyard 1982, 1983).

A variable that influences the formation of consideration sets, apart from involvement, is the decision-making context. Decision making can be memory-based or stimuli-based (or mixed). Very few studies examine the same variable, relation or process in both memory-based and stimuli-based contexts (e.g., Shapiro et al. 1997).

Mittal (1989) defines purchase decision involvement as the extent of interest and concern that customers bring to bear upon a purchase-decision task. Purchase decision involvement is analogous to the situational involvement of Houston and Rothschild (1978), and is considered a mindset, not a response behavior. As such, O'Cass (2000, p. 58) defines product involvement as "the degree a consumer is involved in the product" and purchase decision involvement as "the degree a consumer is involved in the purchase decision".

The current work is located in the B-to-B setting and focuses directly on organizational buying behavior and CR, the constructs of customer satisfaction and loyalty are not examined any further and are not included in the structural model (Mittal and Lee 1989). However, this paper includes the construct of purchase decision involvement and its impact on CR and WOM will be further investigated. Examining the impact of purchase decision involvement on CR aims to enhance our understanding of customer decision making in the B-to-B context. The findings of von Wangenheim (2003) show evidence that involvement in products has virtually no impact on consumer behavior in B-to-B settings, and least of all on WOM. These findings will be referred to and investigated further in the current paper.

Unlike the study of Mittal and Lee (1989), who examined the impact of product involvement and brand-decision involvement in a B-to-C setting, this structural model is based on a combination of both constructs. For this reason, the purchase decision involvement construct used in this work is on a par with three out of six indicators used by Mittal and Lee (1989) in their causal model of consumer involvement. Using the following indicators, the multi-item indicator of purchase decision involvement is measured on a four-point Likert scale:

1. Even if competitors offered the same products as company x, I would prefer the products of company x.
2. I don't care which brand I buy (reverse coding).
3. I care about the outcome of my purchase decision.

In line with the classification criteria of Diamantopoulos et al. (2008) and the criteria evaluations in Sect. 4.2.2, the attribute classification of this construct is formative:

- The above indicators characterize a set of distinct causes which are not interchangeable as each indicator captures a specific aspect of the construct's domain (see also Jarvis et al. 2003; Rossiter 2002).
- Omitting an indicator potentially alters the nature of the construct (Bollen and Lennox 1991).
- There are no specific patterns or magnitudes of intercorrelation between the indicators (for measurement validity of formative constructs, see Sect. 6.2.9).

4.5.6 The Moderating Impact of Culture

A review of the literature reveals several specific shortcomings that have limited the understanding of CR in a global context. No studies are available in the cross-cultural B-to-B context, and existing studies are based on RQ measurement and refer either to "most admired" or "most visible" companies (e.g., Fombrun et al. 2000; Fombrun and Gardberg 2002; Walsh and Wiedmann 2004) or are located in the B-to-C context (e.g., Eberl 2006; Helm 2007; Gardberg 2006). Nevertheless, the studies of Doney and Cannon (1997) and Homburg et al. (2005) on the relationship between national cultures, trust and customer behavior also conclude that different cultural environments impact on customer reactions.

In this study, culture is considered as a moderating variable and evaluated based on Hofstede's (2001) dimensions, although the "failure to address national culture's influence on relationship and knowledge resources jointly has resulted in limited theoretical and managerial insights into how culture influences resources" (Griffith et al. 2006, p. 2). As already discussed in Sect. 3.6.4, trust is expected to be more important in cultures like Australia, Finland, and Germany, scoring low in UAI (Hofstede 2001) and less important in cultures like Russia and Spain, scoring high in UAI. On the other hand, the importance of a supplier's positive reputation is considered to be more important in cultures scoring high in UAI, like Russia and Spain. These assumptions are related to the conclusions of Hofstede (2001) and Griffin (1975), arguing that cultures scoring low in the dimension of uncertainty avoidance (UAI) tend to trust other people more easily. In line with the findings of Hofstede (2001), the impact of direct marketing media is expected to be more substantial in masculine cultures or societies scoring high in IDV (e.g., Australia and Germany).

4.5.7 Reputation Transfer

Reputations are difficult to duplicate because they derive from unique internal features of companies (Fombrun and van Riel 1997). CR is externally perceived and therefore largely outside the direct control of a company's management

(Fombrun and Shanley 1990). According to Schweizer and Wijnberg (1999, p. 261), "transferability of reputation can provide a powerful tool for corporate reputation building". However, it can be assumed that customers from different cultural environments will not react identically.

Considering the central "transfer" between a company's reputation and the new product range, this study therefore investigates other possible impact factors on reputation transfer: direct marketing media, WOM, perceived innovativeness and relationship quality. The perceived fit of the new product to the existing product range is also evaluated. The model also investigates moderating and mediating effects, such as culture.

To find out about this construct, which is seldom considered in studies, the following questions have been included in the survey:

What is you opinion on purchasing products of a certain new product range? Do you agree with the following statements:

- I would purchase them because I trust in the products of this company.
- I would expect the same high standard of product quality as other products of this company.

Attribute classification of this construct is reflective. Items related to the construct of reputation transfer have similar sign and significance of relationships with the antecedents and consequences, and content validity has been established by theoretical considerations (Diamantopoulos and Siguaw 2006; Rossiter 2002).

4.5.8 Word of Mouth

It has often been argued that word of mouth (WOM) can contribute significantly to a company's success in various ways (von Wangenheim and Bayón 2007). In this work, the linkage between WOM, relationship quality, innovativeness, reputation transfer as well as reputation is analyzed.

WOM, the informal advice passed between customers, has a powerful influence on consumer behavior (von Wangenheim 2003). WOM may be positive (PWOM), encouraging brand choice, or negative (NWOM), discouraging brand choice. WOM is often the major reason for brand choice, but the contribution of PWOM and NWOM to this influence is difficult to understand. Moreover, some groups are more responsive to WOM than others (East, Hammond & Lomax, forthcoming).

Although consumers often attribute their brand choice to WOM, it is difficult to observe cases where advice affects brand choice since WOM about a specific category is relatively uncommon, and any effect is often delayed. When evidence is scarce, too much weight may be given to the limited research that is available. In the seminal work of Arndt (1967) it is argued that NWOM has twice as much impact on purchase as PWOM. However, he studied only one brand, and systematic research should be based on all the brands in a category and should include a range of categories. In addition, although the category was familiar, Arndt used a new brand about which there were few expressed opinions. In the absence of direct evidence of the effect of WOM, inferences have been made from experimental work on the impact of positive and negative information. It is well established that negative information usually has more impact on judgment than positive information (Skowronski and Carlston 1989) but this finding may not extend to the relative impact of PWOM and NWOM on brand choice in familiar categories.

The study of Palmatier et al. (2006) shows that relationships have the greatest influence on WOM and recommend that companies depending on WOM strategies for new customers should implement effective relationship commitment programs. The current work investigates the impact of WOM on corporate reputation and reputation transfer success. In a nutshell, the objectives of this study are threefold: to analyze how relationship quality translates into positive WOM, how positive WOM impacts on CR and reputation transfer, and to explore moderating effects, especially in the context of purchase decision involvement.

In line with Helm (2007), the questions related to this reflective multi-item indicator were asked as follows:

- I would recommend the pharmaceutical products of company X
- I would recommend the medical devices of company X

Attribute classification of this construct is reflective. Items related to WOM have similar signs and significance of relationships with the antecedents and consequences as this construct: content validity has been established by theoretical considerations (Diamantopoulos and Siguaw 2006), and convergent and discriminant validity has been assessed empirically. In the literature, the construct of WOM has been measured as a two-item reflective construct (e.g., Ranaweera and Prabhu 2003), as well as a multi-item reflective construct (von Wangenheim 2003; von Wangenheim and Bayòn 2007).

4.5.9 Relationship Quality

In B-to-B settings, suppliers need to understand the nature and the circumstances of their customers because of the unique characteristics of the customers acting as organizations (Rauyruen and Miller 2005; Backhaus and Voeth 2007) Relationship quality is in general construed to be a post-consumption evaluation which depends on perceived quality, value, expectations, and confirmation/disconfirmation – the degree (if any) of discrepancy between actual and expected quality (Anderson and Narus 2004). To evaluate the quality they can expect from a provider of goods, customers rely on the signals that refer to unobservable attributes that affect the ability of a firm to produce quality products (Rauyruen and Miller 2005).

The uncertainty about quality is widespread and an important feature of markets for most company's goods and services (Shapiro 1982). Keller (2003) listed the general dimensions of product quality as follows: Reliability and durability, performance of product operation, conformance quality, serviceability and style and design. Rauyruen and Miller (2005) propose relationship quality to be a construct comprising trust, commitment, satisfaction and service or product quality.

In the context of studies related to reputation, relationship quality does not only refer to products and services, but also to the general quality perception of the company. The Eberl study (2006) contained questions related to quality (proximity to customers, value for money, reliable partner, product quality) and sympathy toward the company (internationally accepted company, top-ranking level, a company the customer can identify with) using two different constructs, which are not clearly unconnected, as both constructs refer, in part, to affective commitment.

To deliver value to customers it is essential that companies have an understanding of the factors that drive customer benefits (Homburg et al. 2004), "customer value must be the central element of every business strategy" (Webster 1992, p. 22). According to Homburg et al. (2004), delivering high customer benefits is a major successfactor in B-to-B settings.

In this work, one multi-item construct related to relationship quality is used. On a four point-Likert-scale, the questions were asked as follows:

- This company offers value for money (Eberl 2006; Helm 2007; Anderson and Narus 2004; Fombrun et al., 2000)
- This company takes my concerns seriously (Rauyruen and Miller 2005)
- I am satisfied with this company (Rauyruen and Miller 2005)

Attribute classification of above constructs is formative:

- Both constructs are viewed as an explanatory combination of its indicators (Fornell and Bookstein 1982; Fornell 1987).
- All indicators represent an independent dimension in its own (Diamantopoulos et al. 2008).
- Causality flows from the indicators to the construct, (Edwards and Bagozzi 2000; Diamantopoulos and Winklhofer 2001).

Following the literature, customer perceived value (Lin et al. 2005), as well as customers' commitment toward retailers (Sanchez-Pérez and Iniesta-Bonillo 2004) have also been formatively measured.

4.5.10 Media-enabled and Personal Direct Marketing

Corporate communication (CC) is an important means of targeting or informing stakeholders (Fombrun and Rindova 1998; Dentchev and Heene 2004) and ascribing to a better reputation. Direct marketing media can be used to influence the interpretations and perceptions of stakeholders (Rindova and Fombrun 1999; Forman and Argenti 2005). Among others, this can also positively or negatively impact the perceived fit of new products to the existing product range (Kumar 2005).

CC is achieved through media-enabled (e.g., the Internet, brochures and mailings) and personal (e.g., symposia, fairs and visits of sales representatives) direct marketing media. In line with the above arguments, the structural model indicates the relationship between both types of direct marketing media and reputation as well as reputation transfer.

Face-to-face communication, meetings during fairs as well as the execution of symposia are very powerful examples of interactive direct marketing (Bruhn 2003; Mann 2004). In addition, in the B-to-B context, sales forces are a major brand-building tool (Gordon et al. 1993). Gordon et al. (1993) claim that purchase choice is also dependent on the company's sales representatives and its relationship with organizational buyers. This is also confirmed by the findings of Kuhn and Alpert (2004): Customers identify with manufacturer's brands and claim to have good relationships with company representatives. To evaluate the use of personal direct media in B-to-B settings, visits of sales representatives and meetings at fairs and symposia are included as indicators in this construct.

Online, or Internet marketing, is a recent tool which includes the use of electronic networks and data, not only to generate sales (e.g., electronic commerce) but also to build and develop relationships between a company and its stakeholders (Klaus and Wagner 2009). Electronic marketplaces are evolving rapidly in both B-to-B and B-to-C settings, and established companies across all types of industrial sectors are striving to improve the effectiveness of interactions between buyers and suppliers on a global scale. To introduce new products, brochures and mailings are frequently used as passive direct marketing tools (Mann 2004). As the empirical study of the current work is also related to the introduction of a new product range, the media-enabled direct marketing tools included in this construct are the Internet, brochures and mailings.

Hofstede (2001), while comparing societies, claims that cultures impact a society's attitude toward direct marketing media. In addition, market entry for new trade marks is more difficult in uncertainty-avoiding countries (in this survey: Russia and Spain). Hence, the cultural impact on the different countries is expected to influence the use of direct marketing media.

The questions related to these two multi-item constructs were asked on a ranking scale as follows:

Which sources do you use to be informed about new products (open question)?

Please indicate how important the following sources are to you by using a one-to-five scale (one meaning not important, five meaning of most important):

- Fairs
- Symposia
- Visits of sales representatives
- The Internet
- Brochures
- Mailings

Attribute classification of the above constructs is formative:

- Both constructs are viewed as an explanatory combination of its indicators (Fornell and Bookstein 1982; Fornell 1987).
- All indicators represent an independent dimension on its own (Diamantopoulos et al. 2008).
- Causality flows from the indicators to the construct (Edwards and Bagozzi 2000, Diamantopoulos and Winklhofer 2001).

Following the literature on direct marketing media, both Internet research abilities (Brock and Zhou 2005) and e-service qualities (Collier and Bienstock 2006) have been formatively measured.

4.5.11 E-Readiness

Culture not only impacts on individuals, by way of determining needs and desires, but it also affects a society's progress in building a digital interaction infrastructure (Ho et al. 2007). This progress is quantified by the country's national e-readiness. According to Klaus and Wagner (2009), e-readiness refers to a country's ability to benefit from the electronic advantages of media like the Internet.

The data on e-readiness are taken from the EIU (2007). E-readiness is quantified by scores from 1 to 10 comprising the following categories: connectivity, business environment, consumer and business adoption, legal and policy environment, social and cultural environment and supporting e-services.

Regarding media-enabled direct marketing media such as the Internet, a strong, positive relationship is expected between the constructs of e-readiness and direct marketing media. E-readiness will be measured exclusively based on the dataset of all five countries, using the e-readiness scores for each of the five countries for correlation.

4.6 Related Hypotheses

In the following subsections, the hypotheses related to the constructs will be introduced. All hypotheses of this survey were developed to clarify the following research questions:

1. Is reputation transfer influenced by reputation? Is this relationship between reputation and reputation transfer significant across all countries and stakeholder groups or related to market leadership?
2. In B-to-B relationships, what factors further influence reputation and reputation transfer? Are these factors identical across countries and stakeholder groups?

3. What role do the media play with regard to corporate reputation, reputation transfer and perceived fit of the new product or product range? Is there a difference regarding countries and stakeholder groups in the use of personal direct marketing media and media-enabled direct marketing media?
4. The use of media varies across the countries. Is there a relationship between the e-readiness score of the different countries and media-enabled direct marketing?
5. Is it really true that purchase decision involvement plays no role in B-to-B buying behavior? Is there a relationship between purchase decision involvement and WOM in cultures with low scores in PDI?
6. What kind of impact does WOM have on reputation and reputation transfer? What factors influence WOM across countries and stakeholder groups?
7. In the B-to-B context, does perceived innovativeness have an impact on both reputation and reputation transfer? Can new products take advantage of the perceived brand characteristics of the parent brand? What about the relationship between perceived innovativeness and WOM?
8. How important is the perceived fit of the new product or product range with regard to reputation transfer success? Does corporate reputation influence this fit across all countries and stakeholder groups? Is perceived fit also influenced in all countries by both direct marketing media?
9. Is there a positive relationship between relationship quality and reputation? Does the attitude toward the company also influence reputation transfer?
10. What about the impact of the national culture of buyers on the factors influencing reputation and reputation transfer? Does national culture influence the impact of a company's reputation on organizational buying decisions?

The following subsections highlight the development of the construct-related hypotheses implemented in the structural model.

4.6.1 Perceived Innovativeness

Several researchers have included the fact that a company is perceived as an innovative company in their construction of components and parameters of corporate reputation (e.g., Schwaiger 2004; van Recom and van Riel 2000; Fombrun et al. 2000; Eberl 2006). This is not only relevant for marketing theory, but also for marketing practice, because companies rely increasingly on the success of new product introductions for future growth and profitability (Steenkamp et al. 1999). Surprisingly, in some empirical studies, the innovativeness of a company as an impact factor on reputation is not included (e.g., Helm 2007).

Deshpandé and Farley (2004) built a framework to examine the impact of organizational culture, market orientation, organizational climate, and innovativeness on a company's performance. Their findings show that in industrial nations, the product pipeline and the range of new products play an important role With reference to reputation transfer, we add that the perception of being an innovative company can be decisive and this fact is expected to be different in the surveyed countries.

To date, our understanding of how culture influences technology acceptance is limited (Srite and Karahanna 2006). According to Hofstede (2001), countries scoring low in IDV and high in UAI focus on control and quality function development rather than on innovativeness. Individualistic cultures typically value personal achievements (Hofstede 1980) and demand greater efficiency, so in individualistic cultures, a company's reputation should be affected more strongly by perceived innovativeness. For this reason, the first hypotheses are laid out as follows:

H1. *The perceived innovativeness of a company is expected to have a strong positive effect on company reputation.*

H1a. *The relationship between perceived innovativeness and reputation is expected to be weaker in cultures scoring high in UAI and low in IDV and MAS(e.g., Russia and Spain)*

H1b. *The relationship between perceived innovativeness and reputation is expected to be stronger in cultures scoring low in UAI and high in IDV and MAS (Australia, Germany).*

Thus, in line with the findings of Hofstede (2001), the author posits that national culture impacts the cultural values an individual holds, which in return influences the attitude towards innovations.

As discussed in Sect. 3.6.3, the Finnish society is based on openness with information and has a strong requirement for technology and fosters openness towards innovations and changes.

H2. *There is a strong positive relationship between perceived innovativeness and reputation transfer in cultures scoring very low in PDI and UAI (Finland).*

H3. *There is a strong positive relationship between perceived innovativeness and WOM.*

4.6.2 Purchase Decision Involvement

Purchase decision involvement refers to the extent to which customers view products as meaningful and engaging objects and as being important to them (O'Cass 2000). Mittal and Lee (1989) argue that consumers can be involved in the product itself (product involvement) or in a purchase decision (decision involvement).

Product involvement has been found to be an antecedent of purchase decision involvement across items such as jeans and fashion clothing, but has not yet tested in the B-to-B context (von Wangenheim 2003). As discussed in Sect. 4.5.5, the construct of purchase decision involvement is built by three out of six indicators of Mittal and Lee (1989). As medical devices (the core competence of the company included in the survey) are mostly high involvement products for doctors and nurses, in the country survey, the relationship between purchase decision involvement and WOM is expected to be positive.

No effect of purchase decision involvement is expected to be significant regarding corporate reputation. Following the literature, the decision-making process of organizational buyers is not influenced by involvement (e.g., von Wangenheim 2003, Giering 2000, Richins and Bloch 1991) and purchase decision involvement is not expected to influence CR. According to Hofstede, societies scoring low in UAI are expected to be open for changes, innovations and for the willingness to take over risks, and generally trust other people, this may also affect the relationship between purchase decision involvement and WOM. As people from cultures scoring high in UAI feel relatively powerless towards external forces and are not allowed to make own decision, there purchase decision involvement is expected to be weaker. In these cultures, no impact of purchase decision involvement on WOM is expected. For further analysis, the following hypotheses related to the construct of purchase decision involvement are developed:

H4. *In cultures scoring low in UAI there is a positive relationship between purchase decision involvement and WOM.*

4.6.3 Relationship Quality

In line with Rindova et al. (2005) and Sharpiro (1982), this work proposes that relationship quality is influenced by the signals that organizations send out when they make their strategic choices about the resources deployed in producing products and services. Stakeholders face uncertainty in evaluating companies as potential suppliers of needed products (Benjamin and Podolny 1999). Reputation influences organizational economic outcomes by alleviating stakeholders' concerns about the quality of a company's products and inducing them to pay price premiums for their products (Sharpiro 1982).

In addition, customers are likely to rely on signals of quality when the products they purchase can only be evaluated with use over time, or require high levels of specialized expertise to evaluate (Rindova et al. 2005, p. 8): "When customers find product quality difficult to evaluate prior to purchase, they may use the quality of inputs and/or the quality of the productive assets a firm uses to convert inputs into outputs to form expectations about the quality of the final product."

According to Keller (2003), the perception of quality of the products already on the market can influence attitude and behavior toward a brand. For this reason, it is considered important in the B-to B context and has been chosen as an impact factor on reputation and reputation transfer.

H5. *There is a positive relationship between the relationship quality and corporate reputation.*

H6. *There is a positive relationship between relationship quality and reputation transfer.*

4.6.4 Word of Mouth

In recent decades, customer satisfaction has featured as one of the most important topics in the marketing literature (Parasuraman et al. 1988, von Wangenheim and Bayón 2007). This development has given rise to a number of conceptual models and empirical studies on quantifying the impact of WOM and product involvement on customer satisfaction (e.g., Anderson and Mittal 2000). The literature suggests that purchasers in the B-to-B setting are not usually very involved in their purchasing decisions (Zaichkowski 1985; Richins and Bloch 1991; von Wangenheim 2003). Nevertheless, a positive relationship between purchase decision involvement, product involvement and WOM is empirically confirmed (e.g., von Wangenheim 2003; Hennig-Thurau and Hansen 2001). Furthermore, the impact of WOM on CR is clear, although according to Dellarocas (2002), not investigated in detail: Buyers and sellers rate one another in Internet-based feedback mechanisms, total quality management concepts in companies require purchasers to rate their satisfaction with suppliers, and users write reviews about products or services of certain companies. The author suggests that all these WOM activities impact on CR.

H7. *There is a strong relationship between relationship quality and WOM.*

H8. *There is a strong, positive relationship between WOM and reputation in market leader countries like Germany, Spain and Finland.*

H9. *There is a strong relationship between WOM and reputation transfer.*

H9a. *This effect is expected to be stronger for the future product users of the new product range.*

H9b. *This effect is expected to be stronger in market leadership countries.*

4.6.5 Perceived Fit

When a company uses an established brand name to introduce a new product as a category extension, the importance of the perceived fit of the new product to the established product range or to the company in general is considered to be extremely high (Tauber 1981; Keller 2003; Schwager 2004; Aaker and Keller 1990; Park et al. 1991). "Perceived similarity, also called perceived fit, is characterized by the number of shared associations (...)" (Czellar 2003).

Understanding how customers judge the goodness of fit between an extension and a parent brand requires suppliers to have an intuitive understanding of exactly which aspects of the new product and the existing brand category the customers will compare (Park et al. 1991). Prior brand-extension research has conceptualized and measured perceived fit as a function of product-similarity judgments in which customers compare some aspects of the existing sets of products with those of the extension product (Schwager 2004; Keller 2003; Madrigal 2000; Tversky, 1977).

Concept-consistency perceptions rely on the extension product's ability to accommodate the brand concept. The results of the study of Park et al. (1991) show that the concept information that is carried with the brand name is taken into account by the customers, which enhances the extension evaluation when the product is consistent with the concept. In surveys referring to brand extension products, the term "fit" was used rather than "being similar". This is due to the findings of Park, Lawson and Milberg (1989) that suggest that fit judgments facilitate detection of the associative relationships among various brands on the basis of not only features but also abstract concepts (see also Fiske 1982). To date, researchers have not given adequate consideration to how a brand-name concept, image or CR affects customers' perception of the fit. Brand concepts position products in the minds of customers (Keller 2003). Reputation concepts are related to past activities of the company and refers to stakeholders' overall evaluation of a company over time (Gotsi and Wilson 2001).

Similarity judgments are primarily based on features. According to Keller (2003), only two out of ten new products are successfully introduced to the market. Keller (2003) cites reasons for product failure: The fit of the product was poor, the product was not new or different, or the product did not go hand in hand with familiarity. To the author's best knowledge, no research has yet been focused on the impact of perceived fit on reputation transfer. Hypotheses are proposed as follows:

H10. *There is a strong positive relationship between the perceived fit of the new product range and reputation transfer.*

H10a. *This effect is expected to be stronger in cultures scoring low in IDV and high in UAI (Spain and Russia).*

H10b. *This effect is expected to be weaker for cultures scoring high in IDV and low in UAI (Australia, Finland and Germany).*

H10c. *As purchasers know best about the existing product portfolio of their supplier, the effect of perceived fit on reputation transfer is expected to be stronger for purchasers and weaker for pharmacists and doctors and nurses.*

4.6.6 Personal and Media-enabled Direct Marketing

The strategic management approaches of the RBV and the knowledge-based view (see Chap. 2) give valuable advice for the subordinated direct marketing approaches of a company, as the goal is to enhance customers' perceived value. According to Grönroos (2000), value is perceived by the customer when using or consuming the goods, services or information offered. The focus on specific customer needs and a general customer-friendly company setting lead to integrated, personalized direct marketing approaches to build relationship equity. If relationship equity is influenced by direct marketing media, is there also a link between direct marketing media, the creation of CR and a successful transfer of reputation? To the author's best knowledge, this impact has not yet been evaluated in the literature. The structural model indicates a relationship between both types of direct marketing media and reputation as well as reputation transfer. Furthermore, some emphasis is placed on possible differences in the cross-cultural use of direct marketing media.

Online, or Internet marketing, builds and develops relationships between a company and its stakeholders (Krafft et al. 2007). Electronic marketplaces are evolving in both B-to-B, and B-to-C settings. However, to introduce new products, brochures and mailings are frequently used as passive direct marketing tools (Mann 2004). Concept consitency perception of the new product range is enhanced by the use of direct marketing media (Schwager 2004).

Face-to-face communication is a powerful example of interactive direct marketing (Bruhn 2003; Mann 2004). As formerly discussed, in the B-to-B context, sales forces are a major brand-building tool (Gordon et al. 1993, Kuhn and Alpert 2004). Personal direct marketing carried out through meetings at symposia and fairs or visits of sales representatives may impact CR and reputation transfer success in these countries. The cultural impact on the different countries is generally expected to influence the use of direct marketing media. As discussed in Sect. 3.6.3, some cultures trust more in media, some others rely on relationships and networks. Therefore, hypotheses are generated as follows:

H11. *The use of direct marketing media varies significantly among the countries and stakeholder groups.*

H11a. *There is a strong positive relationship between direct marketing media and reputation.*

H11b. *There is a strong positive relationship between direct marketing media and reputation transfer.*

H11c. *The impact of direct marketing media on reputation and reputation transfer is expected to be stronger in cultures scoring low in PDI and UAI and high in IDV (Australia, Germany, and Finland).*

H11d. *The impact of direct marketing media on reputation and reputation transfer is expected to be weaker in cultures scoring high in UAI and PDI and low in IDV (Russia and Spain).*

4.6.7 Reputation Transfer

It seems plausible that norms and values linked to Hofstede's dimensions will influence the extent and manner in which the transfer of corporate reputation on new product ranges can take place. As already discussed, the dimension of masculinity versus femininity contrasts the emphasis on attributes such as achievement, assertiveness and material success in high masculinity index cultures with a focus on interpersonal relationships and characteristics such as modesty and caring behavior in cultures with a high femininity index (Hofstede 2001). The studies by Doney et al. (1997) and Schweizer and Wijnberg (1999) suggests a strong femininity dimension in a society's mental programming as supporting the formation of trust via the transference process. They justify their proposition by the higher degree of benevolence present in feminine societies. Hofstede (2001) contrasts benevolence with controlling behavior, an attribute more pronounced in masculine cultures. A relevant hypothesis in this context would then be whether:

H12. *Aculture characterized by a high femininity index (Russia and Finland) provides, relative to a culture with a high masculinity index (Australia and Germany), an environment more conducive to the successful transfer of reputation.*

4.6.8 E-Readiness

E-readiness is progressing around the world, but at different rates. E-ranking shows (EIU 2007) that world region scores for North America and Western Europe are much higher than for Asia-Pacific (e.g., Australia) or Central and Eastern Europe (e.g., Russia). E-readiness ranks and scores for the countries included in the survey are listed in Table 4.7.

Included in the e-readiness ranking is the rapidity with which individuals and businesses can take big digital steps to change how they communicate, share information and work (EIU 2007).

Table 4.7 E-readiness ranking and scores

Country	e-readiness rank (of 69)	e-readiness score (out of ten)
Australia	9	8.46
Finland	10	8.43
Germany	19	8.00
Russia	57	4.27
Spain	26	7.29

Widespread connectivity and access to voice and data communications networks – technology infrastructure – are part of the e-readiness categories in the rankings. The ranks and scores of the countries included in this survey vary significantly. In the light of this, the author predicts that the e-readiness scores will correlate with media-enabled direct marketing. Therefore, the hypothesis is developed as follows:

H13. *There is a strong, positive relationship between e-readiness of different cultures and media-enabled direct marketing activities.*

4.6.9 Reputation

Customers need to hold positive beliefs and favorable attitudes toward the core brand (Aaker 1991; Aaker and Keller 1990). Keller (1993) classified brand associations into attributes, benefits (the personal value customers attach to a product or service) and attitude (like or dislike). There has to be a transfer of favorable associations from the original brand to the extension for the latter to be successful (Aaker and Keller 1990).

The author suggests that in market leader countries-due to a long experience with the company and the products-customer are easier willing to accept new products by transferring the values and beliefs of the reputation of the parent company on the new product range. Thus, the hypothesis is proposed as follows:

H14. *There is a strong relationship between reputation and reputation transfer in market-leader countries (like Germany, Finland and Spain).*

The author considers that reputation also impacts the perceived fit of a new product or product range. Up to now, to the author's best knowledge, this has not been empirically tested. The two hypotheses related to the link between CR, perceived fit and national culture are proposed as follows:

H15. *There is a strong, positive relationship between reputation and the perceived fit of the new product to the existing product range.*

H15a. *The effect is stronger in cultures with high scores in UAI and PDI (Russia and Spain) and weaker in cultures scoring low in UAI and PDI (Australia and Finland)*

4.6.10 Culture

Culture supports openness of communication, involvement in decision making and the sharing of information, and encourages and rewards trustworthy behavior (Hofstede 2001; Firth-Cozen 2004).

Values of customers differ significantly across cultures. Therefore, to argue about cross-cultural commitment and trust, the general importance of a trustful relationship between organizational buyers and their suppliers – and to learn more about the general attitude of organizational buyers – needs to be evaluated. The impact of culture on buying behaviour, according to Hofstede's dimensions, is related to the degree of individualism, masculinity, uncertainty avoidance and power distance in a certain country. In line with de Mooij (1998), the author argues that even if all consumers are offered the same goods, there remain significant differences across the value systems of individual countries. Hofstede (2001) claims that cultures scoring low in the dimension of UAI and PDI tend to trust other people more easily, as these societies are more open and free to make their own decisions. In line with Hofstede (2001) Huff and Kelley (2003) claim that external trust that individuals within an organization have for external partners will be higher for organizations from individual societies than for collective societies. To find out about the question of whether societal culture influences the tendency of individuals and organizations to trust (Huff and Kelley 2003), we propose the following hypothesis:

H16. *With reference to organizational buying behavior, trust in sales representatives and supplier plays a more important role in cultures scoring low in UAI and PDI (Australia, Finland) and a less important role in cultures scoring high in UAI and PDI (Russia, Spain).*

This hypothesis also takes into consideration that, according to Hofstede's findings, Russia and Spain (being feminine societies) have a stronger relationship orientation. This can not be viewed as a contradiction, but as a reason for the lesser importance of trust. As explained by Hofstede (2001, p. 305), this is only true for relationships within peer groups and not regarding externals: "Conceptually, valuing social relationships (culture femininity) converges with relying on external frames of references as guides to behavior..."

The literature suggests that the protection of one's reputation is a force for being trustworthy (Griffin 1975). How decisive and influential is a good CR with regard to the impact on organizational buying decisions. As already discussed in Sect. 3.1.2, Hofstede's (2001) findings on business practices regarding preferential treatment of customers and suppliers implies that the importance and impact of a positive reputation differ across cultures, although this topic is not explicitly discussed in his work. To examine the impact of Hofstede's cultural dimensions on reputation in organizational buying behavior, we propose the following hypothesis:

H17. *With reference to organizational buying behavior, a company's reputation plays a more important role in cultures scoring high in UAI and PDI (Russia, Spain) and a less important role in cultures scoring low in UAI and PDI (Australia, Finland, Germany).*

Table 4.8 Overview of hypotheses

No.	Construct-related hypotheses
H1	The perceived innovativeness of a company is expected to have a strong positive effect on corporate reputation
	H1a This impact of perceived innovativeness on corporate reputation is weaker in cultures scoring high in UAI and low in IDV and MAS (e.g., Russia and Spain)
	H1b The impact of perceived innovativeness on corporate reputation is stronger in cultures scoring high in MAS and IDV and low in UAI (Australia and Germany)
H2	There is a strong positive relationship between perceived innovativeness and reputation transfer in cultures scoring very low in PDI and UAI (Finland)
H3	There is a strong positive relationship between perceived innovativeness and WOM
H4	In cultures scoring low in UAI (Australia, Finland and Germany) there is a positive relationship between purchase decision involvement and WOM
H5	There is a positive relationship between relationship quality and reputation
H6	There is a positive relationship between relationship quality and reputation transfer
H7	There is a strong positive relationship between relationship quality and WOM
H8	There is a positive strong relationship between WOM and reputation in market leader countries like Germany, Spain and Finland
H9	There is a strong positive relationship between WOM and reputation transfer
	H9a.This effect is expected to be stronger for the future product users of the new product range
	H9b. This effect is expected to be stronger in market leadership countries
H10	There is a strong positive relationship between the perceived fit of the new product range and reputation transfer
	H10a. This effect is expected to be stronger in cultures scoring low in IDV and high in UAI (Russia and Spain)
	H10b. This effect is expected to be weaker in cultures scoring high in IDV and low in UAI (Australia, Finland and Germany)
	H10c. As purchasers know best about the existing product portfolio of their supplier, the effect of perceived fit on reputation transfer is expected to be stronger for purchaser and weaker for pharmacists, doctors and nurses
H11	The use of direct marketing media varies significantly among the countries and stakeholder groups
	H11a There is a strong positive relationship between direct marketing media and reputation
	H11b There is a strong positive relationship between direct marketing media and reputation transfer
	H11c The impact of direct marketing media on reputation and reputation transfer is expected to be stronger in cultures scoring low in PDI and UAI and high in IDV (Australia, Germany, and Finland)
	H11d The impact of direct marketing media on reputation and reputation transfer is expected to be weaker in cultures scoring high in UAI and PDI and low in IDV (Russia and Spain)
H12	A culture characterized by a high femininity index (Russia and Finland) provides, relative to a culture with a high masculinity index (Australia and Germany), an environment more conducive to the successful transfer of reputation.
H13	There is a strong positive relationship between E-readiness of different cultures and media-enabled direct marketing activities
H14	There is a strong positive relationship between reputation and reputation transfer in market-leader countries (like Germany, Finland and Spain)
H15	There is a positive relationship between reputation and the perceived fit of the new product to the existing product range

(*continued*)

Table 4.8 (continued)

No.	Construct-related hypotheses
	H15a The effect is stronger in cultures with high scores in UAI and PDI (Russia and Spain) and weaker in cultures scoring low in UAI and PDI (Australia and Finland)
H16	With reference to organizational buying behavior, trust in sales representatives and supplier plays a more important role in cultures scoring low in UAI and PDI (Australia, Finland) and a less important role in cultures scoring high in UAI and PDI (Russia, Spain)
H17	With reference to organizational buying behavior, a company's reputation plays a more important role in cultures scoring high in UAI and PDI (Russia, Spain) and a less important role in cultures scoring low in UAI and PDI (Australia, Finland, Germany)

4.6.11 Overview

To find answers on the research questions related to the structural model and the constructs, this chapter gives an overview of the hypotheses developed (Table 4.8):

4.7 Structural Model of Reputation and Reputation Transfer

Based on the hypotheses developed in this work, a set of formative, reflective and single-item indicators is generated to build the structural model of reputation and reputation transfer.

This model provides this work with a conceptual framework for a quantitative assessment of the impact factors on reputation and reputation transfer. The indicators for the main constructs are based on theories of Fombrun (1996) and Morgan and Hunt (1994). In line with Homburg et al. (2005), this work claims that national culture impacts buying behavior; three out of five of Hofstede's (2001) dimensions and scores for measurement are used.

In the literature, some direct relationships are defined within the communication channels and tools, but how strong the linkages are between media-enabled direct marketing, personal direct marketing, reputation and reputation transfer has not been discussed in detail (Karaosmanoglu and Melewar 2006; Dowling 2001; Dacin and Brown 2002; Wiedmann 2004). Reputation and reputation transfer are expected to be influenced by relationship quality, both direct marketing media, innovativeness and WOM.

In addition, the role of perceived fit of the new product range to the existing range remains unclear: Keller (2003) discusses the necessity of the pre-condition of product-related, or at least category-related, fit for the successful transfer of a company's reputation. Counter-arguments can be found in the study by Klink and Smith (2001), who disagree that brands should not be extended to perceptually distant categories. For this reason, the category fit is considered a possible

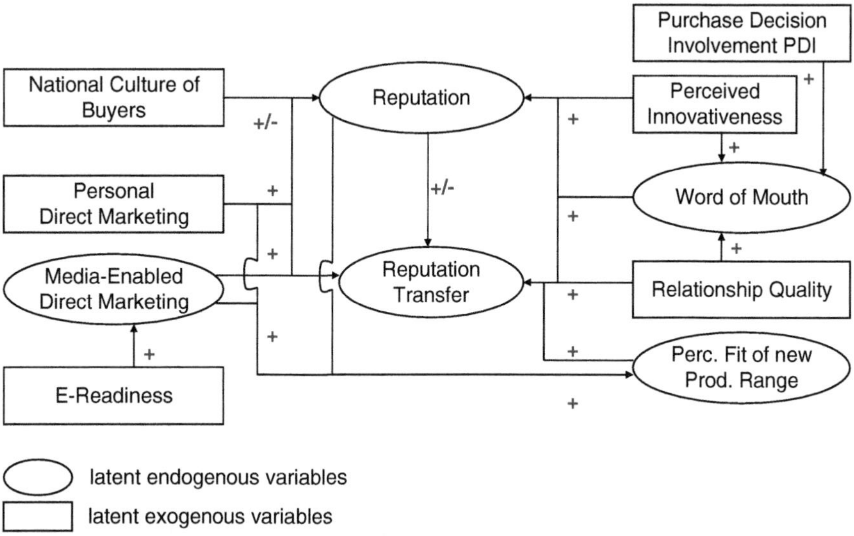

Fig. 4.11 Structural model of reputation and reputation transfer

determinant of reputation transfer success and included in the structural model. A positive relationship between reputation transfer and perceived fit is anticipated.

While influencing the public view and the perception of a company (Fombrun 1996; Dowling 2001), CR is regarded as an impact factor on the perceived fit. Fig. 4.11 depicts the structural model and conjectural relations making up the research hypotheses. Four latent endogenous and six latent exogenous variables are integrated in this structural model.

Dacin and Brown (2002) assert that the research in corporate identity and corporate association areas should focus on the role of direct communications, WOM in third-party communications and emotions and feelings of individuals in understanding how the constituents of organizations build impressions. The author claims that this is also true to understand the impact factors on reputation. Although these internal and external factors have been described by anecdotal articles, and some of them have been studied individually, a comprehensive framework which integrates the above aspects in one model has not yet been tested.

The relationship between industrial product importance, purchase decision involvement and WOM has not been tested empirically to date, but a positive relationship between the two constructs can be argued on the same grounds as the relationship between product involvement and WOM in a consumer setting (von Wangenheim and Bayòn 2007). WOM is estimated to be influenced positively by relationship quality, innovativeness and PDI. The relationship between reputation and reputation transfer is expected to be either positive or negative. For all countries, a positive relationship is estimated between media-enabled direct marketing and e-readiness.

In line with Dowling (2004), the structural model used in this work consists of two major factors to analyze CR: The emotional part of reputation forms the construct itself, based on a company's "personality" (I trust in the products of this company, this company shares expertise as a partner, this company cares for customer opinions) and can also be found in the constructs of "WOM" and "purchase decision involvement" and "relationship quality". A fact-oriented reputation referring to a company's product performance is found in the constructs related to reputation: Reputation transfer (I would expect the same product quality), innovativeness (this company is known for innovative/leading products) and perceived fit of the new product range. Two different types of direct marketing media are integrated in this model in order to learn about the influencing power of the media on a company's reputation and to study cultural differences in the use of direct marketing media. For this reason, the e-readiness scores have also been considered a factor in media-enabled direct marketing.

Chapter 5
Empirical Survey

To define the goals of this research work, the relationship between the above set of constructs was investigated and evaluated based on primary data collection in five countries. This chapter outlines the background and the aim of the study, the required structure of data, the development of the questionnaire, the target groups and countries as well as the plan and structure of the research.

5.1 Markets Under Consideration

"Establishing the pharmaceutical brand position – the advantageous location a product owns in the minds of physicians – is arguably among the most challenging components of marketing development", especially in today's hypercompetitive environment (Vanderveer and Pines 2007, p. 71). The maturation of markets such as pharmaceuticals, medical devices and diagnostics needs superior strategic marketing skills to find competitive advantages in them (Smith 2007). These markets, in which the customer is a physician or related medical professional, have shown double-digit growth rates, high levels of innovation and the penetration of every developed and developing market (Smith 2007). From the 1990s, however, this industry showed all the signs that it was maturing: declining growth rates and fewer launches of new products (IMS Health 2006).

Although considered as an indication of growth for a company, introducing new products and brand extensions may be critical (Kotler and Keller 2006). Generic pharmaceuticals are identical to the branded products, except that they differ in price and have different labels. To replace a successful branded pharmaceutical product after patent expiry, sometimes up to 15 identical generic products are brought onto the market. Being aware that the generic market for pharmaceuticals is still a highly competitive market, the strategic marketing department of a medical devices company decided, in the course of 2006, to carry out an international study on customers' brand perception and the company's reputation. The existing product

C. Falkenreck, *Reputation Transfer to Enter New B-to-B Markets*,
Contributions to Management Science,
DOI 10.1007/978-3-7908-2357-8_5,

range consistes of infusion pumps, cannulas, needles and syringes, intravenous catheters as well as large- and small-volume containers of replacement fluids, among others. The aim of the study was to learn about how the company was perceived by its international customers: Corporate reputation and the perceived fit of the new product range to the existing products in the field of medical devices. Among others, knowledge needed to be extended regarding the manner in which the existing brand and its new corresponding products should be paired (e.g., with an advertising slogan). Branding strategy may influence corporate reputation formation (Gardberg 2006). Is it possible to enter the new market of pharmaceuticals by using the existing reputation of the company? Currently, the traditional approach to pharmaceutical brand positioning involves customers essentially reacting to statements developed by the marketing organization (Vanderveer and Pines 2007). Findings of Kuhn and Alpert (2004) claimed that in the B-to-B context, very few customers pays attention to claims, slogans etc.

A good reputation in an international market consisting of comparable goods may positively affect consumer choices among identical products (Keller 2003). Besides marketer-controlled sources of information, brand associations and reputation can also be created in other ways (Keller 2003). Direct customer experience, information communicated about the brand or product by sales representatives or colleagues, word of mouth, assumptions or inferences from the brand itself (e.g., name or logo) influence a company's image and build its reputation. To build brand equity, to develop marketing programs and to design future communication strategies, knowledge of customers' sources of information needed to be an essential part of the study. The focus of the study was located in the field of direct marketing media to gain a deeper understanding of the various media used by different customers in different countries. Taking into consideration the fact that sources of information may vary from country to country and from stakeholder group to stakeholder group, an international context was required, and up to five different countries should be part of the study.

After discussions with regional heads of different business units, it was decided to include three target groups: purchasers, as they specify the product tenders and buy the goods, pharmacists, as they are involved in the ordering process of injectable drugs, and the users of medical devices and pharmaceutical drugs, i.e., doctors and nurses in hospitals.

5.1.1 Selection of Countries and Definition of Target Groups

To discuss a company's reputation with its customers requires a certain amount of knowledge about the company and its products. The selection of countries to be included in this survey therefore followed three main criteria:

- Years of sales activities of the medical device company in this country,
- Market position and penetration, and

- In order to evaluate the cultural impact, different scores regarding Hofstede's cultural dimensions.

Taking into consideration the market position of the companies in individual countries was very important. On the one hand, the companies' reputations in each country were expected to differ according to market leadership positioning versus follower positioning. On the other hand, certain knowledge on the company and its product range needed to be available via the survey participants. Not knowing the company and its products in this case meant not to be able to judge its reputation.

Market leader countries and follower countries were discussed with the global regional heads of the strategic marketing departments to learn about market structures, sales figures and years of activity in these countries. Finally, the decision was made on three market leader countries (Finland, Germany and Spain) and two follower countries (Australia and Russia), where the market activities did not last longer than 15 years and where customer knowledge of the medical device company existed, although it was rather limited. In Germany, Finland and Spain, market activities last between 50 and 150 years, so customer knowledge about the medical device company was therefore expected to be based on long-lasting customer relationships and product experience.

The only problem regarding the countries selected was the different number of hospitals in each country: Russia was said to have more than 6,000 hospitals, while Germany and Spain had about 4,000 hospitals. According to the literature, Australia had around 1,000 hospitals, whereas Finland only had 100 hospitals. The number of hospitals in each country refers to the population size. As Russia is the biggest country on earth, ten participants were selected from five regions (Western, the Urals, Central, Siberia and Privolzkhy) to ensure that the 50 hospital employees did not all belong to one region.

Regarding Hofstede's dimensions of the countries selected, all the countries differed significantly in at least one out of four dimensions (Table 5.1)

The Australian dimension scores are similar to the US scores: low in UAI, average in PDI, high in MAS and extremely high in IDV. According to Hofstede's research, Germany scores very high in MAS and, like Finland, low in PDI. Russia was chosen because it scores high in UAI and extremely low in IDV.

The study of Newman and Nollen (1996) results in the fact that the UAI dimension may not be a useful dimension for comparative research. They suggest that measuring UAI in the early 1970s may have resulted in higher UAI scores in

Table 5.1 Hofstede's scores in the selected countries

Individualism (IDV) *vs.* collectivism	Masculinity vs. femininity (MAS)	Power distance (PDI)	Uncertainty avoidance (UAI)
Australia: 93	Germany: 72	Russia: 93	Russia: 95
Germany: 73	Australia: 68	Spain: 50	Spain: 80
Finland: 68	Spain: 48	Australia: 32	Germany: 60
Spain: 53	Russia: 36	Germany: 30	Finland: 54
Russia: 39	Finland: 30	Finland: 28	Australia 48

Europe because of the cold war and memories of World War II. Newman and Nollen (1996) also claim that UAI may be irrelevant as a concept in countries labeled as having low scores in UAI, as clarity of policies and direction is a good management practice, regardless of national culture (Denison and Mishra 1995). Using Hofstede's (2001) dimensions, the findings of Homburg et al. (2004) do not support this. Their study indicates that countries scoring high in UAI care more for tangible relationship sources and have low willingness to change (Homburg et al. 2004). Intangibles seem to play a more important role in cultures scoring low in UAI.

Following these discussions, this work is additionally focused on two non-European countries: Regarding the dimension on UAI, Australia scores very low (index of 48), whereas Russia scores very high (index of 95). This work takes into consideration the focus set on intangible assets (corporate reputation) as well as the close relation between caring for sick people and avoiding uncertainty (Firth-Cozens 2004). For this reason, omitting the dimension of UAI in the field of hospital care products can possibly bias the cultural results.

The definition of target groups was related to the customers of the medical device company: purchasers in organizational buying centers (so-called "expert buyers", Darby and Karni 1973), pharmacists and users: doctors and nurses. The coding of the questionnaire ensured that countries, regions and user groups could later be identified in the survey data.

5.1.2 Data

Although cross-cultural studies have been diligently carried out, the core issue of international business relationships – the benefits and the influence of cultural differences on perceptions of these benefits – has largely been ignored (Homburg et al. 2005).

This work aims to examine differences between customers of five countries and looks more closely at possible differences between the various user groups of the products related to this research (purchasers, pharmacists, doctors and nurses). The data were collected using randomly chosen hospital addresses (available from the market research agency, TforG, Belgium, who carried out the telephone survey) in Australia, Germany, Finland, Russia and Spain as a sampling frame. A sample of 250 purchasers, pharmacists, doctors and nurses was randomly selected – 50 participants from each of the five countries. These stakeholder groups were contacted by telephone by TforG and the questionnaire was read out to them.

Data were not only evaluated based on the individual countries, but also summarized in three stakeholder groups: purchasers (purchaser, head of purchasing, expert group member), pharmacists (head pharmacist), and doctors and nurses (head nurse, intensive care unit (ICU) doctor, ICU nurse, anesthetist). Only 5.9% of the participants claimed to have very little knowledge on the product range of the medical device company, and 4.8% did not know the company at all. On the other hand, more than 89% of the purchasers, pharmacists, doctors and nurses claimed to be experienced in both the products and the company.

This questionnaire was pre-tested and re-adjusted in three countries: Germany, Finland and Spain, in order to avoid misunderstandings regarding the content or the general order of the questions, the pre-formulated, standardized answers, and also to check the time required for each telephone interview.

To concentrate on one branch only-medical devices and pharmaceuticals, where all stakeholders are involved in the hospital business-limits the chance of generalizations of data. Nevertheless, to evaluate and compare B-to-B context data across several Western and one Eastern country should make it possible to generalize at least part of the results: the impact of culture, the use of direct marketing media, the influencing role of WOM and relationship quality in the context of reputation and reputation transfer.

5.1.3 Development of Standardized Questionnaire

In September 2007, a telephone survey was conducted with native speakers by an independent market research agency in order to test the derived hypotheses. First, questionnaire items were developed and pre-tested. Working with unobserved latent constructs, single- and multi-item measures with four reflective (reputation, reputation transfer, WOM, Innovativeness), four formative (PDI, perceived quality, personal and media-enabled direct marketing) and four single items (e-readiness, perceived fit, years of product experience, national culture of buyers) to operationalize corporate reputation and reputation transfer were used. The next section provides information about the plan and structure of data collection.

Twenty-four questions and more that 80 sub-questions were asked by native speakers in German, English, Finnish, Russian and Spanish and collected in a CATI (computer-assisted telephone interview) system. All items were measured either on a four-point Likert-type scale with "agree", "somewhat agree", "somewhat disagree" and "disagree" as anchors, or on a 1–5 ranking scale, 1 meaning "I do not use", 5 meaning "I frequently use" with reference to the use of direct marketing media.

The questionnaire was divided into two sections: The first 11 questions were general questions on the use of direct marketing media, customer relationship, consumer behavior and expectations toward suppliers in the field of B-to-B. The company involved in this survey was not mentioned until the 12th question was asked. Questions 12–24 were related to the relationship between the stakeholder groups and the company, the willingness to recommend its products, the attitude toward its existing and future product range as well as expectations and opinions of buyers regarding the company's sales representatives. Without asking for reputational details on a certain company, no general statements can be made on a certain company's reputation, on a company's relationship toward its customers and on the customers' attitude toward the company's existing and future product ranges. The complete questionnaire can be found in Annex 1.

To enhance translation equivalence (Brislin 1980), the German questionnaire was translated into the local languages and back-translated into German to ensure that the concepts were consistent. Native speakers did the translations to ensure that the spelling of specific words was changed to match local usage where necessary, such as Australia.

The pre-test of the questionnaire was carried out at the marketing research agency TforG and included German, Finnish and Spanish participants, three from each country. This pre-test served as an additional check on the translations and the wording of the questions. Some questions contained misunderstandings regarding the alternative answers. Two questions were revised after the pre-test and the time required for each telephone conversation was checked: Each call took about 25–30 min, which is a long period of time for a telephone survey. Nevertheless, as the questionnaire consisted of two parts, it was not possible to shorten it significantly.

The international survey comprised several steps and was conducted over 18 months, including questionnaires, pre-tests and evaluations. The CATI telephone survey was supported by a professional market research agency and took 2 weeks.

5.2 The Measurement Model

Partial Least Squares (PLS) is a powerful method of analysis because of the minimal demands on measurement scales, sample size, and residual distributions. It is primarily intended for causal-predictive analysis in situations of high complexity, but low theoretical information (Jöreskog and Wold 1982). This can also be seen as an advantage as "theory construction is as important as theory verification" (Deshpande 1983, p. 107).

Although PLS can be used for theory confirmation, it can also be used to suggest where relationships might or might not exist and to suggest propositions for later testing (Chin 1998). Compared to the better known factor-based covariance fitting approach for latent structural modeling like LISREL, EQS and AMOS applications, SmartPLS, as well as MPlus applications of the variance-based approach, can handle both types of formative and reflective scales. Formative item weights and reflective item loadings, as well as structural model parameters, can be estimated simultaneously (e.g., Fassott and Eggert 2005; Ringle and Spreen 2007).

The PLS approach is prediction oriented and variance based; latent variable scores are explicitly estimated (Chin 1998). The approach estimates the latent variables as exact linear combinations of the observed measures (Wold 1981). Using the iterative estimation technique (Wold 1981), the PLS approach provides a general model which encompasses, among other techniques, canonical correlation, redundancy analysis, multiple regression, multivariate analysis of variance, and principal components. Sample size can be smaller (Chin 1998); an extreme example is given by Wold (1989) who analyzed 27 variables using two latent constructs with a data set consisting of ten cases.

PLS is considered better suited to explaining complex relationships (Fornell et al. 1990; Fornell and Bookstein 1982). Standard errors need to be estimated via resampling procedures such as jackknifing or bootstrapping (Efron and Gong 1983). The blindfolding procedure omits part of the data matrix for the construct being examined and then estimates the model parameters. This is done a number of times based on the blindfold omission distance. The finite mixture approach can be used to identify certain clusters within the evaluated sample.

Being a limited information method, PLS parameter estimates are less than optimal regarding bias and consistency. The estimates will be asymptotically correct under the joint conditions of consistency (large sample size) and consistency at large (the number of indicators per latent variable becomes large). In this work, this limitation does not influence the empirical results, as sample size varies between 50 and 250 and the number of indicators per latent variable does not exceed three indicators per construct.

5.2.1 Formal Elements

The PLS model consists of endogenous and exogenous constructs. Endogenous constructs have their causal antecedents specified within the model under consideration. The exogenous constructs outside the model are specified exclusively by observed measures or indicators. Endogenous, as well as exogenous, constructs may consist of reflective or formative indicators. The inner relations (inner model, structural model) describe the relation between all constructs (latent variables) corresponding to substantive theory and hypotheses. η represents the vector of the dependent (endogenous) latent variables, ζ is the unexplained variance and ξ is a vector of a exogenous latent variable (Chin 1998).

The weight relations describe the weights between the latent variables and their indicators. The outer relation describes the interrelationship between observed and latent variables, and it defines how each block of indicators relates to its latent variable (Chin 1998). The PLS two-block model presented below consists of one formative exogenous (ξ) and one reflective endogenous (η) construct (Fig. 5.1)

The measurement model consists of the relationship between the constructs and the respective indicators. The extent to which these indicators (x_1, x_2, y_1, y_2) reflect their respective endogenous (η) or exogenous (ξ) construct is determined by the related loadings a, b, c, d (Chin 1998). A one-way causal relationship is estimated between two related variables, constructs ξ and η. As ξ can only explain a portion of the variance in η, the residual variance at this structural level is assumed to reside in ζ. A sample data set can evaluate the parameters for the measurement model (loadings a-d) and structural model (path coefficient p and variance ζ).

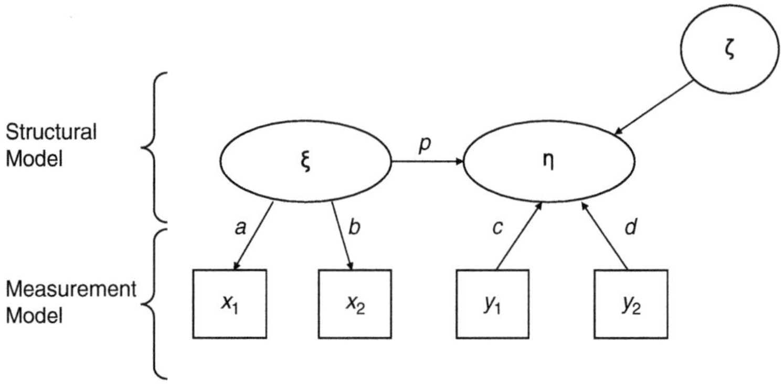

Fig. 5.1 PLS Two-block model, based on Chin (1998)

Table 5.2 Evaluation criteria of PLS structural model based on: Krafft et al. 2005, p. 85; Fornell and Larcker 1981; Chin 1998

Criterion	Definition	Evaluation
Measure (Ausmaß) and significance of PLS path coefficient p	Strength of relationship between the constructs	Standardized betas, reliability of value is tested by a re-sampling bootstrapping procedure (t-values)
t-value	PLS bootstapping procedure Nonparametric approach for estimating the precision of the PLS estimates	Threshold value: above 1.960
R square criterion for predictive relevance	Explained portion of variance of a construct on another construct. Value can be between 0 and 1	Interpretation is identical to that of traditional regression Threshold values are 0.67 (substantial), 0.33 and 0.19 (weak effect), (Chin 1998)
Effect size f^2	Impact of exogenous variable on endogenous variable	$f^2 = \frac{R^2_{incl.} - R^2_{excl.}}{1 - R^2_{incl.}} \,!\, 0$
Stone-Geisser Test Criterion, Q^2 or q^2	Predictive sample re-use technique, developed by Stone (1974) and Geisser (1975) PLS blindfolding procedure	$q^2 = \frac{Q^2_{incl.} - Q^2_{excl}}{1 - Q^2_{incl.}}$ $Q^2 = 1 - \frac{\sum_D E_D}{\sum_D E_D}$ Threshold values: see R^2

5.2.2 *Evaluation Criteria for Indicators and Constructs*

To assess the significance and the explanatory power of the measurement model, certain criteria should be evaluated (see Table 5.2 for an overview). The evaluation criteria can be separated for the structural model as a whole as well as for formative and reflective constructs (Fornell and Larcker 1981). All proposed criteria have been used in this work.

Table 5.3 Evaluation criteria of reflective constructs

Criterion	Definition	Evaluation
Cronbach's Alpha	Threshold ≥ 0.7, Nunally, (1978) ≥ 0.4, for 2–3 indicators, Peter (1997)	$\alpha = \frac{n}{n - 1}\left[1 - \frac{\sum \sigma_i^2}{\sigma_x^2}\right]$
Confirmatory Factor Analysis	Thresholds average variance explained (identical with AVE-values): ≥ 0.5 (Peter 1997) factor loadings > 0.5 (Backhaus et al. 2003, Nunally 1978) significance test of factor loadings: t ≥ 1.96 (Backhaus et al. 2003)	
Average Variance Extracted Fornell and Larcker (1981)	It measures the amount of variance that an LV component captures from its indicators relative to the amount due to measurement error. As well as the composite reliability measure, the AVE is only applicable to reflective constructs	$AVE = \frac{\sum \lambda_i^2 \operatorname{var} F}{\sum \lambda_i^2 \operatorname{var} F + \sum \theta_{ii}}$ According to Diamantopoulos and Siguav (2002), the threshold for the AVE is > 0.5, factor loadings should be > 0.7. λ_i ,F and θ_{ii} are factor loading, factor variance, and unique/error variance, respectively
Composite reliability of construct (Werts, Linn and Jöreskog 1974)	Internal consistency for a given block of indicators This measure does not assume equivalence among the measures with its assumption that all indicators are equally weighted (Chin 1998)	$\rho_c = \frac{(\sum \lambda_I)^2 \operatorname{var} F}{((\sum \lambda_I)^2 \operatorname{var} F + \sum \theta_{ii})}$ Referring to Hulland (1999) the threshold value for the composite reliability is > 0.70
Cross-loadings	Test of discriminant validity, calculation of correlation between latent variable component score and other indicators of the model	If an indicator loads higher with other latent variables, the appropriateness is recommended to be reconsidered, and reflection of construct is unclear

The Tables 5.3 and 5.4 list the criteria generally proposed for reflective and formative constructs (Chin 1998; Diamantopoulos and Siguaw 2006; Ringle et al. 2006).

The criteria for acceptable psychometric properties require that (1) internal consistency exceed 0.70; (2) loading in a confirmatory factor analysis exceed 0.50, (3) loadings are greater than cross-loadings, and (4) the square root of the average variance extracted (AVE) exceeds the inter-construct correlations (Chin 1998; Fornell and Larcker 1981).

In an overview, the evaluation criteria for structural models proposed by Herrmann, Huber and Kressmann (2006 see also Chin and Newsted 1999, p. 312 and Chin 1998, p. 318) show once again the different models and their validation criteria. The table also separates between validation criteria for formative versus reflective constructs.

The (Table 5.5) offers an overview of how the different validation criteria are related to reflective or formative constructs as well as of different threshold values referring either to the measurement model or to the structural model. It makes it

Table 5.4 Evaluation criteria of formative constructs

Criterion	Definition	Evaluation
Content validity of construct	Ensures that the formation of formative constructs generated by index construction is performed in a reliable way, (Diamantopoulos and Winklhofer, 2001; Diamantopoulos and Siguaw, 2006; Bagozzi et al. 1981)	Pre-test of indicators with experts regarding content, parsimony and criterion validity
Variance Inflation Factor, VIF	Testing multicollinearity of constructs using an adjusted R value (Diamantopoulos and Siguaw 2006).	$\text{VIF} = \frac{1}{1-R^2}$ Using standardized weights of formative constructs followed by SPSS regression analysis. Threshold value: < 12.

clear that especially with regard to the validation of constructs, completely different measures are used.

5.2.3 Creation of SmartPLS Structural Model

The structural model shown below presents all endogenous and exogenous constructs: (Fig. 5.2)

5.2.4 Treatment of Missing Values

Data were captured subject to a number of standard procedures to check for missing values and multivariate normality. The analysis of data revealed an average number of missing values, and no systematic pattern of missing values was identified. Missing values in the constructs are treated with the standardized procedure of SmartPLS (Kristensen and Eskildsen 2005), which is considered to be robust (Chatelin et al. 2002).

5.2.5 Content Validity of Reflective Constructs

In a reflective scale, all observed indicators are viewed as being caused by some underlying common dimension or construct (Bagozzi et al. 1981; Fornell and Bookstein 1982). Unlike items used in a formative scale, each item in a reflective scale is assumed to share a common context, which is the underlying construct of interest. An increase in the value of the construct leads to an increase in the value for all the items representing the construct.

Table 5.5 Validation criteria of PLS models

Measurement model			Structural model		Selection of model
	Reflective constructs	Formative constructs			
Weights	Irrelevant	No guidelines	Structural Parameters	No guidelines	Group comparison (see Chin, 1998)
Loadings	> 0.8	Irrelevant	T-values	Two-way paths > 1.98	f^2 test
t-Value	One-way paths > 1.66	Two-way paths > 1.98	R^2	> 0.19	Changes in Stone-Geissers Q^2 (Redun-dancy)
Multicollinearity	irrelevant	Variance Inflation Factor < 10	Multicollinearity	Variance Inflation Factor < 10	
Prediction validity	Stone-Geissers Q^2 (Redundancy) > 0			Stone-Geissers Q^2 (Redundancy) > 0	
Uni-dimensionality	Crossloadings	Irrelevant			
Discriminancy	Fornel-Larcker Criterion	Correlation of construct (<0.9)			

Source: adapted from Hermann et al. (2006) based on Chin and Newsted (1999) and Chin (1998)

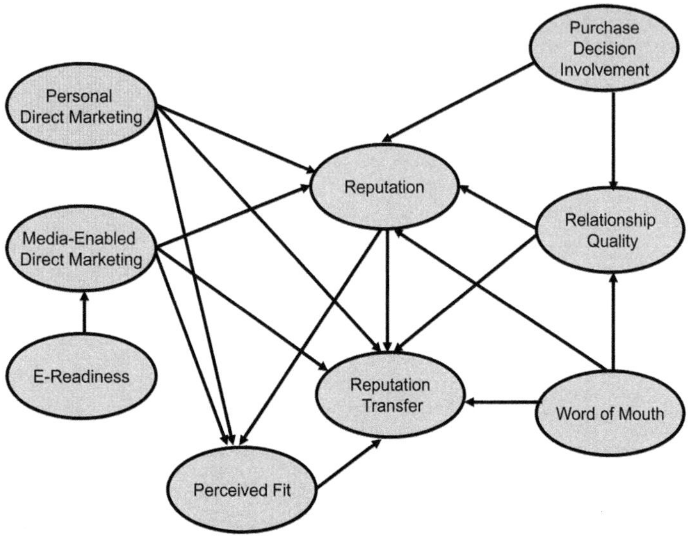

Fig. 5.2 SmartPLS structural model

The data were analyzed with a structural-equation-model approach using a SmartPLS algorithm. Measurement tests for each construct were carried out first: Cronbach's Alpha values and a confirmatory factor analysis. These confirmatory methods provide a comprehensive means for assessing and modifying theoretical models (Anderson and Gerbing 1988). The results indicate acceptable psychometric reliability and validity. No indicators needed to be eliminated, as the loadings did not fall below the threshold of 0.4 (Hulland 1999).

To assess the significance and the explanatory power of the structural model, one must consider not only theory, but also measurement (Fornell and Larcker 1981). The determination of the statistical significance of individual parameter estimates can only be solved by using additional measurement testing methods (Bagozzi et al. 1981). The discriminant validity of the reflective variables is evaluated based on the Fornell-Larcker criterion (Fornell and Larcker 1981) and on the cross-loadings of all indicators generating the reflective constructs (Bollen and Lennox 1991).

Chapter 6
Results and Findings

The evaluation of research data starts with the presentation of some general findings on the importance of CR and external trust to international purchasers in organizational relationships. Subsequently, a detailed data analysis of ten different measurement criteria is carried out. A synopsis of these criteria can be found in Sect. 6.1, followed by the assessment of research hypotheses in Sect. 6.4. An overview presenting the different structural models according to countries and stakeholder groups can be found in Sect. 6.2.12; fit measures and significant paths are integrated. The findings related to countries and stakeholder groups are summarized in Sect. 6.4, followed by the discussion of research questions.

6.1 Synopsis of Measurement Criteria

During the evaluation phase of the data-sets of different countries and stakeholder groups, the following criteria have been examined and measured (Table 6.1):

To evaluate the goodness of a structural model, it is not generally recommended that all criteria need to be fulfilled simultaneously: "Fit indices should not be regarded as measures of usefulness of a model. They contain some information about the lack of fit of a model, but none about plausibility" (Browne and Cudeck 1993, p. 157, see also Peter 1999).

6.2 Model Validation

Data were subject to a number of standard procedures to check for missing values and multivariate normality. The analysis of data revealed an average number of missing values, but no systematic pattern of missing values was identified. The data were then analyzed in several separate, but sequentially related steps. A correlation analysis was conducted to learn about the nature and direction of relationships

C. Falkenreck, *Reputation Transfer to Enter New B-to-B Markets*,
Contributions to Management Science,
DOI 10.1007/978-3-7908-2357-8_6,

between different scales, as well as the strength of association. Understanding these strengths of theses relationships was the basis for the application of the structural model. In a final step, the data were analyzed, utilizing SmartPLS 2.0 (M3) Beta. The purpose of the data analysis was to test the theoretical model development empirically. A PLS path model can be validated at three levels (Tenenhaus et al. 2004):

- The quality of the measurement model
- The quality of the structural model
- Each structural regression equation

The results of this analysis are reported in the following chapters. Sample sizes, effect sizes, power of statistical tests and significance levels are discussed to provide consistency in the results. An overview of all evaluated measurement criteria can be found in Sect. 6.3. Although Tenenhaus et al. (2004) propose to also evaluate a global criterion of goodness-of-fit as the geometric mean of the average communality and the average R^2, the author declines to do so. This measurement criterion refers solely to reflective structural models (Amato et al. 2004) and can, moreover, be manipulated easily by using single-item constructs, where the communality is always = 1. This positively impacts on the goodness of fit.

Table 6.1 Evaluation criteria of reflective and formative constructs and structural model

Criterion	Threshold value	Valid for reflective constructs	Valid for formative constructs	Valid for structural model
Multi-collinearity	VIF < 10		(√)	
Significant weights and loadings	≥ 0.1 ≥ 0.7 für p= 0.05	√	√	
Content validity	Confirmatory factor analysis (≥ 0.5) Pretest with experts	√		
AVE	≥ 0.5 (Diamantopoulos and Siguaw 2002)	√	√	
Cronbach's alpha	≥ 0.7 (Nunally 1978) ≥ 0.4 (Peter, 1997)	√		
Cross loadings	Test of discriminant validity	√		
Composite reliability	≥ 0.7	√		
t-value	≥1.96	√	√	√
Significance of paths	Reliability tested by a re-a sampling bootstrapping procedure	√	√	√
R^2	≥ 0.19 (Chin)			√
Effect size f^2	>0			√
Stone-Geisser test Q^2 or q^2	≥ 0			√
Bonferroni-Holm's Proc.				√
Fornell–Larcker criterion	A construct should share more variance with its measures than it shares with the other constructs	√		

6.2.1 Examination of Sample Size

It is essential to have an adequate sample size in order to apply the PLS latent variable modeling approach. In this survey, sample sizes consisted of a total of 250 participants in five countries, i.e., 50 participants from each country. There were four indicators per construct (reputation, purchase decision involvement, relationship quality, personal and media-enabled direct marketing), and three (reputation transfer, innovativeness, WOM). In addition, three single-item indicators were used: perceived fit, culture (based on Hofstede's scores for each country) and e-readiness (EIU 2007 e-readiness rankings).

Based on their findings, Chin et al. (1996) have developed a rule of thumb indicating that a tenfold sample size related to the number of indicators of the most substantial construct. The maximum number of indicators in this survey is three, which results in a maximum sample size of 30. As the present study consists of a maximum of 250 and minimum of 50 samples, the required sample size is given.

6.2.2 Moderating Effects on Reputation Transfer

To test possible moderating effects on reputation transfer, the following constructs have been evaluated:

Surprisingly, as shown in Table 6.2, except for Finland, no significant moderating effects on reputation transfer were found. In Finland, the only direct positive path coefficients related to reputation transfer were perceived innovativeness, WOM, perceived quality and media-enabled direct marketing. In addition, moderating effects were positive regarding relationship quality, which was moderated on reputation transfer through WOM.

Table 6.2 Moderating effects on reputation transfer

Moderating effects on reputation transfer	Rel. quality moderated by WOM	Media-enabled DM moderated by relationship quality	Personal DM moderated by relationship quality	Reputation moderated by WOM	Purchase decision involvement moderated by WOM
All	n.s.	n.s.	n.s.	n.s.	n.s.
Australia	n.s.	n.s.	n.s.	n.s.	n.s.
Germany	n.s.	n.s.	n.s.	n.s.	n.s.
Finland	0.116 (2.340)	n.s.	n.s.	0.085 (2.307)	n.s.
Russia	n.s.	n.s.	n.s.	n.s.	n.s.
Spain	n.s.	n.s.	n.s.	n.s.	n.s.
Purchaser	n.s.	n.s.	n.s.	n.s.	n.s.
Pharmacists	n.s.	n.s.	n.s.	n.s.	n.s.
Doctors and nurses	n.s.	n.s.	n.s.	n.s.	n.s.

A positive, significant path coefficient refers to the link between reputation and reputation transfer: the effect of reputation on reputation transfer was moderated through the predictor variable of WOM. This is remarkable because, as presented later in the evaluation of the Finnish dataset, there was no direct effect of reputation on reputation transfer: As Finnish customers openly discuss and recommend the products, reputation has a positive impact on reputation transfer through WOM.

6.2.3 Moderating Effects on Reputation

Regarding all countries and stakeholder groups, moderating effects of moderator variables on personal and media-enabled direct marketing media on reputation have been evaluated, as the direct path coefficients show only little significance and vary greatly across countries. Both direct marketing media do not affect the strength of the relation between relationship quality or WOM as a predictor variable and reputation as the criterion variable, and no significant path coefficients were found.

Furthermore, in Australia, Spain, Russia, and Finland, as well as in all stakeholder groups, no moderating effects on reputation were found regarding the moderator variable of purchase decision involvement through the predictor variable of WOM. Positive, significant values were only found evaluating the German dataset (path coefficient 0.260, t-value: 2.240) (Fig.6.1).

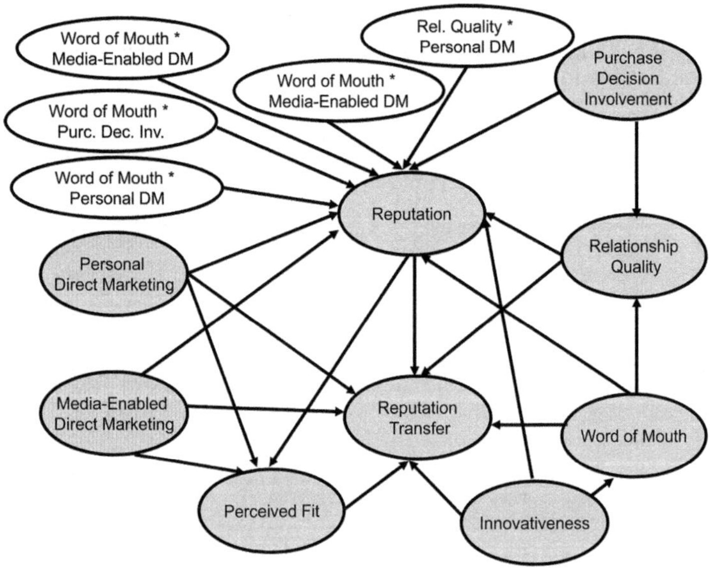

Fig. 6.1 PLS structural model including moderating effects on reputation

Purchase decision involvement affects the strength of the relation between WOM as a predictor variable and reputation as the criterion variable. This is remarkable because, as presented later in the evaluation of the German dataset, the direct effect of purchase decision involvement on reputation was not significant.

6.2.4 Mediating Effects

The following mediating effects (for calculations, see Sect. 4.3) were found and verified by calculating the VAF-value (variance accounted for). A VAF-value of 0.5 indicates that 50% of the effect of the exogenous variable on the endogenous variable is based on the mediator variable (Eggert et al. 2005). (Fig 6.2)

The following table shows that in only three countries, a significant mediator effect related to the above mediator model was found. With reference to the Finnish VAF-value >1, effects of multicollinearity (see Sect. 6.2.10) referring to the construct of media-enabled DM caused statistical suppressor effects (Table 6.3).

Suppression is defined as a variable which increases the predictive validity of another variable (or set of variables) by its inclusion in a regression equation (MacKinnon et al. 2000). However, it was suggested recently that suppression should be viewed as adding interest to the results, rather than as a confound or problem (Shrout and Bolger 2002).

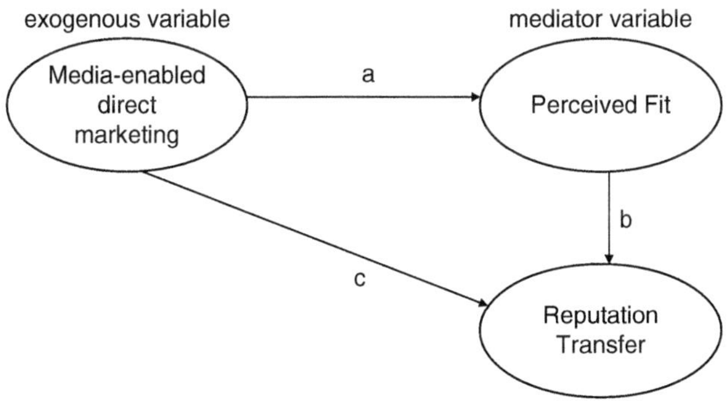

Fig. 6.2 Mediator model

Table 6.3 VAF-values of mediating effects

Country	Significant VAF-value	Interpretation
Russia	0.776	77.6% of the effect of media DM on reputation transfer is based on mediator perceived fit
Australia	0.983	98.3% of the effect of media DM on reputation transfer is based on mediator perceived fit
Finland	2.274	VAF >1: statistical suppressor effect due to multicollinearity in construct "media-enabled DM"

Table 6.4 List of evaluated mediator effects on reputation transfer and reputation

Exogenous variable	Mediator variable	Endogenous variable	Findings
Relationship quality	WOM	Reputation transfer	Significant mediating effects regarding all countries (VAF-value of 0.691) and Germany (VAF-value of 0.942)
Innovativeness	WOM	Reputation transfer	Significant mediating effects in Russia (VAF-value of 0.576)
Purchase decision involvement	WOM	Reputation	No significant mediating effects

In addition, the following mediator-models have been evaluated on all countries and stakeholder groups (Table 6.4):

Surprisingly, as listed in the above table, only very few countries show mediating effects regarding the mediator variable of WOM. Nevertheless, taking into consideration the general importance of WOM for CR and reputation transfer, the findings are valuable. With reference to the evaluation of the Russian structural model in Sect. 6.2.12, Russia does not show a significant path correlation between innovativeness and reputation transfer. Thus, this effect is mediated through WOM and can nonetheless have an impact on reputation transfer success.

The above findings also influence the construct relationships of the German structural model. As seen in Sect. 6.2.12, there is no direct significant impact of relationship quality on reputation transfer. At a first glance, reputation transfer is exclusively influenced by media-enabled direct marketing and WOM. The impact of relationship quality on reputation transfer is mediated through WOM and therefore also has to be taken as an influencing factor on reputation transfer. The same is true with regard to the evaluation of the "all countries" dataset.

6.2.5 Reliability and Content Validity of Reflective Constructs

To assess the significance and the explanatory power of the measurement model, certain criteria need to be evaluated. The following table refers to the outer loadings of the reflective constructs.

The outer loadings vary around the threshold value of 0.7 (Diamantopoulos and Siguaw, 2002). Critical values were found in relation to the indicator "shares expertise" in Germany and Spain (0.6084 and 0.6620). For further information on the research data, the outer loadings of the stakeholder groups of purchasers, pharmacists, as well as doctors and nurses, can be found in the Annex.

The following Tables 6.5 and 6.6 give an overview on the quality criteria of all reflective constructs: average variance extracted (AVE), Cronbach's alpha, composite reliability and confirmatory factor analysis.

Table 6.5 Outer loadings of reflective constructs

Constructs	Indicators	All countries	Aus	Fin	Ger	Rus	Spain
Innovativeness	Innovative prod.	0.8898	0.9129	0.9071	0.9024	0.7573	0.9019
	Leading prod.	0.8864	0.9398	0.6982	0.8840	0.8790	0.9554
Reputation	Cares for cust. opinion	0.8195	0.8736	0.8587	0.6858	0.6935	0.8207
	Shares expertise	0.8150	0.7835	0.9093	0.6084	0.8587	0.6620
	I trust in products	0.8083	0.8683	0.8670	0.9050	0.7402	0.6867
WOM	Would recommend Medical Dev.	0.9297	0.8506	0.8629	0.9539	0.9768	0.9346
	Would recommend Pharma	0.9200	0.8719	0.8788	0.9393	0.9790	0.9054
RepTransfer	Would purchase it	0.9147	0.9034	0.9585	0.9451	0.9890	0.9317
	Expect same quality	0.8650	0.8715	0.9646	0.5895	0.9885	0.9120

Table 6.6 Overview, quality criteria reputation

Reputation	Cronbach's α	Composite reliability	AVE	Confirmatory factor analysis (three indicators)
Threshold	>0.7 (Nunally 1978) >0.4 (Peter 1997)	>0.7 (Hulland 1999)	>0.5	Indicator-reliability > 0.4 (Bagozzi and Baumgartner 1994)
All	0.746	0.8551	0.6636	0.826, 0.788, 0.829
Australia	0.800	0.8725	0.7271	0.774, 0.700, 0.708
Germany	0.642	0.7839	0.6529	0.668, 0.922, 0.696
Finland	0.852	0.9103	0.7739	0.857, 0.859, 0.921
Russia	0.653	0.8100	0.6059	0.763, 0.843, 0.725
Spain	0.551	0.7688	0.5577	0.717, 0.447, 0.890
Purchaser	0.798	0.8807	0.7225	0.878, 0.813, 0.858
Pharmacists	0.637	0.8037	0.5851	0.786, 0.737, 0.771
Doctors and nurses	0.782	0.8725	0.7259	0.836, 0.841, 0.879

The overview of the quality criteria separated by the data of all countries (sample size: n=250), the five different countries (sample size of each country: n=50), purchasers (n=58), pharmacists (n=65) and users (n=110) shows that all average variance extracted scores (AVE) are above the threshold value of 0.5 (Fornell and Larcker 1981). The AVE-value measures the amount of variance that a latent variable component captures from its indicators relative to the amount due to measurement errors. The composite reliability values, (the internal consistency) of all reflective constructs exceed the threshold value of 0.7 (Hulland 1999).

Cronbach (1951) viewed reliability, including internal consistency measures, as the proportion of test variance that was attributable to group and general factors. Specific item variance, or uniqueness, was considered an error. Following the literature on Cronbach's alpha values, two different threshold values exist (>0.7: Nunally 1978, >0.4: Peter 1997), depending on the number of indicators used per construct.

In this study, as constructs consist of up to three constructs, a threshold Cronbach's alpha value of >0.4 (Peter 1997) is sufficient. Generally, most of all indicators nevertheless exceed the threshold value of >0.7 (Nunally 1978). When a measure has other desirable properties, such as a meaningful content coverage of some domain and reasonable unidimensionality, a low Cronbach's alpha value may not be a major impediment to its use (Schmitt 1996) (Table 6.7).

The German and the pharmacist dataset show low Cronbach's alpha values. However, in line with the findings of Peter (1997), a value exceeding 0.4 is still acceptable. Finland and Russia show very high Cronbach's alpha values. All other quality criteria referring to the construct of reputation transfer come up to the threshold values. All values related to the confirmatory factor analysis exceed the threshold value of 0.4 and fulfill this criterion (Table 6.8).

Surprisingly, referring to the construct of "perceived innovativeness" for Finland and Russia, low but still acceptable Cronbach's alpha values are found (Peter 1997). Referring to the confirmatory factor analysis, Germany shows one very low value not exceeding the threshold value of 0.4. All other quality criteria of the construct "perceived innovativeness" comply with the threshold values (Table 6.9).

Table 6.7 Overview, quality criteria of reputation transfer

Reputation transfer	Cronbach's α	Composite reliability	AVE	Confirmatory factor analysis (two indicators)
All	0.741	0.8841	0.7943	0.891, 0.891
Australia	0.731	0.8706	0.7652	0.765, 0.765
Germany	0.453	0.7562	0.7906	0.993, 0.401
Finland	0.918	0.9609	0.9255	0.962, 0.962
Russia	0.977	0.9887	0.9776	0.989, 0.989
Spain	0.824	0.9189	0.8517	0.904, 0.938
Purchaser	0.730	0.8805	0.7871	0.887, 0.887
Pharmacists	0.651	0.8487	0.7426	0.862, 0.862
Doctors and nurses	0.712	0.8706	0.7767	0.881, 0.881

Table 6.8 Overview, quality criteria of perceived innovativeness

Perceived innovativeness	Cronbach's α	Composite reliability	AVE	Confirmatory factor analysis (two indicators)
All	0.732	0.8819	0.7887	0.888, 0.888
Australia	0.836	0.9125	0.6649	0.815, 0.815
Germany	0.747	0.8876	0.7841	0.728, 0.377
Finland	0.500	0.7890	0.7025	0.838, 0.838
Russia	0.523	0.8037	0.7105	0.843, 0.843
Spain	0.846	0.9266	0.8768	0.932, 0.940
Purchaser	0.736	0.8836	0.7988	0.894, 0.894
Pharmacists	0.687	0.8561	0.9371	0.697, 0.747
Doctors and nurses	0.809	0.9125	0.8439	0.919, 0.919

Table 6.9 Overview, quality criteria of WOM

WOM	Cronbach's α	Composite reliability	AVE	Confirmatory factor analysis (two indicators)
All	0.831	0.9221	0.8556	0.925, 0.925
Australia	0.652	0.9263	0.7418	0.861, 0.861
Germany	0.884	0.9452	0.8971	0.938, 0.955
Finland	0.681	0.8627	1.0000	1.000, 1.000
Russia	0.954	0.9776	0.9635	0.982, 0.982
Spain	0.820	0.9173	0.8478	0.904, 0.938
Purchaser	0.771	0.8962	0.8926	0.945, 0.945
Pharmacists	0.932	0.9663	0.9918	0.996, 0.996
Doctors and nurses	0.841	0.9263	0.8777	0.937, 0.937

With regard to the quality criteria of WOM, all results were in line with the threshold values. Russia and Spain show very high Cronbach's alpha values, whereas the values of Australia and Finland are relatively weak.

To assess whether the interaction effect and main effects were significant, a bootstrap resampling procedure (Efron and Tibshirani 1993) was performed. The results of 500 resamples confirm or disconfirm validity of the path coefficients. All valid path coefficients and t-values are included in the tables in Sect. 6.2.12.

6.2.6 *R-Square and Q^2 Predictive Relevance of Structural Model*

"No proper overall goodness of fit measures exist for models estimated using PLS" (Hulland 1999, p. 202). Non-parametric tests like R^2 for dependent variables, the Q^2 cross-validation test (Stone-Geisser) and f^2 explaining the strength of effects are used (Fornell and Bookstein 1982; Krafft et al. 2005) and discussed in detail in this chapter.

Cross-validated R-square (i.e., Stone-Geisser's Q^2) between each endogenous latent variable and its own manifest variables can be calculated automatically in SmartPLS, Stone-Geisser's Q^2 by blindfolding and R^2 by running the PLS procedure (Chatelin et al. 2002). The significance levels of the regression coefficients can be computed using the Student's t statistic and cross-validation methods like bootstrapping. The bootstrap samples are built by reasampling with replacements from the original sample. The procedure yields samples consisting of the same number of cases as in the original sample.

The R^2 value is obtained because the case values of the latent variables (LV) are determined by the weight relations (Chin 1998), and the interpretation is identical to that of traditional regression. The changes in R^2 are explored to see whether the impact of a particular independent LV on a dependent LV has substantial impact. According to Chin (1998), an R^2 value > 0.67 is "substantial", 0.33 is "moderate" and 0.19 is a "weak" value. According to Fassott (2003), a value of 0.586 can be regarded as "very satisfactory". R^2 for the endogenous variable "reputation" varies

Table 6.10 R^2 and Q^2 values of different countries and stakeholder groups

R^2 threshold >0.19, Q^2 threshold >0	Reputation R^2 Q^2		WOM R^2 Q^2		Reputation transfer R^2 Q^2		Perceived fit R^2 Q^2		Media. DM, all
All	0.445	0.277	0.174	0.140	0.630	0.497	0.056	0.062	R^2
Australia	0.515	0.027	0.169	0.112	0.797	0.632	0.314	0.349	0.207
Germany	0.551	0.137	0.533	0.469	0.465	0.259	0.049	0.046	Q^2
Finland	0.661	0.449	0.275	0.212	0.929	0.836	0.230	0.209	0.072
Russia	0.422	0.114	0.411	0.367	0.891	0.879	0.294	0.294	
Spain	0.511	0.137	0.152	0.119	0.697	0.584	0.070	0.048	
Purchaser	0.546	0.297	0.101	0.101	0.873	0.672	0.098	0.088	
Pharmacist	0.568	0.257	0.101	0.073	0.649	0.481	0.386	0.284	
Docs & nurses	0.461	0.266	0.388	0.321	0.510	0.310	0.068	0.035	

between 0.431 for Russia and 0.661 for Finland, and therefore explains between 43% and 66% of the variance of this construct. Most of the R^2 values related to "reputation" can be regarded as very satisfactory.

The R^2 values for the endogenous variable of "reputation transfer" are even more substantial and vary between 0.510 for the stakeholder group of doctors and nurses and 0.929 for Finland, which explains more than 92% of the variance of this construct. Most of the R^2 values can be qualified as "substantial" (see Table 6.10).

The call for a significantly high squared correlation of endogenous variables can be regarded as reasonable if the scientific objective comprises explaining the respective endogenous variable completely (Homburg and Baumgartner 1995). In the case where the scientific objective is focused on the explanation of the causal relationship between the constructs, the retention of a given threshold value of the variance explained is not mandatory (Homburg and Baumgartner 1995). This is true for the R^2 values of WOM and perceived fit. Only the causal relationships between the endogenous constructs of WOM and perceived fit vis-à-vis the constructs reputation and reputation transfer is in the focus of this research work. This study does not aim to explain the variables of WOM and perceived fit completely. Falling below the threshold value of 0.19 is therefore acceptable for the constructs of WOM and perceived fit.

The above indicated Q^2 value refers to the quality of each structural equation and is measured by the cross-validation redundancy index (i.e., Stone-Geisser's Q^2). This results from the predictive sample reuse technique as developed by Stone (1974) and Geisser (1975). It represents a synthesis of cross-validation and function fitting with the perspective that "the prediction of observables or potential observables is of much greater relevance than the estimation of what are often artificial construct parameters" (Geisser 1975, p. 320). This technique is based on R^2, but without losses in the degrees of freedom. The idea behind the test of Stone and Geisser is to omit, or "blindfold", one case at a time, to re-estimate the model parameters on the basis of the remaining cases, and to reconstruct or predict omitted case values on the basis of re-estimated parameters.

The value of Q^2 needs to be >0. A negative value in this context means that the model is misleading, as the trivial prediction in terms of sample means is superior to the prediction derived from the tested model relation (Wold 1982; Seltin and Keeves 1994). As all Q^2 values exceed the threshold value and are not negative, all variables have fulfilled the Q^2 cross-validation test of Stone and Geisser (see Table 6.10).

In addition, with regard to the datasets of all countries and stakeholder groups, all effect sizes f^2 exceed the threshold value of >0. To avoid double presentation of measurement data, the effect sizes f^2 can be found together with the significant path coefficients in the evaluation of hypotheses data (see Sect. 6.3).

6.2.7 *Cross Loadings*

According to Chin (1998), another test of discriminant validity can be obtained by calculating the correlations between latent variable (LV) component scores and other indicators besides its own block.

If an indicator loads higher with other LVs than the one it is intended to measure, the researcher may wish to reconsider its appropriateness because it is unclear which construct or constructs it is actually reflecting (Chin 1998). Furthermore, the loading of each block of indicators is expected to load higher for its respective LV than indicators for other LVs (Table 6.11 and 6.12).

Table 6.11 Cross-loadings of reflective constructs: All countries

Cross-loadings: all countries	Perceived innovativeness	Reputation transfer	Reputation	Word of mouth
Innovative products	0.8897	0.1612	0.4648	0.2027
Cares for cust. opinions	0.4161	0.2407	0.8194	0.2382
Shares expertise	0.4232	0.1170	0.8139	0.1646
Trust in products	0.4069	0.2375	0.8093	0.3345
Leading products	0.8864	0.1880	0.4406	0.2143
Recommend Med. Dev.	0.2463	0.4630	0.3113	0.9287
Recommend pharma	0.1865	0.5242	0.2534	0.9210
Would purchase it	0.2536	0.9147	0.2422	0.5666
Expect same quality	0.0783	0.8650	0.1923	0.3625

Table 6.12 Cross-loadings of reflective constructs: Australia

Cross-loadings: Australia	Perceived innovativeness	Reputation transfer	Reputation	Word of mouth
Innovative products	0.9128	0.1579	0.2385	0.2203
Cares for cust. opinions	0.2145	0.2487	0.8723	0.4143
Shares expertise	0.1828	0.0176	0.7839	0.0259
Trust in products	0.3036	0.4105	0.8692	0.4656
Leading products	0.9399	0.2516	0.2859	0.1997
Recommend Med. Dev.	0.1590	0.2516	0.3755	0.8631
Recommend pharma	0.2298	0.4233	0.3755	0.8597
Would purchase it	0.2664	0.8784	0.3212	0.5832
Expect same quality	0.3194	0.9034	0.2370	0.5779

With reference to the loadings listed above, all items load significantly on their respective factors, with no cross-loadings and no correlated measurement errors. Discriminant validity for reflective constructs perceived innovativeness, reputation, reputation transfer and WOM can be assumed (Bollen and Lennox 1991; Diamantopoulos and Siguaw 2006) for the datasets of all countries and Australia.

Table 6.14 refers to the Finnish dataset and reveals a weak value for the second indicator of the construct "perceived innovativeness". Nevertheless, no other indicator loaded higher on this construct than the two that were intended to be measured. Therefore, this test of discriminant validity is also fulfilled for Finland (Table 6.13).

Table 6.14 (Germany) indicates that loadings on the construct of reputation and reputation transfer were weaker in comparison to other countries. As for the construct of reputation transfer, no other indicator loaded higher on this construct than the two that were intended to be measured. This is not the case regarding the construct of reputation: Haphazardly, one indicator related to the construct of WOM (recommend Medical Devices.) load higher with the construct of reputation than any of the other three indicators (shares expertise). As this only occurs with the German dataset, this matter will not be further followed up.

Table 6.13 Cross-loadings of reflective constructs: Finland

Cross-loadings: Finland	Perceived innovativeness	Reputation transfer	Reputation	Word of mouth
Innovative products	0.9069	0.4706	0.6982	0.5030
Cares for cust. opinions	0.6796	0.4285	0.8588	0.4900
Shares expertise	0.6573	0.2696	0.9095	0.2357
Trust in products	0.6611	0.3299	0.8666	0.3799
Leading products	0.6987	0.2091	0.5152	0.1932
Recommend Med. Dev.	0.4173	0.3593	0.4425	0.8665
Recommend pharma	0.3980	0.5982	0.3018	0.8754
Would purchase it	0.4505	0.9586	0.3608	0.4973
Expect same quality	0.4170	0.9646	0.3953	0.5616

Table 6.14 Cross-loadings of reflective constructs: Germany

Cross-loadings: Germany	Perceived innovativeness	Reputation transfer	Reputation	Word of mouth
Innovative products	0.9025	0.2541	0.1298	0.3487
Cares for cust. opinions	0.0367	0.2783	0.6808	0.4085
Shares expertise	0.1428	0.0228	0.6168	0.3122
Trust in products	0.1142	0.4678	0.9050	0.6189
Leading products	0.8839	0.2753	0.0881	0.2980
Recommend Med. Dev.	0.3531	0.5868	0.6372	0.9540
Recommend pharma	0.3332	0.5173	0.5712	0.9392
Would purchase it	0.3294	0.9450	0.4540	0.6161
Expect same quality	0.0510	0.5895	0.1282	0.1898

Table 6.15 Cross-loadings of reflective constructs: Russia

Cross-loadings: Russia	Perceived innovativeness	Reputation transfer	Reputation	Word of mouth
Innovative products	0.7573	0.1948	0.4966	0.1813
Cares for cust. opinions	0.2729	0.2028	0.6963	−0.0042
Shares expertise	0.6657	0.2577	0.8589	0.4031
Trust in products	0.3621	0.3112	0.7379	0.2898
Leading products	0.8789	0.2788	0.4941	0.4943
Recommend Med. Dev.	0.4081	0.4580	0.3057	0.9768
Recommend Pharma	0.4468	0.4276	0.3525	0.9790
Would purchase it	0.2653	0.9890	0.3248	0.4260
Expect same quality	0.3167	0.9885	0.3406	0.4692

Table 6.16 Cross-loadings of reflective constructs: Spain

Crossloadings Spain	Perceived innovativeness	Reputation transfer	Reputation	Word of mouth
Innovative products	0.9028	0.1076	0.0739	−0.1438
Cares for cust. opinions	0.2156	0.2198	0.8196	0.2323
Shares expertise	−0.0139	0.1319	0.6649	0.1065
Trust in products	0.0835	−0.0660	0.6855	0.2099
Leading products	0.9548	0.0025	0.1812	−0.1890
Recommend Med. Dev.	−0.2642	0.2779	0.2307	0.9296
Recommend pharma	−0.0610	0.3002	0.2460	0.9112
Would purchase it	0.1545	0.9317	0.1649	0.3169
Expect same quality	−0.0788	0.9120	0.0904	0.2573

As far as the cross-loadings of the Russian and Spanish dataset are concerned, all indicators loaded highest with the construct that was intended to be measured (Table 6.15).

Interestingly the cross-loadings of Russia regarding "perceived innovativeness" are much weaker compared to the cross-loadings of Spain, Germany and Australia. On the other hand, the cross-loadings of the indicators of "Word of Mouth" are much higher than the cross-loadings of all other countries. Also, with regard to the cross-loadings, the data-sets of the single countries differ substantially (Table 6.16).

Generally, in this study, the calculation of the correlations between LV component scores and other indicators besides its own block, show that the indicators reflect the construct they are intended to measure. The additional cross-loadings of purchasers, pharmacists and users can be found in Annex 1.

6.2.8 Fornell–Larcker Criterion

To analyze the validity and to exclude measurement errors of structural equation models with unobserved variables, the Fornell–Larcker criterion is used (Fornell and Larcker 1981). This testing system is based on measures of shared variances within the structural model, measurement model, and overall model. First of all, the tables below show that the average variance extracted (AVE) is above the threshold value of 0.5 (Diamantopoulos and Siguaw 2002). The AVE is sensitive to a lack of convergent validity and can therefore be used to assess discriminant validity (Fornell and Larcker 1981): If the shared variance is not large enough to warrant interpretation in terms of operational significance, the model is rejected, regardless of its statistical significance.

AVE scores greater than 0.50 indicate that a higher amount of variance in the indicators is captured by the construct compared to that accounted for by measurement error (Fornell and Larcker 1981; Diamantopoulos and Siguaw 2006). The tables show that, as required, each of the squared measures of the SmartPLS correlation matrix does not exceed the AVE-values. Following the definitions of the Fornell–Larcker criterion, it is fulfilled for all observed countries and stakeholder groups (Table 6.17and 6.18).

With reference to the dataset of "all countries" and "Australia", Tables 6.19 and 6.20 show that the AVE-values exceed the threshold value of 0.5. Furthermore, none of the squared measures of the SmartPLS correlation matrix exceeds the AVE-value. The Fornell–Larcker criterion is fulfilled for these countries.

Table 6.17 Fornell–Larcker criterion, data of all countries

All countries	Perceived innovativeness	Reputation transfer	Reputation	Word of mouth
Perc. innovativeness	1.0000	0,0386	0,2600	0,0551
Reputation transfer	0,0386	1.0000	0,0607	0,2839
Reputation	0,2600	0,0607	1.0000	0,0936
Word of mouth	0,0551	0,2839	0,0936	1.0000
AVE	0.7887	0.7924	0.6629	0.8554

Table. 6.18 Fornell–Larcker criterion, data of Australia

Australia	Perceived Innovativeness	Reputation Transfer	Reputation	Word of Mouth
Perc. innovativeness	1.0000	0,0508	0.0813	0.0508
Reputation transfer	0.0508	1.0000	0.0910	0.3201
Reputation	0.0813	0.0910	1.0000	0.1595
Word of mouth	0.0508	0.3201	0.1595	1.0000
AVE	0.8390	0.7713	0.6950	0.8628

Table 6.19 Fornell–Larcker criterion, data of Finland

Finland	Perceived innovativeness	Reputation transfer	Reputation	Word of mouth
Perc. innovativeness	1.0000	0.2029	0.5771	0.2188
Reputation transfer	0.2029	1.0000	0.1552	0.3045
Reputation	0.5771	0.1552	1.0000	0.1816
Word of mouth	0.2188	0.3045	0.1816	1.0000
AVE	0.6553	0.9247	0.7719	0.7585

Table 6.20 Fornell–Larcker Criterion, data of Germany

Germany	Perceived innovativeness	Reputation transfer	Reputation	Word of mouth
Perc. innovativeness	1.0000	0.0874	0.0147	0.1318
Reputation transfer	0.0874	1.0000	0.1861	0.3427
Reputation	0.0147	0.1861	1.0000	0.4114
Word of mouth	0.1318	0.3427	0.4114	1.0000
AVE	0.7979	0.6203	0.5543	0.8961

Table 6.21 Fornell–Larcker criterion, data of Spain

Spain	Perceived innovativeness	Reputation transfer	Reputation	Word of mouth
Perc. innovativeness	1.0000	0.0024	0.0215	0.0333
Reputation transfer	0.0024	1.0000	0.0208	0.0981
Reputation	0.0215	0.0208	1.0000	0.0663
Word of mouth	0.0333	0.0981	0,0663	1.0000
AVE	0.8634	0.8499	0.5279	0.8472

Table 6.22 Fornell–Larcker criterion, data of Russia

Russia	Perceived innovativeness	Reputation transfer	Reputation	Word of mouth
Perc. innovativeness	1.0000	0.0864	0.3602	0.1916
Reputation transfer	0.0864	1.0000	0.1132	0.2047
Reputation	0.3602	0.1132	1.0000	0,1154
Word of mouth	0.1916	0.2047	0.1153	1.0000
AVE	0.6730	0.9776	0.5890	0.9563

The datasets of Finland and Germany also exhibit AVE-values exceeding 0.5. Nevertheless, regarding the German, Russian, and Spanish datasets, the construct of reputation exhibits only a relatively low AVE-value (0.52–0.58) compared to other country values. While exceeding 0.9, the Finnish AVE-value of reputation transfer score is extremely high.

The Russian dataset shows that the AVE-values exceed the threshold value of 0.5; very high AVE-values can be found with the constructs of WOM and reputation transfer. The overview of the Fornell–Larcker criteria of the different stakeholder groups can be found in Annex 2 (Table 6.21 and 6.22).

6.2.9 *Reliability and Content Validity of Formative Constructs*

According to Bollen and Ting (2000), it is difficult to establish the causal priority between a latent variable and its indicators. Formative scales are used when a construct is viewed as an explanatory combination of its indicators (e.g., Fornell and Bookstein 1982; Diamantopoulos and Winklhofer 2001). In this case, the construct is defined as a total weighted score across all the items, where each item represents an independent dimension in its own. An increase in the value of one indicator results in a higher score for the overall scale, regardless of the value on the other indicators (Fassott and Eggert 2005). The final score for the construct is the sum of the weighted scores on all items. A good formative scale exhausts the entire domain of the construct. The items should collectively represent all the relevant aspects of the related construct: "scale development and index construction as alternative approaches to deriving multi-item measures can produce substantially different operationalization of the same construct," (Diamantopoulos and Siguaw 2006). Formative constructs do not need to correlate or have an internal consistency (Diamantopoulos and Winklhofer 2001; Chin 1998).

Typically, in marketing studies, formative indicators are tested for their validity using a theoretical rationale and expert opinion (e.g., Rossiter 2002). In this study, formative indicators have been presented and discussed with 13 regional heads and five members of the strategic marketing department, responsible for the marketing of hospital care products of the company involved in the empirical research. This pre-test was not limited to the five countries included in the survey, but covered all regional heads globally.

Criterion validity of formative constructs can be measured using the content validity to test multicollinearity.

6.2.10 Multicollinearity

As discussed before, criterion validity of formative constructs is difficult to measure. One measurement method is to use content validity to test multicollinearity. High levels of multicollinearity in a formative measure can be problematic because the influence of each indicator on the latent construct cannot be distinctly determined (Bollen 1989; Diamantopoulos and Siguaw 2006). This chapter examines the possible multicollinearity of the formative measures used in this survey.

As shown in the above table, related to the data of "all countries", the variance inflation factor (VIF)-value of one indicator, which is part of the formative construct of purchase decision involvement indicates a VIF-value exceeding the threshold value of 10. The evaluation of the structural model based on the "all countries" data reveals that there are no significant path correlations influencing this construct.

As shown in the following Table 6.23, related to the data of "Germany", the VIF-value of one indicator, which is part of the formative construct of media-enabled direct marketing, indicates a VIF exceeding the threshold value of 10. The evaluation of the structural model based on the German dataset reveals that there are significant path correlations in the structural model influencing this construct. Therefore, the problem of multicollinearity in this construct needs to be taken into consideration (Table 6.24).

Table 6.23 Quality criteria of formative constructs: evaluation of data, "all countries"

All countries	Indicators	Weights	Std. Error	t-values >1.660	VIF <10
Purchase decision involvement	Same features	0.879	0.000	1.320	110.0
	Brand imp.	−0.037	0.092	2.590	1.008
	Purch. dec.	0.535	0.098	0.085	1.020
Relationship quality	Value for money	0.5020	0.112	2.267	1.879
	Concerns	0.3845	0.087	2.479	1.876
	Satisfied	0.4555	0.053	2.177	1.289
Personal DM	Fairs	1.1107	0.000	0.722	1,000
	Symposia	−0.4303	0.026	0.1567	0.998
	Visits SR	−0.4236	0.018	0.820	1.004
Media-enabled DM	Brochures	1.0239	0.020	1.796	1.002
	Internet	−0.1250	0.210	0.231	1.047
	Mailings	−0.0614	0.488	0.114	1.025

Table 6.24 Quality criteria of formative constructs: evaluation of data "Germany"

Germany	Indicators	Weights	Std. error	t-values	VIF <10
Purchase decision involvement	Same features	0.911	0.000	4.081	korr. R^2= 1
	Brand imp.	−0.153	1.094	0.581	1.001
	Purch. dec.	0.514	0.667	2.045	0.980
Relationship quality	Value for money	−0.026	2.872	0.202	3.508
	Concerns	0.649	0.132	4.996	2.625
	Satisfied	0.584	0.158	4.874	1.347
Personal DM	Fairs	0.852	0.018	1.745	8.772
	Symposia	0.037	1.169	0.112	0.991
	Visits SR	−0.470	0.052	1.037	1.165
Media-enabled DM	Brochures	0.542	0.017	1.448	125,0
	Internet	0.328	0.342	1.098	1.101
	Mailings	0.639	1.032	3.929	0.992

As indicated in the above Table 6.25 related to the Spanish dataset, the VIF-value of one indicator, which is part of the formative construct of personal direct marketing, indicates a VIF-value exceeding the threshold value of 10. The evaluation of the structural model based on the Spanish dataset reveals that there are significant path correlations in the structural model influencing this construct. Therefore, the problem of multicollinearity in this construct needs to be taken into consideration. No evaluations can be made regarding the use of the direct marketing medium "visits of sales representatives" in the Spanish market.

The following Table 6.26, related to the Finnish dataset, indicates two VIF-values exceeding the threshold value of 10. One indicator is part of the formative construct of media-enabled direct marketing, and the other refers to the construct of purchase decision involvement. The evaluation of the structural model based on the Finnish dataset reveals that there are significant path correlations in the structural model influencing both constructs.

Table 6.25 Quality criteria of formative constructs: evaluation of data "Spain"

Spain	Indicators	Weights	Std. error	t-values	VIF <10
Purchase decision involvement	Same features	0.802	0.000	4.712	korr. R^2= 1
	Brand imp.	0.375	0.818	1.859	0.980
	Purch. dec.	0.815	1.936	1.361	1.001
Relationship quality	Valuefor money	0.607	0.131	4.834	3.861
	Concerns	0.430	0.209	2.947	2.155
	Satisfied	0.514	0.185	4.229	2.028
Personal DM	Fairs	0.041	0.453	0.075	0.993
	Symposia	0.743	0.177	1.041	1.110
	Visits SR	0.709	0.025	1.752	30.30
Media-enabled DM	Brochures	0.353	0.133	0.479	1.179
	Internet	1.000	0.001	1.382	1.000
	Mailings	0.770	0.080	0.982	0.990

Table 6.26 Quality criteria of formative constructs: evaluation of data "Finland"

Finland	Indicators	Weights	Std. error	t-values	VIF <10
Purchase decision involvement	Same features	0.784	0.062	1.480	20.40
	Brand imp.	0.648	0.347	1.426	1.213
	Purch. dec.	0.689	0.830	1.430	0.981
Relationship quality	Value for money	0.597	0.085	4.142	2.950
	Satisfied	0.637	0.068	4.828	4.166
	Concerns	−0.098	0.725	0.504	1.623
Personal DM	Symposia	1.076	0.088	1.419	1.032
	Fairs	−0.987	0.068	1.111	1.610
	Visits SR	0.846	0.037	1.444	4.348
Media-enabled DM	Brochures	0.111	1.048	0.614	1.157
	Internet	0.529	0.207	1.785	1.054
	Mailings	0.837	0.028	3.526	35.71

Considering the problem of multicollinearity, no evaluations will later be made regarding the use of the direct marketing medium "mailings" and the indicator "same features" in the Finnish market.

The above Table 6.27 refers to the Australian dataset and indicates no VIF-values exceeding the threshold value of 10. Regarding the dataset of Australia, the levels of multicollinearity do not exceed the threshold value.

The next Table 6.28 is related to the Russian dataset and indicates three VIF-values exceeding the threshold value of 10. The evaluation reveals multicollinearity, but no significant path correlations in the structural model influencing the construct of purchase decision involvement. Another indicator is part of the formative construct of media-enabled direct marketing, while the other refers to the construct of personal direct marketing. The evaluation of the structural model based on the Russian dataset reveals that there is no significant path correlations in the structural model influencing the latter construct.

Nevertheless, a significant path correlation was found influencing the construct of media-enabled direct marketing, where the levels of multicollinearity exceed the threshold value regarding the direct marketing medium of the "Internet".

Table 6.27 Quality criteria of formative constructs: evaluation of data "Australia"

Australia	Indicators	Weights	Std. error	t-values	VIF <10
Purchase decision involvement	Same features	0.339	0.060	1.628	1.812
	Brand imp.	−0.051	0.295	0.340	1.032
	Purch. dec.	0.797	0.672	1.152	3.436
Relationship quality	Value for money	−0.385	0.157	0.247	3.460
	Satisfied	0.884	1.211	1.113	1.972
	Concerns	−0.110	0.075	2.852	2.132
Personal DM	Symposia	0.493	0.163	1.675	2.105
	Fairs	0.320	5.411	1.083	1.023
	Visits SR	0.588	0.103	5.644	2.083
Media-enabled DM	Brochures	1.269	0.016	3.049	1.375
	Internet	−0.846	0.018	1.943	1.996
	Mailings	−0.129	0.166	0.503	1.669

Table 6.28 Quality criteria of formative constructs: evaluation of data "Russia"

Russia	Indicators	Weights	Std. error	t-values	VIF <10
Purchase decision involvement	Same features	0.561	0.044	1.271	18.18
	Brand imp.	0.636	0.212	1.367	1.102
	Purch. dec.	0.785	1.768	1.939	1.029
Relationship quality	Value for money	0.722	0.075	5.942	7.812
	Satisfied	0.547	0.184	3.594	1.968
	Concerns	0.102	1.265	1.006	1.131
Personal DM	Fairs	1.083	0.004	1.887	500.0
	Symposia	−0.350	0.347	0.576	1.002
	Visits SR	0.432	0.186	1.277	1.020
Media-enabled DM	Brochures	−0.457	0.116	1.470	1.280
	Internet	0.514	0.019	1.892	22.22
	Mailings	0.600	0.126	2.048	0.989

Unfortunately, only the Australian dataset does not reveal certain indicators causing multicollinearity problems. Six indicators exceed the VIF threshold value, the influence of these indicators on the respective formative construct cannot be accurately judged. Anyway, in half of the cases, no significant path correlations related to the said constructs were found. About 92% of all indicator values do not exceed the VIF threshold value of 10 and fulfill the measurement criterion.

6.2.11 Summary of Content Adequacy of Formative Constructs

Content adequacy provides evidence about the construct validity. Construct validity is the degree to which an assessment instrument measures the targeted construct (Diamantopoulos et al. 2008).

According to Diamantopoulos and Siguaw (2006, p. 276), for formative measures "no hard and fast rules can be offered". Thus, one has to reconcile the theory-driven conceptualization of the measure. As already discussed in Sect. 4.1 (C-OAR-SE procedure), interviews with two marketing research experts about the classification of objects and attributes were carried out. Based on these discussions, one object was defined to be concrete singular. Other objects were defined to be formative (purchase decision involvement, both direct marketing constructs, as well as relationship quality). Following the recommendations of Diamantopoulos and Winklhofer (2001), to specify "the nature and the direction of the relationship between constructs and measures" (Edwards and Bagozzi 2000, p. 156) and to support this empirically ensures the nomologic validity of constructs-although always making the right choice is "far from simple" (Diamantopoulos and Siguaw 2006, p. 265).

Content validation of formative constructs involves the refinement of the targeted construct to avoid multi-collinearity. In this survey, the problem of multi-collinearity partially occurs with single countries or stakeholder groups. For example, no multi-collinearity occurs within the Australian data-set, once within the Spanish, German and all countries data-set, while Russia shows three indicators exceeding the recommended threshold value. Nevertheless, as a concession to keep comparable constructs across all countries, this refinement of indicators has not been carried out. The problem of multi-collinearity each time occurs with different indicators, constructs and countries.

Additionally, the weights, standard errors and t-values of the formative constructs have been evaluated (see Sect. 6.2.10). Unfortunately, t-values do only exceed the value of 1.66 for half of all indicators evaluated in five countries and stakeholder groups, and outer weights also sometimes were low- but this always refers to different indicators, constructs, countries and stakeholder groups. Therefore, eliminating weak significant indicators in one country limits the comparability of data.

6.2.12 Structural Model, Evaluated by Country and Stakeholder Groups

In this chapter, the final structural model including path coefficients, related t-values, as well as the effect sizes R^2 and Q^2 are vizualized by countries and stakeholder groups. Significant differences are presented.

As already discussed in Sect. 6.2.6, the call for a significantly high squared correlation of endogenous variables can be regarded as reasonable, if the scientific objective comprises to explain the respective endogenous variable completely (Homburg and Baumgartner 1995). In this study, the scientific objective is focused on the explanation of the causal relationship between the constructs, the retention of a given threshold value of the variance explained is therefore not mandatory (Homburg and Baumgartner 1995). This refers to the R^2 values of WOM and perceived fit, as only the causal relationships between the endogenous constructs of WOM and perceived fit toward the constructs reputation and reputation transfer should be explained. With reference to the following data-sets, to fall below the threshold value of 0.19 is therefore acceptable for the constructs of WOM and perceived fit.

The following results on country- and stakeholder group indicate that the use of direct marketing media differs substantially within these groups. This is due to the fact that in the "all country" data relationships regarding paths and t-values of both types of direct marketing media are very inconsistent. Nontheless, the construct of media-enabled direct marketing shows a significant R^2 value (0.207) of 20% of the variance explained. Different e-readiness scores form this construct, indicating the use of electronic media in the five countries included in the survey.

6.2.12.1 All Countries

The following Table 6.29 and Fig. 6.3 are related to the data of "all countries" and displays considerable predictive power: More than 60% of the variance of reputation transfer was explained (R^2 of 0.630) through WOM and perceived fit. Similarly, about 45% of the variance of reputation (R^2 of 0.445) was explained. Interestingly, this was exclusively achieved by the constructs relationship quality and perceived innovativeness. Two other endogenous variables-WOM and perceived fit-show only low R^2-values.

There is a strong positive relationship between reputation and the perceived fit of brand or product. Relationship quality shows positive paths towards reputation and WOM. In this data-set, no direct marketing media show significant paths and t-values regarding the constructs reputation, reputation transfer, and perceived fit.

6.2.12.2 Australia

The data set of Australia shows displays considerable predictive power: regarding the construct of reputation transfer: More than 79% of the variance of reputation transfer was explained (R^2 of 0.797) exclusively through personal direct marketing media and perceived fit. Media-enabled direct marketing activities show no significant correlations towards reputation and reputation transfer, but there is a positive relationship between media-enabled direct marketing and perceived fit of new brand or product. No moderating effects reveal significant paths, but 98.3% of the effect of media-enabled direct marketing on reputation transfer are based on mediator perceived fit (see Sect. 6.2.4). Indirectly, media-enabled marketing activities are positively influencing reputation transfer through perceived fit. 31% of the

Table 6.29 All countries, significant paths

All Countries	t-values	Path coefficients
E-readiness → Media-enabled direct marketing	2.290	0.454
Perceived Fit → Reputation transfer	7.277	0.644
Perceived Innovativeness → Reputation	2.994	0.337
Relationship Quality → Reputation	3.963	0.439
Relationship Quality → Word of mouth	2.951	0.370
Reputation → Perceived fit	2.056	0.236
Word of Mouth → Reputation transfer	2.553	0.248

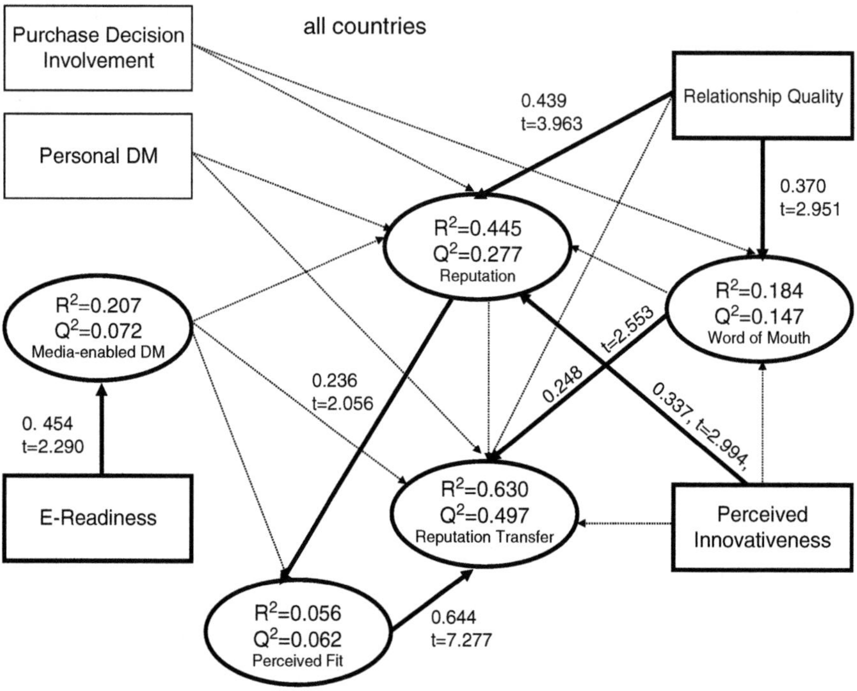

All Countries	t-values	path coefficients
E-readiness-> Media-enabled Direct Marketing	2.290	0.454
Perceived Fit -> Reputation Transfer	7.277	0.644
Perceived Innovativeness -> Reputation	2.994	0.337
Relationship Quality -> Reputation	3.963	0.439
Relationship Quality -> Word of Mouth	2.951	0.370
Reputation -> Perceived Fit	2.056	0.236
Word of Mouth -> Reputation Transfer	2.553	0.248

Fig. 6.3 All countries, significant paths

variance of perceived fit (R^2 of 0.314) is explained by media-enabled direct marketing activities. Similarly, about 51% of the variance of reputation (R^2 of 0.515) is explained exclusively through the construct of relationship quality. Interestingly, in Australia this is the only significant path on reputation. There is also no significant relationship between reputation and reputation transfer (Fig. 6.4 and Table 6.30).

Perceived innovativeness exclusively shows one significant path related to WOM, but no impact on reputation and reputation transfer. Although WOM is strongly influenced by the constructs of relationship quality, perceived innovativeness and purchase decision involvement, this explains only 21% of the variance of WOM. The weak explanatory power of WOM in the Australian data set does not lead to positive or negative significant paths towards reputation or reputation transfer.

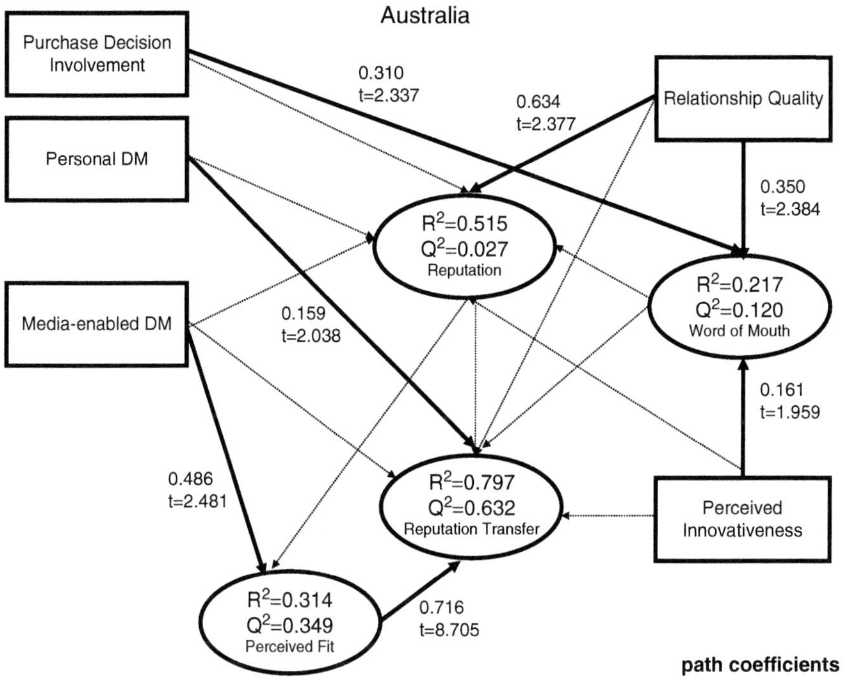

Australia	**t-values**	**path coefficients**
Innovativeness -> WOM	1.959	0.161
Media-enabled Direct Marketing -> Perceived Fit	2.481	0.486
Perceived Fit -> Reputation Transfer	8.705	0.716
Personal Direct Marketing -> Reputation Transfer	2.038	0.159
Purchase Decision Involvement -> WOM	2.337	0.310
Relationship quality -> WOM	2.384	0.350
Relationship quality -> Reputation	2.377	0.634

Fig. 6.4 Australia, significant paths

Table 6.30 Australia, significant paths

Australia	t-values	Path coefficients
Innovativeness → WOM	1.959	0.161
Media-enabled direct marketing → Perceived fit	2.481	0.486
Perceived Fit → Reputation transfer	8.705	0.716
Personal Direct Marketing → Reputation transfer	2.038	0.159
Purchase decision involvement → WOM	2.337	0.310
Relationship quality → WOM	2.384	0.350
Relationship quality → Reputation	2.377	0.634

6.2.12.3 Finland

In comparison to the other data evaluations, Finland shows the highest rate of significant paths (Fig. 6.5 and Table 6.31).

In comparison to the other data evaluations, Finland shows the highest rate of significant paths. The Finish structural model displays considerable predictive power regarding the construct of reputation transfer: More than 92% of the variance

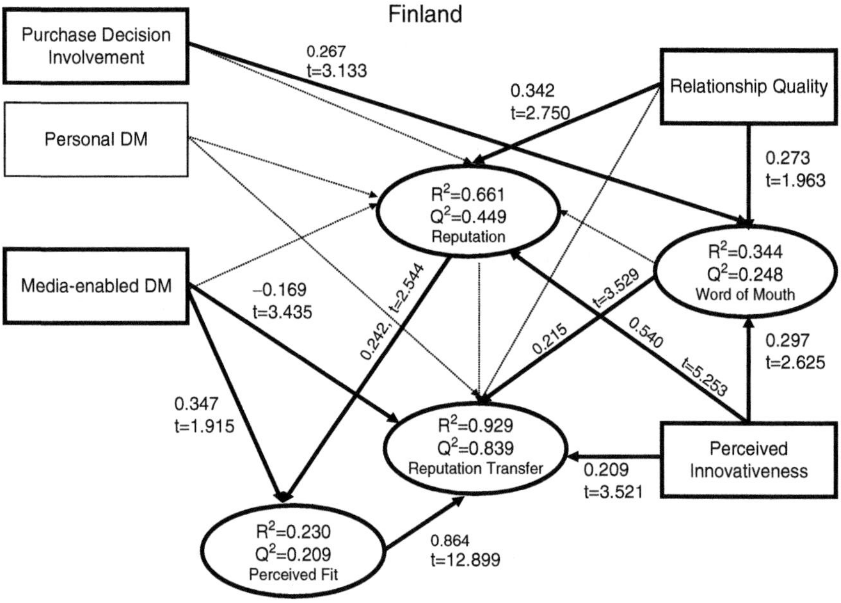

Finland	t-values	path coefficients
Innovativeness -> WOM	2.625	0.297
Innovativeness -> Reputation Transfer	3.521	0.209
Innovativeness -> Reputation	5.353	0.540
WOM -> Reputation Transfer	3.529	0.215
Media-enabled Direct Marketing -> Perceived Fit	1.915	0.347
Media-enabled Direct Marketing -> Rep. Transfer	3.435	–0.169
Perceived Fit -> Reputation Transfer	12.899	0.864
Reputation -> Perceived Fit	2.544	0.242
Purchase Decision Involvement -> WOM	3.133	0.267
Relationship quality -> WOM	1.963	0.273
Relationship quality -> Reputation	2.750	0.342

Fig. 6.5 Finland, significant paths

Table 6.31 Finland, significant paths

Finland	t-values	Path coefficients
Innovativeness → WOM	2.625	0.297
Innovativeness → Reputation transfer	3.521	0.209
Innovativeness → Reputation	5.353	0.540
WOM → Reputation Transfer	3.529	0.215
Media-enabled Direct Marketing → Perceived fit	1.915	0.347
Media-enabled Direct Marketing → Rep. transfer	3.435	−0.169
Perceived Fit → Reputation transfer	12.899	0.864
Reputation → Perceived fit	2.544	0.242
Purchase Decision Involvement → WOM	3.133	0.267
Relationship quality → WOM	1.963	0.273
Relationship quality → Reputation	2.750	0.342

of reputation transfer was explained (R^2 of 0.929) through WOM, perceived innovativeness, perceived fit, and media-enabled direct marketing.

Similarly, about 66% of the variance of reputation (R^2 of 0.661) was explained. Interestingly, this was exclusively achieved by relationship quality and perceived innovativeness. On the other hand, reputation only shows significant impact on perceived fit. In comparison to all other countries and stakeholder groups and related to both above constructs, the Finnish data set shows the highest explanatory power. There is no significant relationship between reputation and reputation transfer.

About 34% of the variance of WOM was explained (R^2 of 0.344) through significant paths from relationship quality, perceived innovativeness and purchase decision involvement. WOM exclusively shows significant paths to reputation transfer.

Relationship quality shows a strong positive relationship towards reputation and also towards WOM. In the data-set output "Finland", only media-enabled direct marketing media show significant paths and t-values. There is a negative relationship between media-enabled direct marketing and reputation transfer, but a positive relationship between media-enabled direct marketing and perceived fit. The evaluation of mediating effects shows positive effects of media-enabled direct marketing through perceived fit on reputation transfer, unfortunately, statistical suppressor effects due to multi-collinearity in construct "media-enabled DM" led to interpretation problems. Personal direct marketing shows no significant paths at all. The R^2 value of perceived fit (0.230) indicates a moderate impact value of 23%. This percentage of the variance is explained by reputation and media-enabled direct marketing.

6.2.12.4 Germany

In comparison to other countries, the German data set shows the weakest highest explanatory power regarding reputation and reputation transfer-but the strongest explanatory power of WOM: Only 46.5% of the variance of reputation transfer is explained (R^2 of 0.465) through WOM and media-enabled direct marketing (Fig. 6.6 and Table 6.32).

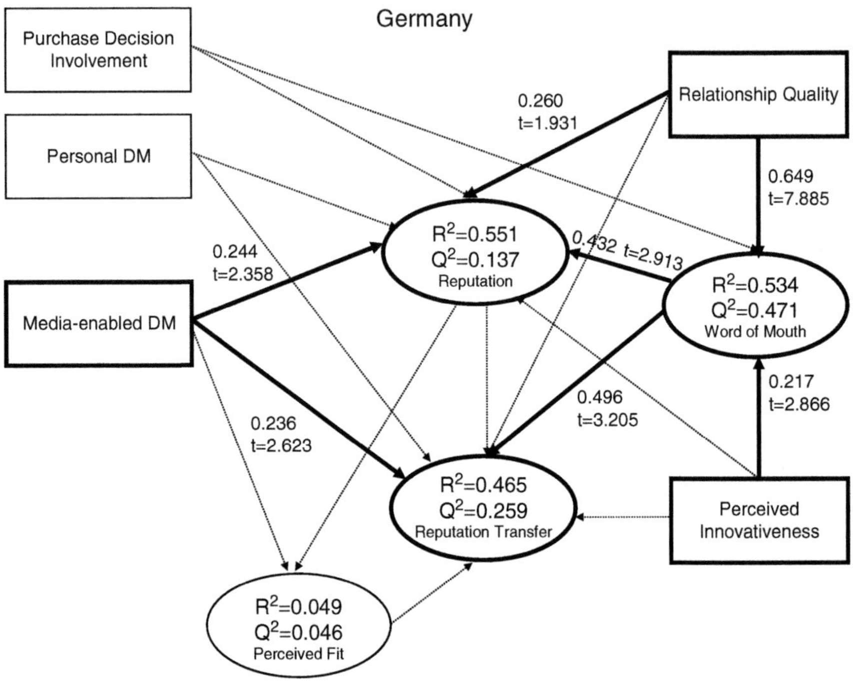

Germany	**t-values**	**path coefficients**
Innovativeness -> WOM	2.866	0.217
WOM -> Reputation Transfer	3.205	0.496
WOM -> Reputationr	2.913	0.432
Media-enabled Direct Marketing -> Reputation	2.358	0.244
Media-enabled Direct Marketing -> Reputation Transfer	2.623	0.236
Relationship quality -> WOM	7.855	0.649
Relationship quality -> Reputation	1.931	0.260

Fig. 6.6 Germany, significant paths

Table 6.32 Germany, significant paths

Germany	t-values	Path coefficients
Innovativeness → WOM	2.866	0.217
WOM → Reputation transfer	3.205	0.496
WOM → Reputationr	2.913	0.432
Media-enabled Direct Marketing → Reputation	2.358	0.244
Media-enabled Direct Marketing → Reputation transfer	2.623	0.236
Relationship quality → WOM	7.885	0.649
Relationship quality → Reputation	1.931	0.260

Similarly, about 55% of the variance of reputation (R^2 of 0.551) is explained. This is exclusively achieved by relationship quality and WOM. Interestingly, just like the Australian data set, the German data shows no significant relationships between reputation and perceived fit or reputation and reputation transfer.

Like with all other countries and stakeholder groups included in this survey, relationship quality shows a significant path towards reputation. About 53% of the variance of WOM was explained (R^2 of 0.534) exclusively through significant paths from relationship quality and perceived innovativeness. Additionally, the relatedness between relationship quality and WOM is much stronger in comparison to all other countries and stakeholder groups. With regard to significant path coefficients, the German data-set differs substantially from all other country data: Only in this structural model WOM indicates a strong positive relationship towards both constructs, reputation transfer and reputation. Moreover, Germany is the only country, where perceived fit does not show a significant relationship towards reputation transfer. Additionally, the construct of perceived innovativeness shows no impact on reputation and reputation transfer, but on WOM. Interestingly, Germany is the only country, where media-enabled direct marketing activities have significant impact on both constructs, reputation and reputation transfer. On the other hand, purchase decision involvement shows no impact on reputation or on WOM.

6.2.12.5 Spain

The following model displays strong predictive power regarding the construct of reputation transfer: More than 69% of the variance of reputation transfer is explained (R^2 of 0.697) through reputation, perceived fit, and personal direct marketing. Similarly, about 51% of the variance of reputation (R^2 of 0.511) is achieved by significant paths of relationship quality, perceived innovativeness, and personal direct marketing. In comparison to other countries, Spain shows the strongest relationship between relationship quality and reputation (Fig. 6.7 and Table 6.33).

In comparison to all other countries and stakeholder groups, the Spanish data set shows the strongest relationship between reputation and reputation transfer-interesting to see that the latter is a negative one. Spain is the only country, where innovativeness as well as WOM show no relationship towards reputation and reputation transfer at all. About 26% of the variance of WOM was explained (R^2 of 0.260) through significant paths from relationship quality and purchase decision involvement.

Relationship quality shows a strong positive relationship towards reputation and also towards WOM. With regard to the Spanish data-set output, only personal direct marketing media show significant paths and t-values towards reputation and reputation transfer. Media-enabled direct marketing shows not significant paths towards any of the constructs included in the structural model. Compared to all other countries and stakeholder groups, the Spanish R^2 value of perceived fit (0.070) is the lowest value of all, no variance can be explained, although there is a strong positive relationship between reputation and perceived fit.

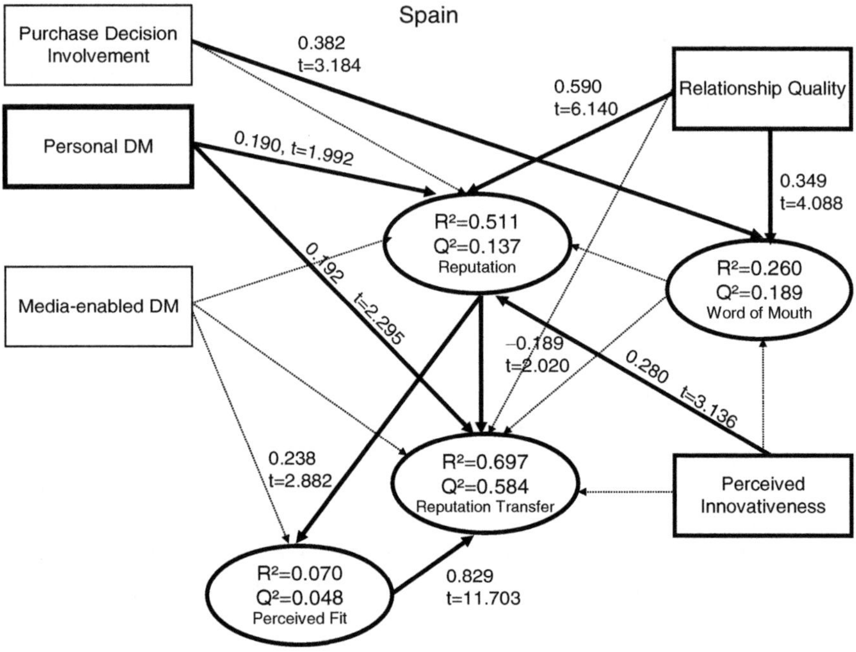

Fig. 6.7 Spain, significant paths

Table 6.33 Spain, significant paths

Spain	t-values	Path coefficients
Innovativeness → Reputation	3.136	0.280
Personal Direct Marketing → Reputation	1.992	0.190
Personal Direct Marketing → Reputation transfer	2.295	0.192
Perceived Fit → Reputation transfer	11.703	0.829
Reputation → Perceived fit	2.882	0.238
Reputation → Reputation transfer	2.020	−0.189
Purchase Decision Involvement → WOM	3.182	0.382
Relationship quality → WOM	4.088	0.349
Relationship quality → Reputation	6.140	0.590

6.2.12.6 Russia

The Russian structural model displays strong predictive power regarding the construct of reputation transfer. The relationship between two other constructs and reputation transfer explains more than 89% of the variance (R^2 of 0.891): perceived fit and WOM. Only about 42% of the variance of reputation (R^2 of 0.422) was explained, achieved by relationship quality and perceived innovativeness.

Compared to the other country data, Russia shows the strongest relationship between reputation and perceived fit, but the weakest R^2 value of variance of reputation explained. In line with all other countries in this survey, in Russia relationship quality shows a strong positive relationship towards reputation as well as towards WOM. Regarding the use of direct marketing media, only media-enabled direct marketing show one significant path and t-value, related to perceived fit. Additionally, this relationship is negative. This relationship as well as a positive relationship between reputation and perceived fit leads to an R^2 value of perceived fit (0.294) amounting a moderate variance explained of 29% (Fig. 6.8 and Table 6.34).

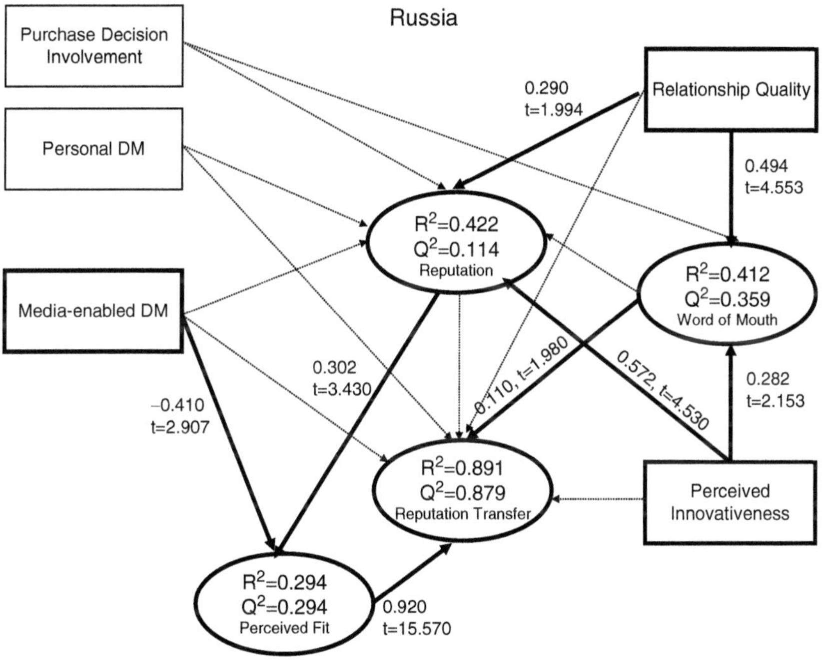

Russia	t-values	path coefficients
Innovativeness -> WOM	2.153	0.282
Innovativeness -> Reputation	4.530	0.572
WOM -> Reputation Transfer	1.980	0.110
Media-enabled Direct Marketing -> Perceived Fit	2.907	−0.410
Perceived Fit -> Reputation Transfer	15.570	0.920
Reputation -> Perceived Fit	3.430	0.302
Relationship quality -> WOM	4.553	0.494
Relationship quality -> Reputation	1.994	0.290

Fig. 6.8 Russia, significant paths

Table 6.34 Russia, significant paths

Russia	t-values	Path coefficients
Innovativeness → WOM	2.153	0.282
Innovativeness → Reputation	4.530	0.572
WOM → Reputation transfer	1.980	0.110
Media-enabled Direct Marketing → Perceived fit	2.907	−0.410
Perceived Fit → Reputation transfer	15.570	0.920
Reputation → Perceived fit	3.430	0.302
Relationship quality → WOM	4.553	0.494
Relationship quality → Reputation	1.994	0.290

Perceived innovativeness shows strong positive correlations towards WOM and reputation. About 41% of the variance of WOM was explained (R^2 of 0.412) through significant paths of constructs relationship quality and perceived innovativeness. In Russia, no significant relationship exist between purchase decision involvement and WOM.

6.2.12.7 Stakeholder Groups

All three stakeholder groups reveal the following identical findings:

- No significant relationships can be found between both direct marketing media and perceived fit, reputation and reputation transfer.
- There is no impact of purchase decision involvement on WOM or on reputation.

6.2.12.8 Purchasers

Although in this structural model related to the data of 58 purchasers of five different countries displays there are existing only four significant paths, the variances explained of reputation and reputation transfer are substantial: The relationship between two other constructs and reputation transfer explains more than 87% of the variance (R^2 of 0.873): perceived fit and reputation (Fig. 6.9 and Table 6.35).

About 54% of the variance of reputation (R^2 of 0.546) is explained by relationship quality and perceived innovativeness. Here, compared to all other countries and stakeholder groups, purchasers show the strongest correlation between perceived innovativeness and reputation. As no significant path coefficients are related to WOM and perceived fit at all, the R^2 values are weak.

6.2.12.9 Pharmacists

Evaluating the data of the structural model related to 65 pharmacists of all five countries, significant impact of relationship quality on reputation, reputation

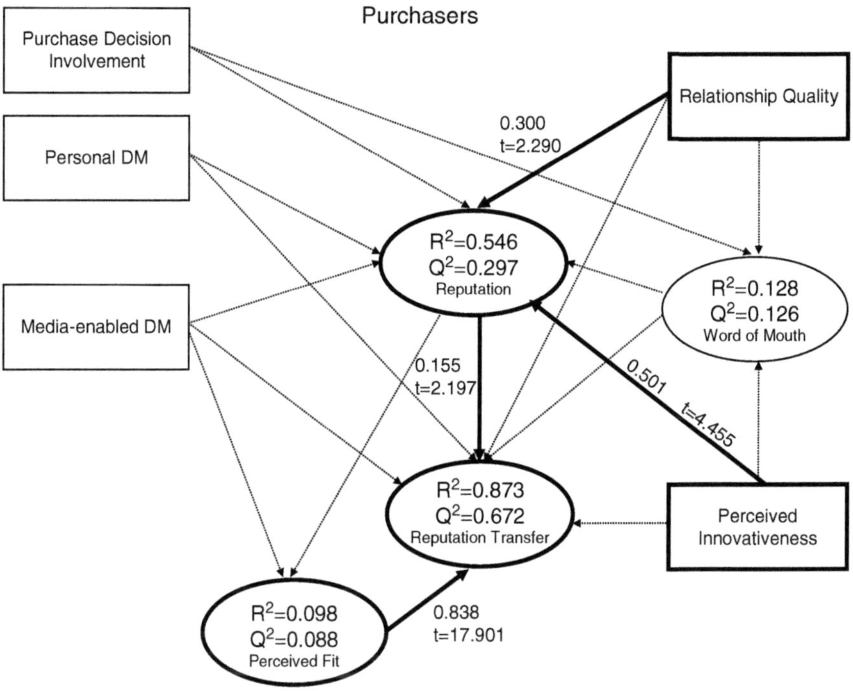

Purchasers	**t-values**	**path coefficients**
Innovativeness -> Reputation	4.455	0.501
Perceived Fit -> Reputation Transfer	17.901	0.838
Reputation -> Reputation Transfer	2.197	0.155
Relationship quality -> Reputation	2.290	0.141

Fig. 6.9 Purchasers, significant paths

Table 6.35 Purchasers, significant paths

Purchasers	t-values	Path coefficients
Innovativeness → Reputation	4.455	0.501
Perceived Fit → Reputation transfer	17.901	0.838
Reputation → Reputation transfer	2.197	0.155
Relationship quality → Reputation	2.290	0.141

transfer and WOM was found. The relationship between two other constructs and reputation explains more than 56% of the variance (R^2 of 0.568): relationship quality and perceived innovativeness (Fig.6.10 and Table 6.36).

Additionally, in comparison to all other countries and stakeholder groups, the pharmacist-data shows the only significant path between relationship quality and reputation transfer.

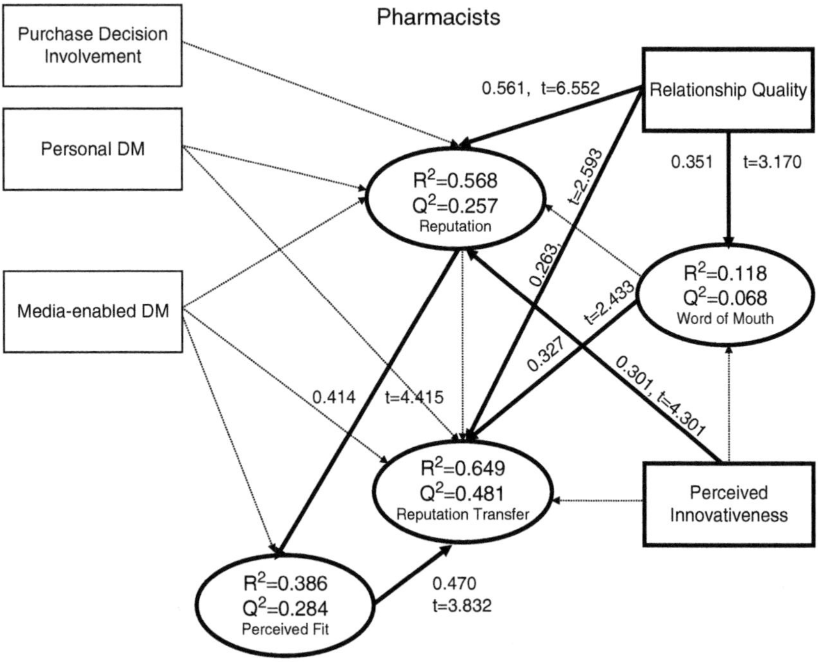

Pharmacists	**t-values**	**path coefficients**
Innovativeness -> Reputation	4.301	0.301
WOM -> Reputation Transfer	2.433	0.327
Perceived Fit -> Reputation Transfer	3.832	0.470
Reputation -> Perceived Fit	4.415	0.414
Relationship quality -> Reputation Transfer	2.593	0.263
Relationship quality -> WOM	3.170	0.351
Relationship quality -> Reputation	6.552	0.561

Fig. 6.10 Pharmacists, significant paths

Table 6.36 Pharmacists, significant paths

Pharmacists	t-values	Path coefficients
Innovativeness → Reputation	4.301	0.301
WOM → Reputation Transfer	2.433	0.327
Perceived Fit → Reputation Transfer	3.832	0.470
Reputation → Perceived Fit	4.415	0.414
Relationship quality → Reputation Transfer	2.593	0.263
Relationship quality → WOM	3.170	0.351
Relationship quality → Reputation	6.552	0.561

This structural model displays strong predictive power regarding the construct of reputation transfer. More than 64% of the variance (R^2 of 0.649) was explained by the impact of WOM, relationship quality and perceived fit. As only one significant path coefficient of relationship quality is related to WOM, the R^2 value of 0.118 is weak and can be neglected. Nevertheless, there is a positive relationship between the constructs of WOM and reputation transfer.

In line with the output of data of purchasers, doctors and nurses, no significant relationships can be found between direct marketing media and perceived fit, reputation and reputation transfer. Also, there is no impact of purchase decision involvement on WOM or on reputation. On the first glance there does not seem to be a relationship between reputation and reputation transfer, the path coefficient is not significant. Nevertheless, there is a strong relationship between reputation and perceived fit, which explains more than 38% of the variance of the latter (R^2 of 0.386) and additionally leads to a significant path between perceived fit and reputation transfer. A test of moderating effects (moderator variable: reputation, predictor variable: perceived fit) did not indicate significant results.

6.2.12.10 Doctors and Nurses

The following model is related to the data of 110 product users of all five countries. Although only four significant relationships exist, it displays considerable predictive power: More than 50% of the variance of reputation transfer was explained (R^2 of 0.510) through WOM and perceived fit. Similarly, about 46% of the variance of reputation (R^2 of 0.461) was explained. Interestingly, this was exclusively achieved by relationship quality.

One other endogenous variables, perceived fit, shows only weak R^2-values (0.068), but, on the other hand, indicates a strong relationship towards reputation transfer. Additionally, there is a strong positive relationship between relationship quality and WOM, which leads to a variance explained of 39% (Fig. 6.11 and Table 6.37).

In the data-set output of "doctors and nurses", no direct marketing media show significant paths and t-values. Interestingly, the construct of perceived innovativeness in this important stakeholder group does no show significant relationships, neither to WOM, nor to reputation and reputation transfer.

6.3 Assessment of Research Hypotheses

To test the hypotheses, path analysis with observed (manifest) variables using SmartPLS 2.0 was carried out. Additionally, the effect size f^2 (Chin, 1998) was calculated.

Hypothesis *H1* predicted that the perceived innovativeness of a company has a strong positive effect on company reputation. As obvious from Table 6.38, this hypothesis is supported by a significant positive relationship between innovativeness

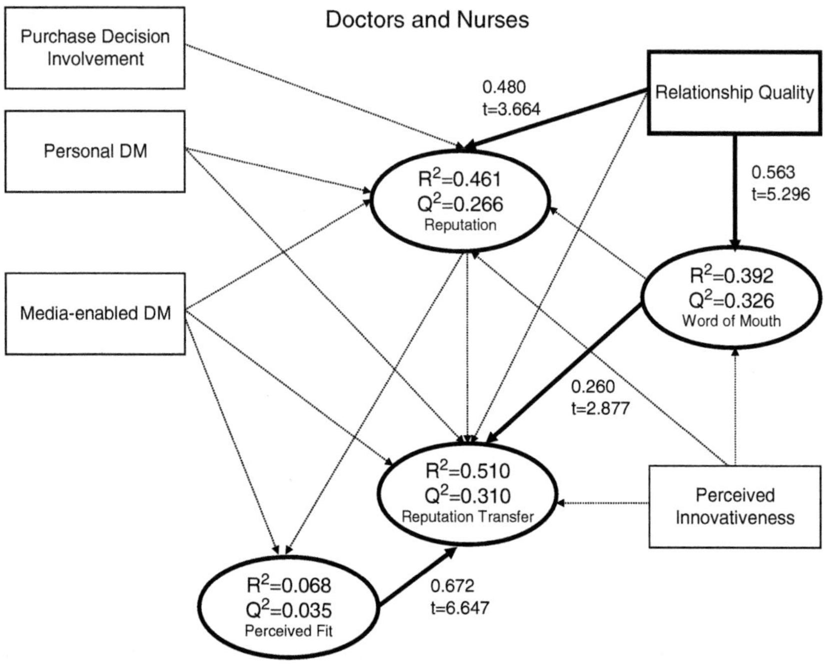

Pharmacists	**t-values**	**path coefficients**
Innovativeness -> Reputation	4.301	0.301
WOM -> Reputation Transfer	2.433	0.327
Perceived Fit -> Reputation Transfer	3.832	0.470
Reputation -> Perceived Fit	4.415	0.414
Relationship quality -> WOM	3.170	0.351
Relationship quality -> Reputation	6.552	0.561

Fig. 6.11 Doctors and nurses, significant paths

Table 6.37 Doctors and nurses, significant paths

Pharmacists	t-values	Path coefficients
Innovativeness → Reputation	4.301	0.301
WOM → Reputation transfer	2.433	0.327
Perceived Fit → Reputation transfer	3.832	0.470
Reputation → Perceived fit	4.415	0.414
Relationship quality → WOM	3.170	0.351
Relationship quality → Reputation	6.552	0.561

and reputation in six out of nine tested countries or stakeholder groups. All six paths were significant at the $p<0.05$ level, the perceived innovativeness of a company is theorized to be important for CR in the B-to-B setting.

Table 6.38 Direct impact of innovativeness on reputation

H1. Direct impact of innovativeness on reputation	Path coefficient	t-value	f^2 value
Threshold values	>0.1	> 1,96	>0.02 weak, >0.15 moderate >0.35 substantial
All	0.337	2.994	0.164
Australia	n.s.	n.s.	n.a.
Germany	n.s.	n.s.	n.a.
Finland	0.540	5.253	0.457
Russia	0.572	4.530	0.399
Spain	0.280	3.136	0.140
Purchaser	0.501	4.455	0.454
Pharmacists	0.301	4.301	0.155
Doctors and Nurses	n.s.	n.s.	n.a.

In comparison to other countries, Finland shows the strongest t-values and the most significant effect size. This fact may be traced back to the findings of Hofstede (2001) regarding its very low scores in PDI: the strong need for technology fosters openness towards innovations and changes. Disregarding the cultural impact, openness towards innovations may explain the important impact of innovativeness on reputation within the stakeholder group of purchaser and pharmacists.

Regarding the strength of relationship, a weaker path correlation and a weak effect size f^2 is found in the Spanish data-set. This supports hypothesis *H1a*, predicting that in cultures scoring high in UAI and low in IDV, the relationship between perceived innovativeness and reputation is weaker. On the other hand, findings referring to the Russian data-set do not support this claim: t-values of Russia are the second strongest, also regarding the effect size f^2, the value is substantially.

Hypothesis *H1b* predicted that in cultures scoring high in MAS and IDV and low in UAI, (in this survey: Germany, Australia) the relationship of perceived innovativeness on reputation is stronger. This hypotheses can not be supported. The German and Australian data-set shows not path correlation between innovativeness and reputation. In both cultures scoring high in IDV, perceived innovativeness of a company does not have an impact on CR. Therefore, no cultural impact related to Hofstede's dimensions of IDV and UAI can be confirmed regarding the relationship between perceived innovativeness and reputation.

Hypothesis *H2* predicted that there is a strong positive relationship between perceived innovativeness and reputation transfer in cultures scoring very low in PDI and UAI (Finland). Except for Finland, no significant correlation was found between innovativeness and reputation transfer. Hypothesis H2 is therefore accepted: The perceived innovativeness of a company is no antecedent of reputation transfer of a new product or product range in a cross-national context-except for cultures which are as open towards changes and foster innovations. This result may therefore also be true for other Scandinavian countries sharing the same cultural dimensions as Finland (Table 6.39).

Hypothesis *H3* predicted that there is a strong positive relationship between perceived innovativeness of a company and WOM. This hypothesis is supported by a significant positive relationship between innovativeness and WOM in four out of nine tested countries or stakeholder groups. Only four paths were significant at the $p<0.05$ level, effect sizes were weak. Interestingly, no stakeholder group shows significant relationships between innovativeness and WOM,but-except for Spain-this effect exists regarding the other countries included in the survey. The perceived innovativeness of a company is theorized to have an important impact on WOM on a country level (Table 6.40).

Hypothesis *H4* predicts that in cultures scoring low in UAI there is a positive relationship between purchase decision involvement and WOM. This hypothesis is partially supported with reference to the countries involved in the survey: three out of five countries show positive significant paths between purchase decision involvement and WOM: Australia and Finland-scoring low in UAI- and Spain. Moreover, Spain shows the strongest relationship between the above constructs. In Germany, there is no relationship between purchase decision involvement and WOM, although this culture is scoring low in UAI.

Table 6.39 Direct impact of innovativeness on reputation transfer

H2. Direct impact of innovativeness on rep. transfer	Path coefficient	t-value	f^2 value
All	n.s.	n.s.	n.a.
Australia	n.s.	n.s.	n.a.
Germany	n.s.	n.s.	n.a.
Finland	0.209	3.521	0.239
Russia	n.s.	n.s.	n.s.
Spain	n.s.	n.s.	n.a.
Purchaser	n.s.	n.s.	n.a.
Pharmacists	n.s.	n.s.	n.a.
Doctors and Nurses	n.s.	n.s.	n.a.

Table 6.40 Significant paths of innovativeness on WOM

H3. Direct impact of innovativeness on WOM	Path coefficient	t-value	f^2 value
All	n.s.	n.s.	n.s.
Australia	0.161	1.959	0.028
Germany	0.217	2.866	0.099
Finland	0.297	2.625	0.077
Russia	0.282	2.153	0.120
Spain	n.s.	n.s.	n.a.
Purchaser	n.s.	n.s.	n.a.
Pharmacists	n.s.	n.s.	n.a.
Doctors and Nurses	n.s.	n.s.	n.a.

Table 6.41 Significant paths of purchase decision involvement on WOM

H4. Direct impact of purchase decision inv. on WOM	Path coefficient	t-value	f^2 value
All	n.s.	n.s.	n.a.
Australia	0.310	2.337	0.061
Germany	n.s.	n.s.	n.a.
Finland	0.267	3.133	0.105
Russia	n.s.	n.s.	n.a.
Spain	0.382	3.184	0.442
Purchaser	n.s.	n.s.	n.a.
Pharmacists	n.s.	n.s.	n.a.
Doctors and Nurses	n.s.	n.s.	n.a.

Table 6.42 Significant paths of relationship quality on reputation

H5. Direct impact of relationship quality on reputation	Path coefficient	t-value	f^2 value
All	0.439	3.963	0.253
Australia	0.634	2.377	0.371
Germany	0.260	1.931	0.077
Finland	0.342	2.750	0.118
Russia.	0.290	1.994	0.062
Spain	0.529	6.140	0.400
Purchaser	0.300	2.920	0.141
Pharmacists	0.561	6.552	0.449
Doctors and Nurses	0.480	3.664	0.170

Additionally, no stakeholder groups show significant relationships between these constructs. In Australia, Finland and Spain, purchase decision involvement is theorized to possibly have an impact on reputation in the B-to-B setting.

To the author's best knowledge, up to 2008, the impact of purchase decision involvement on WOM has not been evaluated in a cross-cultural context, but on stakeholder's level in Germany (von Wangenheim 2003). So, the German results of this study are in line with the findings of von Wangenheim (2003): No relationship between stakeholder and WOM as well as no relationship in Germany between purchase decision involvement and WOM (Table 6.41).

Hypothesis *H5* suggests that there is a positive relationship between relationship quality and reputation. This hypothesis is supported, all countries and stakeholder groups show positive significant paths between relationship quality and reputation. Path coefficients as well as effect sizes were stronger in Australia and Spain and weaker in Germany and Russia. Pharmacists, doctors and nurses show more substantial paths coefficients than purchasers. Thus, relationship quality is theorized to have an impact on reputation in the B-to-B setting (Table 6.42).

Hypothesis *H6* predicted that there is a positive relationship between relationship quality and reputation transfer. This hypothesis is not supported, all countries and two stakeholder groups show no significant paths between relationship quality and reputation transfer. Except for the stakeholder group of pharmacists, relationship quality is theorized not to have an impact on reputation transfer in the B-to-B setting (Table 6.43).

Table 6.43 Significant paths of relationship quality on reputation transfer

H6. Direct impact of relationship quality on reputation transfer	Path coefficient	t-value	f^2 value
All	n.s.	n.s.	n.a.
Australia	n.s.	n.s.	n.a.
Germany	n.s.	n.s.	n.a.
Finland	n.s.	n.s.	n.a.
Russia	n.s.	n.s.	n.a.
Spain	n.s.	n.s.	n.a.
Purchaser	n.s.	n.s.	n.a.
Pharmacists	0.263	2.593	0.131
Doctors and Nurses	n.s.	n.s.	n.a.

Table 6.44 Significant Paths of Relationship Quality on WOM

H7. Direct impact of relationship quality on WOM	Path coefficient	t-value	f^2 value
All	0.370	2.951	0.144
Australia	0.350	2.384	0.140
Germany	0.649	7.885	0.859
Finland	0.273	1.963	0.073
Russia	0.494	4.553	0.372
Spain	0.349	4.088	0.139
Purchaser	n.s.	n.s.	n.a.
Pharmacists	0.315	3.170	0.103
Doctors and Nurses	0.563	5.296	0.435

Hypothesis *H7* suggested that there is a strong relationship between relationship quality and WOM. This hypothesis is supported, eight out of nine countries and stakeholder groups show positive significant paths between relationship quality and reputation. The strongest paths coefficients as well as substantial effect sizes can be found in the German and Russian data-set. Interestingly, doctors and nurses show strong significant paths and effect sizes-whereas purchasers do not show no significant impact at all between relationship quality and reputation. Nevertheless, relationship quality is theorized to have an impact on WOM in the B-to-B setting (see Table 6.44).

Hypothesis *H8* suggests that in market leader countries like Germany, Spain and Finland, there is a strong positive relationship between WOM and reputation. This Hypothesis is not supported (see Table 6.45). Only the German data-set shows a positive significant path between WOM and reputation. Therefore, WOM is not considered to have an impact on reputation-no matter, if the countries are market leader or follower countries.

Hypothesis *H9* suggests that there is a strong relationship between WOM and reputation transfer. This hypothesis is supported by a significant positive relationship between WOM and reputation transfer in six out of nine tested countries or stakeholder groups. All six paths were significant at the $p < 0.05$ level, therefore WOM is theorized to be important for reputation transfer in the B-to-B setting.

Table 6.45 Significant paths of WOM on reputation

H8. Direct impact of WOM on Reputation	Path coefficient	t-value	f^2 value
All	n.s.	n.s.	n.s.
Australia	n.s.	n.s.	n.s.
Germany	0.432	2.913	0.226
Finland	n.s.	n.s.	n.a.
Russia	n.s.	n.s.	n.a.
Spain	n.s.	n.s.	n.a.
Purchaser	n.s.	n.s.	n.a.
Pharmacists	n.s.	n.s.	n.a.
Doctors and Nurses	n.s.	n.s.	n.a.

Table 6.46 Significant paths of wom on reputation transfer

H9. Direct impact of WOM on reputation transfer	path coefficient	t-value	f^2 value
All	0.248	2.553	0.121
Australia	n.s.	n.s.	n.a.
Germany	0.496	3.205	0.187
Finland	0.215	3.529	0.422
Russia	0.110	1.980	0.074
Spain	n.s.	n.s.	n.a.
Purchaser	n.s.	n.s.	n.a.
Pharmacists	0.327	2.433	0.273
Doctors and Nurses	0.260	2.877	0.094

This effect was predicted to be stronger *H9a* for the future product users of the new product range. With reference to Table 6.46, the future users of pharmaceuticals-pharmacists as well as doctors and nurses-show significant positive relationship between the constructs of WOM and reputation transfer. On the other hand, the stakeholder group of purchasers show no significant paths between these constructs. This hypothesis is supported.

Hypothesis *H9b* suggested that in comparison to follower countries, in market leadership countries there is a strong relationship between WOM and reputation transfer. In this study, market leader countries are Germany, Spain and Finland. A significant positive relationship between WOM and reputation transfer can be found in Germany and Finland, especially the latter shows substantial effect sizes whereas Germany shows the highest path coefficient. No significant path coefficient can be found with regard to the Spanish data-set. Therefore, this hypothesis is only partially supported.

Hypothesis *H10* predicts a positive relationship between the perceived fit of the new product range and reputation transfer. This hypothesis is supported by a significant positive relationship between perceived fit and reputation transfer in eight out of nine tested countries or stakeholder groups. All eight paths were significant at the $p<0.05$ level, therefore perceived fit is theorized to be very important for reputation transfer in the B-to-B setting. The f^2 and t-values found in the relationship between perceived fit and reputation transfer were the highest effect sizes and values of all evaluated relationships. Surprisingly, market leader country Germany does not show a significant relationship between these both constructs. In Germany, the perceived fit of a new product to the existing product range is unimportant for the transfer of reputation.

H10a. This effect is expected to be stronger in cultures scoring low in IDV and high in UAI (Spain and Russia) and *H10b*. weaker for cultures scoring high in IDV and low in UAI (Australia and Germany). With reference to Table 6.47, Spain and Russia show much higher t-values and path coefficients than Australia. Germany shows no relationship at all between perceived fit and reputation transfer. Therefore, H10a and H10 b both are supported. Hypothesis *H10c* suggests that the stakeholder group of purchasers has the best knowledge regarding the existing product portfolio of its suppliers. Therefore the effect of perceived fit on reputation transfer is predicted to be stronger for purchaser in comparison to pharmacists and doctors and nurses. Path coefficient as well as t-value and f^2 value was much higher for purchasers than for pharmacists and doctors and nurses. This hypothesis is also supported.

Hypothesis *H11* suggested that the use of direct marketing media varies significantly among the countries and stakeholder groups.

This hypothesis is supported for all countries and stakeholder-groups: Above Table 6.48 indicates the percentages mentioned by the participants. Answers refer to "media is of most importance" or "important" to be informed about new products. As hypothesized, the use of direct marketing media varies significantly among the different countries.

Table 6.47 Significant paths of perceived fit on reputation transfer

H10. Direct impact of perceived fit on reputation transfer	Path coefficient	t-value	f^2 value
All	0.664	7.277	0.867
Australia	0.716	8.705	1.083
Germany	n.s.	n.s.	n.a.
Finland	0.864	12.899	7.535
Russia	0.920	15.570	4.962
Spain	0.829	11.703	1.683
Purchaser	0.838	17.901	3.118
Pharmacists	0.470	3.832	0.424
Doctors and Nurses	0.672	6.647	0.573

Table 6.48 Use of direct marketing media

Direct marketing media	Australia	Germany	Finland	Russia	Spain
Fairs	38%	40%	44%	43%	12%
Symposia	30%	46%	44%	37%	14%
Internet	42%	16%	50%	41%	26%
Brochures	26%	48%	72%	41%	6%
Mailings	44%	40%	72%	10%	10%
Visits of Sales Reps.	38%	48%	58%	45%	18%

Goodness-of-fit tests from grouped data constitute a classical problem in inference. Thus, Pearson's (1900) chi-squares test-the most commonly used test statistic for testing goodness-of-fit as well as the calculation of the φ-coefficient to derive a measure of association between the countries and the direct marketing media was carried out.

With reference to a null hypothesis assuming that there is no relationship between the different countries and the use of direct marketing media, the chi-square test prooves the likelyhood that the above variations were due just to random chance alone. The results in annexe 9.6 show that there exists a relationship, which generally is exceeding the requested φ-coefficient threshold value of 0.3. Additionally, allmost all chi-square values are significant on a predetermined alpha level of significance (5% error level).

Evaluating the data-set of different stakeholder groups, 66% of all pharmacists claim that the Internet is the most important media used for information on new products-this is only true for 46% of doctors and nurses and 52% of the purchasers. On the other hand, users like doctors and nurses show strong interest in symposia and fairs: 60% of all user claim that this medium is important/most important to them. Only 32% of all pharmacists and 28% of the purchasers judge fairs and symposia as important or most important. Due to the substantial difference in the user habits, no significant path correlations are expected related to the direct marketing media use of the stakeholder groups (see Table 6.48). To evaluate the data regarding hypotheses H11a and H11b, the results have been split up in relationships between reputation, reputation transfer and both kinds of direct marketing media (media-enabled and personal) to focus on detailed differences in the country results.

Hypotheses *H11a* and *H11b* suggested that the impact of direct marketing media on reputation and reputation transfer is expected to be stronger in cultures scoring low in PDI and UAI and high in IDV. This hypothesis is not supported, except for Germany, all countries and stakeholder-groups show no significant paths between media-enabled direct marketing and reputation. Therefore, media-enabled direct marketing is theorized not to have an important impact on reputation in the B-to-B setting.

As obvious from Table 6.49, except for Germany, no significant paths between media-enabled direct marketing and reputation were found. As listed in Table 6.50, Spain is the only country showing a significant correlation between personal direct marketing media and reputation. This result is in line with the findings of Hofstede (2001) that networks and personal contact in business relationships is more important in cultures scoring high in UAI. Remarkably, while comparing the general results on the use of direct marketing media, Spanish participants show the lowest percentages regarding "visits of sales representatives" (18 %). Taking into consideration that com-pared to the other countries, all Spanish percentages are low and just ranging between 10 and 26 %, this result is nevertheless acceptably high. On the other hand, Russia shows no significant correlations between personal direct marketing media and reputation at all, although 45 % of all participants list the

Table 6.49 Significant paths of media-enabled direct marketing on reputation

H11. Direct impact of media-enabled DM on reputation	Path coefficient	t-value	f^2 value
All	n.s.	n.s.	n.s.
Australia	n.s.	n.s.	n.s.
Germany	0.244	2.358	0.136
Finland	n.s.	n.s.	n.s.
Russia	n.s.	n.s.	n.s.
Spain	n.s.	n.s.	n.s.
Purchaser	n.s.	n.s.	n.s.
Pharmacists	n.s.	n.s.	n.s.
Doctors and Nurses	n.s.	n.s.	n.s.

Table 6.50 Significant paths of personal direct marketing on reputation

H11. Direct impact of personal DM on reputation	Path coefficient	t-value	f^2 value
All	n.s.	n.s.	n.a.
Australia	n.s.	n.s.	n.a.
Germany	n.s.	n.s.	n.a.
Finland	n.s.	n.s.	n.a.
Russia	n.s.	n.s.	n.a.
Spain	0.190	1.992	0.067
Purchaser	n.s.	n.s.	n.a.
Pharmacists	n.s.	n.s.	n.a.
Doctors and Nurses	n.s.	n.s.	n.a.

importance of "visits of sales representatives" as a source to be informed about new products.

Hypothesis *H11c* predicts that the impact of direct marketing media on reputation and reputation transfer is stronger in cultures scoring low in PDI and UAI and high in IDV (e.g., Australia, Germany and Finland). This hypothesis is supported. Germany and Finland show significant paths between media-enabled direct marketing and reputation transfer, whereas the Australia data-set reveals a positive relationship between personal direct marketing media and reputation transfer, although the effect size is weak. Germany additionally positively correlates between media-enabled direct marketing media and reputation. Direct marketing media are theorized to have an important impact on reputation and reputation transfer in cultures low in PDI and UAI and high in IDV (Table 6.51).

Due to a higher level of decision-making authority (Hofstede 2001), the impact of media-enabled direct marketing media on reputation transfer is expected to be stronger in cultures scoring low in PDI (Germany and Finland). Media-enabled direct marketing therefore is theorized to have an impact on reputation transfer in cultures with low scores in Hofstede's dimension PDI. Surprisingly, with regard to the Finnish data-set, the relationship between media-enabled direct marketing and reputation transfer is negative. In Finland, media-enabled direct marketing

Table 6.51 Significant paths of personal direct marketing on reputation transfer

H11. Direct impact of personal DM on reputation transfer	Path Coefficient	t-value	f^2 value
All	n.s.	n.s.	n.a.
Australia	0.159	2.038	0.059
Germany	n.s.	n.s.	n.a.
Finland	n.s.	n.s.	n.a.
Russia	n.s.	n.s.	n.a.
Spain	0.192	2.295	0.099
Purchaser	n.s.	n.s.	
Pharmacists	ns	n.s.	
Doctors and Nurses	n.s.	n.s.	

Table 6.52 Significant paths of media-enabled direct marketing on reputation transfer

H11. Direct impact of media-enabled DM on rep. transfer	Path coefficient	t-value	f^2 value
All	n.s.	n.s.	n.a.
Australia	n.s.	n.s.	n.a.
Germany	0.236	2.623	0.115
Finland	−0.169	3.435	0.366
Russia	n.s.	n.s.	n.a.
Spain	n.s.	n.s.	n.a.
Purchaser	n.s.	n.s.	n.a.
Pharmacists	n.s.	n.s.	n.a.
Doctors and Nurses	n.s.	n.s.	n.a.

activities have a strong negative impact on reputation transfer, effect size is substantial (Table 6.52).

Hypothesis *H11 d* suggested that the impact of direct marketing media on reputation and reputation transfer is weaker in cultures scoring high in UAI and PDI and low in IDV (e.g., Russia and Spain). This hypothesis is partially supported: Russia shows no significant relationships between media-enabled direct marketing and reputation or reputation transfer. Spain shows no relationship between direct marketing media and reputation transfer, but a weak significant path correlation with low effect sizes between personal direct marketing and reputation as well as reputation transfer.

Hypothesis *H12* suggests that in feminine cultures like Russia and Finland there is a strong relationship between reputation and reputation transfer. This hypothesis is not supported. Both countries show no relevant path correlation at all.

Nevertheless, with reference to Finland, the impact of CR on reputation transfer is moderated positively through WOM.

As far as the stakeholder groups are concerned purchasers show a positive relationship between reputation and reputation transfer. Reputation is theorized to have a impact on reputation transfer in the B-to-B setting.

With reference to hypothesis H 14, the impact of reputation on reputation transfer can either be positive or negative-but in this study no cultural impact can be confirmed. Surprisingly, having a look at countries who value CR more than trust

(Spain and Russia) only Spain shows correlations between reputation and reputation transfer-negative relationships, though (Table 6.53). This fact will later be discussed.

Hypothesis *H13* suggests that there is a strong positive relationship between E-readiness of different cultures and media-enabled direct marketing activities.

This hypothesis was developed on the one hand to verify the media-enabled direct marketing data-set. On the other hand, the impact of different levels of e-readiness in the five countries is supposed to influence the use of electronic media like mailings and the Internet.

With reference to the following significant path correlation in the following table, E-readiness is theorized to have a impact on media-enabled direct marketing in the B-to-B setting (Table 6.54).

Hypothesis *H15* predicts that there is a positive relationship between reputation and the perceived fit of the new product to the existing product range. This hypothesis is supported by a significant positive relationship between reputation and perceived fit in five out of nine tested countries or stakeholder groups. All five paths were significant at the $p<0.05$ level, reputation is theorized to be important for the fit perception of new products in the B-to-B setting.

As the effect is stronger in cultures with high scores in UAI and PDI (Russia and Spain) and weaker in cultures scoring low in UAI and PDI (Australia and Finland), hypothesis *15a* is supported, too (Table 6.55).

As already discussed (see Sect. 3.3.4 and 4.6.5), Eberl (2006) has also carried out an empirical research on the relationship between reputation and perceived fit. In his study he uses a reputation measure consisting of two separate constructs: sympathy and competence. His survey was carried out on the German B-to-C market and this hypothesis was not supported. In this study, Germany also showed no significant relationship between both constructs. Nevertheless, the impact of reputation on reputation transfer is significantly high in some other countries.

Table 6.53 Significant path of reputation on reputation transfer

H14. Direct impact of reputation on reputation transfer	Path coefficient	t-value	f^2 value
All	n.s.	n.s.	n.a.
Australia	n.s.	n.s.	n.a.
Germany	n.s.	n.s.	n.a.
Finland	n.s.	n.s.	n.a.
Russia	n.s.	n.s.	n.a.
Spain	−0.189	2.020	0.145
Purchaser	0.155	2.197	0.212
Pharmacists	n.s.	n.s.	n.a.
Doctors and Nurses	n.s.	n.s.	n.a.

Table 6.54 Significant path of E-readiness on media-enabled DM

Direct impact of E-readiness on media-enabled DM	path coefficient	t-value
All countries	0.454	2.290

Table 6.55 Significant path of reputation on perceived fit

H15. Direct impact of reputation on perceived fit	Path coefficient	t-value	f^2
All	0.236	2.058	0.055
Australia	n.s.	n.s.	n.a.
Germany	n.s.	n.s.	n.a.
Finland	0.242	2.544	0.063
Russia	0.302	3.430	0.101
Spain	0.238	2.882	0.062
Purchaser	n.s.	n.s.	n.a.
Pharmacists	0.414	4.415	0.423
Doctors, Nurses	n.s.	n.s.	n.a.

This again shows, how decisive a cross-cultural evaluation of datasets on CR is regarding the definition of its impact factors.

In line with Hofstede (2001) hypothesis *H 16* predicts that trust in sales representatives and supplier is more important in cultures scoring low in UAI and PDI (Australia, Finland) and less important in cultures scoring high in UAI and PDI (Russia, Spain).

For all countries, a test of inference (Pearson's (1900) chi-square (χ^2) test of independence) as well as the calculation of the φ-coefficient to derive a measure of association between the variables "countries" as well as trust and reputation was carried out. With reference to a null hypothesis assuming that there is no relationship between the different countries, trust and reputation, the chi-square test prooves the likelyhood that the variations evaluated in hypotheses *H16* and *H17* were due just to random chance alone. The results in annexe 9.6 show that there exists a relationship, which generally is exceeding the requested φ-coefficient threshold value of 0.3. Additionally, allmost all chi-square values are significant on a predetermined alpha level of significance (5% error level).

Huff and Kelley (2003) claimed that external trust that individuals within an organization have for external partners will be higher for organizations from individual societies than for collective societies.

This study supports all findings. Asked for the importance of a trustful relationship with their supplier, 83.3% of the German participants, as well as 67.7% of the Finnish and 73.3% of the Australian participants, argue that trust is decisive to them. On the other hand, only 13.7% of the Russian and 36% of the Spanish organizational stakeholders think that a trustful relationship is decisive (Fig. 6.12).

According to Hofstede (2001), Australia (index of 93), Germany (index value 73) and Finland (index of 68) score high in IDV. Referring to an index value of 39, Russia scores extremely low in IDV and Spain shows an average IDV index of 53. Also, in the context of this cross-cultural study, trust for external partners is more substantial in organizations from individual societies scoring low in UAI like Australia, Germany and Finland, than for collective societies scoring high in UAI like Spain and Russia. Although there are market-leader (Finland, Germany, Spain) and follower countries (Russia, Australia), it is clear that the above results are not influenced by the market situation in hospital care. The importance of trust and

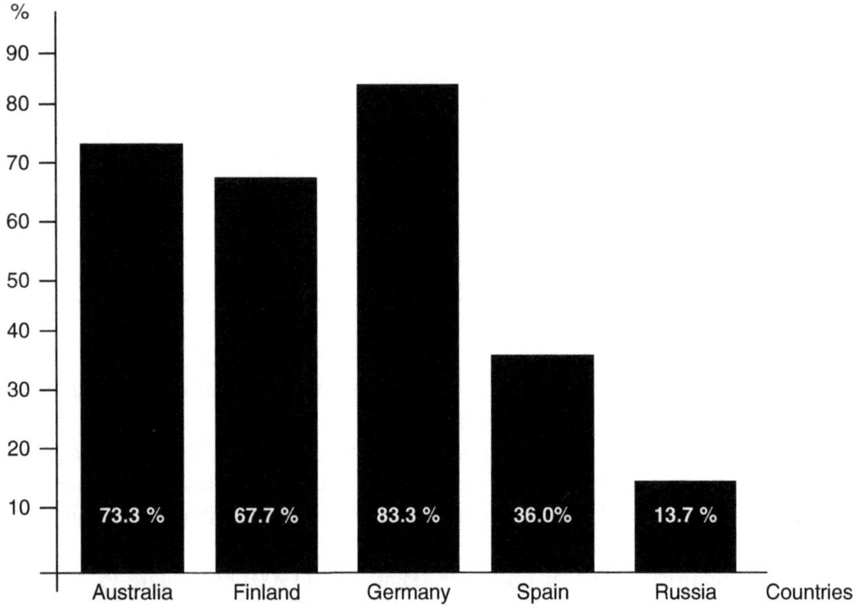

Fig. 6.12 Decisiveness of a trustful relationship to the supplier

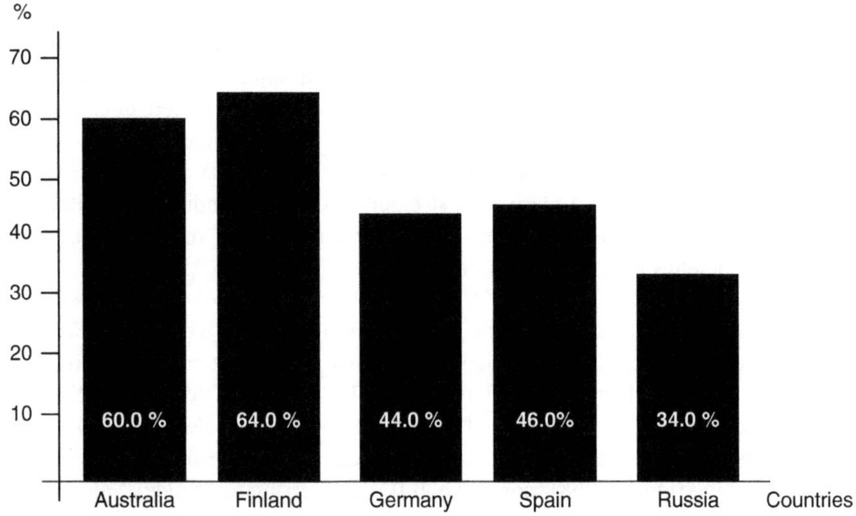

Fig. 6.13 Importance of trust in the recommendations of sales representatives

positive reputations of a supplier is clearly related to the cultural impact of the respective countries (Fig. 6.13).

Regarding the importance of trust in the recommendations of sales representatives of certain suppliers, Finland and Australia (scoring low in UAI) show much higher rates of importance than Russia and Spain (scoring high in UAI). For the German participants of this survey-scoring average in UAI-trust in the recommendations of sales representatives is not as important as it is for Australian or Finnish purchasers and users. Hypothesis 16 is supported by a significant positive relationship between the importance of trust and Hofstede's cultural dimensions.

Hypotheses *H17* suggests that with reference to organizational buying behavior, reputation is more important in cultures scoring high in UAI and PDI (Russia, Spain) and less important in cultures scoring low in UAI and PDI (Australia, Finland, Germany).

Interestingly, significant cultural differences were found: Only 41 % of the German participants agree that CR is somewhat important (25%) or decisive (16%) while deciding about new supplier or products, whereas 72,8 % of the Russian and 90.0 % of the Spanish organizational buyers think that CR is a somewhat important or decisive factor on their buying decision.

Unfortunately, Hofstede's (2001) dimensions offer no insights regarding the importance of CR in different cultures. Figure 6.14 lists the results of the general importance of a supplier's positive reputation. For 74.2% (43.7% + 30.5%) of the purchasers, pharmacist, doctors and nurses involved in the organizational buying process, a good CR is somewhat important or decisive with regard to purchasing decisions. Only about 5% of the survey participants had no opinion on that subject. This shows that even in the B-to-B context, characterized by tender businesses, comparable products and a general lower level of involvement (von Wangenheim 2003; Backhaus and Voeth 2007), the intangible asset of CR is a valuable one. Nevertheless, to learn about possible cultural differences, the data needed to be further evaluated by country.

The above results lead to the conclusion that a positive reputation of the supplier is more important in collective societies scoring high in UAI like Russia and Spain and less important in individual societies scoring low in UAI like Australia,

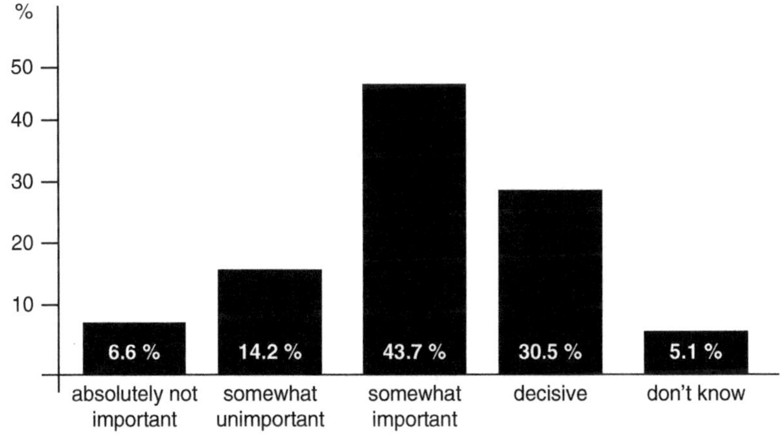

Fig. 6.14 Importance of a suppliers' positive reputation

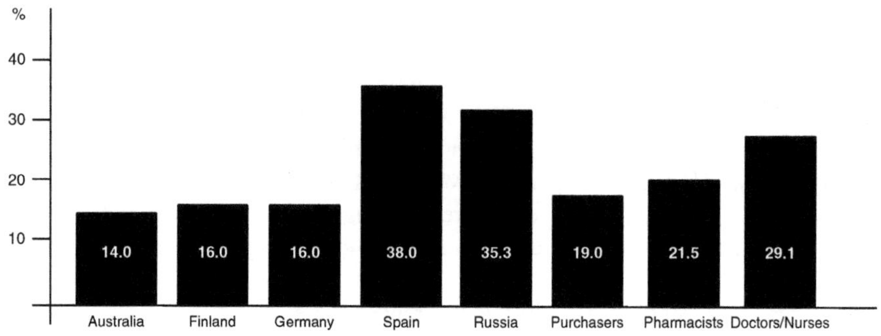

Fig. 6.15 Decisiveness of a good reputation of the supplier

Germany and Finland. This is an important issue-bearing in mind that most of the actual research on CR is focused on the individual US society. Hypothesis H17 is supported by a significant positive relationship between reputation and Hofstede's cultural dimension of UAI. Disregarding the possible cultural impact, the users of the products (in this survey: doctors and nurses) care more for a suppliers reputation than purchasers and pharmacists. Interestingly, 60% of all pharmacists additionally claim a good reputation to be "somewhat important" to them, as quoted above, additionally 21.5% think it is decisive. This leads to the conclusion-although not directly visible in above Fig. 6.15, a good reputation of a supplier is generally important for the stakeholder group of pharmacists.

6.4 Findings related to Countries and Stakeholder Groups

Before the highlights and particularities of the single countries and stakeholder groups are discussed, first of all, an overview on the fulfillment of the construct-related hypotheses is given. Derived from theory and actual literature, 17 hypotheses and eleven sub-hypotheses were developed. All in all, 20 of them are now judged to be fulfilled (Table 6.56).

To the author's best knowledge, the construct of reputation has never been before designed based exclusively on relationship- and knowledge resources-and has never before tested-implemented in one study-in five countries and three stakeholder groups. Additionally, the cultural impact on reputation, perceived fit and reputation transfer has been evaluated in detail in a B-to-B context. Several findings are in line with the study of Hofstede (2001), whose dimensions still can be regarded as a useful tool to compare cultural effects across countries.

In this study, most conclusions on reputational impact factors could only be drawn by splitting up customer-related research data by countries. While comparing the results of the aggregated data-set with the country results and the outcomes of the three stakeholder groups, certain influencing factors remain invisible and therefore unconsidered. This especially refers to the differences in use of direct

Table 6.56 Overview on the fulfillment of hypotheses

No.	Construct-related hypotheses	Fulfilled
H1.	The perceived innovativeness of a company has a strong positive effect on corporate reputation	+
	H1a. This impact of perceived innovativeness on corporate reputation is weaker in cultures scoring high in UAI and low in IDV and MAS (e.g., Russia and Spain)	-/+
	H1b. The impact of perceived innovativeness on corporate reputation is stronger in cultures scoring high in MAS and IDV and low in UAI (Australia and Germany)	-
H2.	There is a strong positive relationship between perceived innovativeness and reputation transfer in cultures scoring very low in PDI and UAI (Finland)	+
H3.	There is a strong positive relationship between perceived innovativeness and WOM	-/+
H4.	In cultures scoring low in UAI (Australia, Finland and Germany) there is a positive relationship between purchase decision involvement and WOM	-/+
H5.	There is a positive relationship between relationship quality and reputation	+
H6.	There is a positive relationship between relationship quality reputation transfer	-
H7.	There is a strong positive relationship between relationship quality and WOM	+
H8.	There is a strong positive relationship between WOM and reputation in market leader countries like Germany, Spain and Finland	-/+
H9.	There is a strong positive relationship between WOM and reputation transfer	+
	H9a.This effect is expected to be stronger for the future product users of the new product range	+
	H9b. This effect is expected to be stronger in market leadership countries	-/+
H10.	There is a strong positive relationship between the perceived fit of the new product range and reputation transfer.	+
	H10a. This effect is expected to be stronger in cultures scoring low in IDV and high in UAI (Russia and Spain)	+
	H10b. This effect is expected to be weaker in cultures scoring high in IDV and low in UAI (Australia, Finland and Germany).	+
	H10c. As purchasers know best about the existing product portfolio of their supplier, the effect of perceived fit on reputation transfer is expected to be stronger for purchaser and weaker for pharmacists, doctors and nurses	+
H11.	The use of direct marketing media varies significantly among the countries and stakeholder groups	+
	H11a. There is a strong positive relationship between direct marketing media and reputation	+
	H11b. There is a strong positive relationship between direct marketing media and reputation transfer	
	H11c. The impact of direct marketing media on reputation and reputation transfer is expected to be stronger in cultures scoring low in PDI and UAI and high in IDV (Australia, Germany, and Finland)	
	H11d. The impact of direct marketing media on reputation and reputation transfer is expected to be weaker in cultures scoring high in UAI and PDI and low in IDV (Russia and Spain)	-/+
H12	A culture characterized by a high femininity index (Russia and Finland) provides, relative to a culture with a high masculinity index (Australia and Germany), an environment more conducive to the successful transfer of reputation	-/+
H13	There is a strong positive relationship between E-readiness of different cultures and media-enabled direct marketing activities	+
H14	There is a strong positive relationship between reputation and reputation transfer in market-leader countries (like Germany, Finland and Spain)	-/+

(*continued*)

Table 6.56 (continued)

No.	Construct-related hypotheses	Fulfilled
H15	There is a positive relationship between reputation and the perceived fit of the new product to the existing product range	+
	H15a. The effect is stronger in cultures with high scores in UAI and PDI (Russia and Spain) and weaker in cultures scoring low in UAI and PDI (Australia and Finland)	+
H16	Trust in sales representatives and supplier plays a more important role in cultures scoring low in UAI and PDI (Australia, Finland) and a less important role in cultures scoring high in UAI and PDI (Russia, Spain)	+
H17	A company's reputation plays a more important role in cultures scoring high in UAI and PDI (Russia, Spain) and a less important role in cultures scoring low in UAI and PDI (Australia, Finland, Germany)	+

marketing media and to the construct of purchase decision involvement. Regarding the above mentioned constructs, no significant path correlation was found with reference to the data-sets of all countries, purchasers, pharmacists as well as doctors and nurses.

Referring to the Theory of Commitment and Trust (Morgan and Hunt 1994), both factors impact on reputation and reputation transfer in different ways. In some cultures, social networks and trust in the company and in the recommendations of sales representatives are more important than reputation. On the other hand, reputation also does play a more important role in cultures scoring low in UAI- and a less important role in those cultures relying on trust-and scoring high in UAI. Following the results of this study and in line with Hofstede's (2001) findings, a cultural impact on the use of and the trust in direct marketing media is confirmed. Commitment towards the company and suppliers is weak in cultures scoring high in IDV (Australia, Germany). In collectivist cultures, commitment and trust is more important within social networks (Russia, Spain). These "social networks" may also include sales representatives of certain suppliers and are (together with WOM) replacing the influence of direct marketing media on information about new products.

As discussed before, resources, representing what can be done by the company and the competitive environment, representing what should be done to compete effectively in satisfying customer needs, are both essential in the strategy-development process (Priem and Butler 2001). Following the findings of this study, CR can be considered as a superior resources in cultures scoring high in UAI, like Russia and Spain. Also, with regard to the knowledge-based view, customers in the B-to-B setting appreciate that the supplier shares expertise as a partner. This indicator is more important in Finland and Russia (feminine cultures) and less important in Australia, Germany and Spain (masculine cultures).

Interestingly, the importance of trust and reputation on relationship behavior varies between countries and stakeholder groups: Opposite to trust, reputation is more important in uncertainty avoiding countries scoring high in power distance. Possibly, due to similar cultural scores, this result can be extended on all Latin countries (e.g., South America, Portugal). In these countries, Hofstede's (2001) dimension of UAI score high, indicating the society's low level of tolerance for uncertainty. All these societies do not readily accept changes and are very risk adverse. To purchase products from a company having a positive CR may reduce risks. Also, taking into consideration the effect of not accepting changes and risks, long-term buyer-seller relationships as well as customer commitment are important. Additionally, users like doctors and nurses rely on a good reputation of the supplier.

The impact of innovativeness on reputation is strong across all countries and stakeholder groups, no cultural influence can be confirmed. Only Australia, Germany and-surprisingly-the stakeholder group of doctors and nurses do not show significant impact of innovativeness on reputation. On the other hand, the relationship between innovativeness and reputation transfer is practically non-existent and only visible in Finland.

Regarding the construct of purchase decision involvement, a cultural impact could not be confirmed-although its impact on WOM is remarkably strong in some countries. Then again, no relationship was found between the constructs of purchase decision involvement and reputation. In line with Hofstede (2001), a cultural impact on the use of and the trust in direct marketing media is confirmed.

The following subsections focus on different findings referring to the five countries and three stakeholder groups. Scientific and managerial implications are provided.

6.4.1 Findings Related to all Countries

In comparison to the single-country data-sets, probably caused by the cultural differences between the countries, several constructs do not show significant relationships towards other constructs. This especially refers to the use of direct marketing media, but also to purchase decision involvement. By only evaluating the disaggregated analysis, several conclusions resulting from this study could not be drawn. Surprisingly, the outer loadings of all reflective constructs are higher with reference to the complete data-set. Nevertheless, this does not lead to sufficient significant path correlations. Regarding the data-set of all countries, only two paths are influencing reputation:

- Relationship quality and
- Innovativeness
- Reputation transfer is influenced by perceived fit in eight out of nine groups and by WOM in six out of nine groups

Finally, the author concludes that paths significant across all countries are valid at least in all Western-type countries and not influenced by cultural differences. This especially refers to the construct of relationship quality, which positively influences reputation and WOM, and the construct of perceived fit.

6.4.1.1 Cross-Cultural Managerial Implications

Only little managerial recommendations can be given based on the aggregated data-set. It is useful to invest in the enhancement of relationship quality as being the cross-culturally important impact factor on reputation. This leads to the conclusion that-no matter in which country new products or product ranges shall be introduced,

- Relationship quality as well as
- Perceived fit (and WOM in a limited way) are decisive
- Generally, in line with Keller (2003), the fit perception is important
- It can not be recommended to rely on the use of “one global direct marketing medium” cross-culturally: in some countries social networks as well as WOM are even more important than any other direct marketing media
- In some countries, trust is more essential than CR- and vice versa

As already discussed before, it is indispensable to have information on the use of direct marketing media, before launching the product in certain countries.

6.4.2 Australia

The cultural dimensions of Australia are characterized by a high level of individuality, loosely knit social frameworks, and a focus on privacy. Although trust is easier developed in lower-UAI societies like Australia (Hofstede 2001) and companies from this cultural type engage in relationships, they also tend to restrain themselves from fully trusting in partners, to whom they are not strongly tied by cultural norms to group goals (Griffith et al. 2006). Full commitment to its interorganizational partners is difficult to achieve (Hofstede 2001).

6.4.2.1 Scientific Implications for Australia

As far as the Australian data-set is concerned, all outer loading are scoring high. Australia is the only country, where both types of direct marketing media have impact on other constructs included in the structural model.

- In Australia, the perceived fit of the new product has a strong positive impact on reputation transfer success.
- Although direct marketing media do not impact directly on reputation, they are influencing reputation transfer as well as the fit perception.

Additionally, the construct of perceived fit serves as a mediator of media-enabled direct marketing on reputation transfer. Reputation is exclusively influenced by relationship quality. Together with perceived innovativeness and purchase decision involvement, the latter has also a positive impact on WOM. Surprisingly, the Australian research results indicate that WOM does not have a positive influence either on reputation or on reputation transfer.

6.4.2.2 Managerial Implications for Australia

Australia is much less price-sensitive as the other Western-type cultures included in this survey. To inform about new products,

- Australian customers rely on direct marketing media and on fit perceptions than on personal recommendations, WOM has no impact on reputation or or reputation transfer.
- With regard to Australian customer relations in the B-to-B setting, direct marketing media are judged to be the key influencing factor on reputation, reputation transfer and perceived fit.

Additionally, in this country, the strong influencing factor of relationship quality needs to be taken under consideration, reputation in Australia is exclusively influenced by this construct. Reputation has no direct impact on reputation transfer, in Australia trust in the supplier is more important than a positive CR. As personal direct marketing media are directly influencing reputation transfer, a trustful relationship between the sales representatives and the customers is key to success. The fit perception of the new product can nevertheless been influenced using brochures, the Internet or mailing: facts count more than WOM.

6.4.3 Finland

According to Hofstede (2001) Finland is a very feminine country with low hierarchy levels. Characterized by openness towards changes and innovations as well as decentralized decision structures, the Finnish research results reveal the importance of relationship quality, innovativeness as well as WOM on a company's reputation and on reputation transfer.

6.4.3.1 Scientific Implications on Finland

In Finland not only WOM, but additionally innovativeness impacts positively on reputation transfer. Interestingly, with reference to the construct of "perceived innovativeness" this country distinguishes explicitely between "leading" and "innovative" products. Furthermore, the impacts of the constructs relationship quality and reputation have an indirect impact on reputation transfer-moderated through WOM. Finnish customers positively discuss and recommend products. WOM is therefore judged to be the key influencing factor on reputation transfer.

Unlike the findings of von Wangenheim (2003) as well as Feick and Price (1987), concluding that buying behavior of industrial purchasers as well as WOM is not determinated by purchase decision involvement, the results of this cross-cultural study for Finland (as well as for Australia and Spain) indicate a strong positive relationship between purchase decision involvement and WOM.

6.4.3.2 Managerial Implications for Finland

Reviewing the use of direct marketing media,

- The Finnish B-to-B customers prefer to rely on media-enabled direct marketing sources, such as the Internet, brochures and mailings. These media are have a strong positive impact on the perceived fit of new products.
- Study results show that the impact of media-enabled direct marketing media on reputation transfer is negative and that Finnish customers rely on trust in the recommendations of sales representatives. Therefore, to transfer the positive reputation of a company on new products, the trustful relationship between sales representatives and customers is essential.
- Results of a second study based on the same data-set also reveal a positive impact of media-enabled direct marketing on relationship quality.
- Personal direct marketing is of minor importance

Thus, if a company wants to extent their product range in Nordic countries like Finland by using its good reputation, this company should rely on media-enabled direct marketing actions. Additionally, in this country, the strong influencing factor of WOM needs to be taken under consideration.

6.4.4 Germany

According to Hofstede (2001), Germany is a very masculine culture with low hierarchy levels, focused on individual benefits. Advertising is seen as a useful source of new product information.

The German research results reveal the importance of relationship quality on reputation and WOM. WOM is also influenced by the perceived innovativeness of the company involved, no significant correlations is found between purchase decision involvement and WOM. On the other hand, the construct of perceived innovativeness neither influences reputation nor reputation transfer directly. Additionally, Germany is the only country where WOM impacts on both, reputation and reputation transfer. The impact of relationship quality on reputation transfer is existing indirectly, moderated through WOM.

6.4.4.1 Scientific Implications for Germany

Following the research question referring to a to successful transfer of a company's reputation on a new product range, this may not be possible on the German market:

- The fit perception of the new product range is lacking and, additionally, can not be influenced either by a company's reputation, or by any direct marketing media (although Germany is "home market" and market leader country of the company involved in this survey).
- In Germany, reputation is generally considered to be of minor importance and has no direct impact on reputation transfer.
- Although reputation transfer is positively influenced by WOM and media-enabled direct marketing, the customers do not agree that the new product range fits to the existing portfolio.

Evaluating the outer loadings of the construct of reputation transfer, the quality perception of the new product range is lacking: German customers are the only ones who do not expect the same high product quality standard compared to the already existing core products (0.5895 compared to the outer loadings of the other countries, which are scoring much higher: between 0.8715–0.9885).

Coming back to the differences in a customer's view of CR, in Germany trust is much more important than reputation:

- A trustful relationship to the supplier is very important to the German B-to-B customers, more than 83% of all survey participants agree to that.
- In line with above findings and with reference to the construct of reputation, the outer loading referring to the indicator of "I trust in the products of this company" scores much higher (0.9050) compared to the other two indicators of this construct (0.6858 and 0.6084, see Table 6.5).

6.4.4.2 Managerial Implications for Germany

Reviewing the use of direct marketing media, the German B-to-B customers prefer to rely on media-enabled direct marketing sources, such as the Internet, brochures and mailings. Also note that Germany is the only country where media-enabled direct marketing is able to influence both, reputation and reputation transfer. No path is significant related to the constructs of personal direct marketing media. Results of a second study based on the same data-set also reveals a positive impact of media-enabled direct marketing on relationship quality.

Thus, if a company wants to extent their product range in masculine countries with low hierarchy levels and the disposition to take over risks by using its good reputation, this company should bear in mind the problem of the fit perception. Possibly, countries with these cultural dimensions are more critical and only influenceable through direct marketing media and WOM. Therefore, in Germany, the strong influencing factor of WOM needs to be taken under consideration.

As in Germany (as well as in Australia and Finland) trust in the supplier and in the recommendation of its sales representatives is more important than CR, trust-enhancing activities may positively influence a customer's relationship. This may be one reason, why reputation is not related at all to the construct of reputation transfer in these countries.

6.4.5 *Russia*

Following the findings of Hofstede (2001), Russia is a feminine, very hierarchical and centralized country. Russian people are said to dislike decisions based on uncertainty and are characterized by high uniformity, high conservatism, high secrecy (Salter and Niswander 1995) and stronger interpersonal and interorganizational ties (Money et al. 1998).

6.4.5.1 Scientific Implications for Russia

Evaluating the Russian data-set, one of the outer loadings of the indicators forming the construct of reputation scores low: Russia is not much of the opinion that the company involved in this survey really cares for customers opinions. On the other hand, Russia scores highest with regard to the indicators of reputation transfer (0.9890 and 0.9885).

Although perceived innovativeness of a company is an important feature, new products-like all innovations placed on the Russian market-need to be supported from upper hierarchy levels to be successful.

- Social networks are important: Instead of direct marketing media, WOM is directly influencing reputation transfer, but does not show any impact on reputation.
- In line with the findings of Hofstede (2001), in Russia the impact of any direct marketing media is weak
- No significant path correlations were found between reputation and reputation transfer
- Perceived fit of the new product is positively influenced by reputation as well as by media-enabled direct marketing´
- The Internet as well as brochures and mailings can be used to influence the fit perception. Thus, these media need to include padding information instead of focusing exclusively on facts and figures (Hofstede, 2001)

In Russia, brand names and a company's positive reputation value more than trust in the suppliers, the outer loadings for "I trust in products of this supplier" are relatively weak. Relationship quality as well as perceived innovativeness have a positive impact on reputation.

6.4.5.2 Managerial Implications for Russia

If a company wants to extent its product range in feminine countries with strong hierarchy levels and no disposition to take over risks, it is possible to use its good reputation. Although CR is influencing reputation transfer through the construct of perceived fit, WOM and CR are the essential factors with reference to the successful transfer of reputation.

The use of direct marketing media is limited, moreover, media enabled direct marketing sources like the Internet, brochures and mailings are even able to influence the fit perception of the new product in a negative way.

As in Russia (as well as in Spain) CR is much more important than trust in the supplier and sales representatives, a customer's relationship relies on a company's CR while deciding on purchasing products in the B-to-B context. Relationship quality as well as the perceived innovativeness of a company are positively influencing CR. Russian customers want have the feeling that a company is offering value for money and take their concerns seriously. To enhance a company's reputation in Russia is more important than focus on direct marketing media, if reputation transfer shall be successful.

6.4.6 Spain

According to Hofstede (2001) Spain is an average society regarding the dimension of MAS and dislikes decisions based on uncertainty. Hierarchy levels are relatively strong, commitment of employees towards the organization is low, as personal relationships prevail over task and company. Findings of Hofstede (2001) claim that persons in low IDV societies do not believe in advertising, innovations are less important.

6.4.6.1 Scientific Implications for Spain

In line with Hofstede's (2001) findings and especially in comparison to the Finnish results,

- Perceived innovativeness does not play an important role. Spain is the only country, where this construct has no impact on WOM.
- The impact of perceived innovativeness on reputation is weak and non-existent with reference to reputation transfer, although the outer loadings of the construct "perceived innovativeness" are higher (0.9019 and 0.9554) than in any other country included in this survey.
- In Spain CR is generally more important than trust, in this survey the reputation of the company involved is not as high compared to the other countries.

Evaluating the outer loadings of the construct of reputation, values related to the indicators of "I trust in the products of this company" (0.6620) as well as "this company shares expertise as a partner" (0.6867) are much lower compared to other countries. These low scores on two out of three indicators show that the reputation of the company involved in the research is inferior compared to the other countries. This also influences the relationship between reputation and reputation transfer in a negative way and leads to the conclusion that

- Reputation transfer can just be carried out successfully, if the company in general owns a positive reputation
- And is possible only in cultures, where reputation is more important than trust.

6.4.6.2 Managerial Implications for Spain

With reference to the results of the study,

- Media-enabled direct marketing sources do neither influence reputation, reputation transfer nor the perceived fit of the new products to the existing product range.
- Personal direct marketing media like fairs, symposia or visits of sales representatives have a significant influence on both, reputation and reputation transfer.
- It can not be recommended to refer to the “perceived innovativeness”, if a company wants to positively enhance their reputation on the Spanish market

Compared to other countries, the impact of relationship quality is very strong, not only regarding a company’s CR, but also with reference to WOM. Interestingly, although influenced by relationship quality and purchase decision involvement, WOM does not show any significant impact on any of the constructs involved in the structural model. If a company wants to extent its product range in Spain,

- Personal direct marketing media should be used,
- Activities like the participation in fairs and symposia as well as visits of sales representatives have a positive impact on reputation and reputation transfer.
- In Spain CR is much more important than trust in the supplier and its sales representatives.
- Relationship quality as well as the perceived innovativeness of a company are positively influencing CR. There is a strong positive relationship between reputation and the perceived fit of the new product range, although-surprisingly-the direct impact of reputation on reputation transfer is negative.

6.4.7 Purchasers

Although only very little path correlations in this stakeholder group are significant, the results are very interesting:

- Organizational purchasers are the only group in this survey, where reputation directly positive impacts on reputation transfer.
- With reference to this stakeholder group, a transfer of reputation is a very good opportunity, even without the round-about-way via perceived fit.

This is a very interesting result, taking into consideration that except for this stakeholder group, the direct link between reputation and reputation transfer is non-existent (all countries, Australia, Germany, Finland, Russia, pharmacists, doctors and nurses) or-even worse-negative (Spain). So,

- If a company is focused on extending its product range and organizational purchasers are its target group, using a company's positive reputation is very well possible.
- Thus, as far as the direct marketing media are concerned, the country results additionally need to be taken under consideration.
- As already discussed before, relationship quality as well as innovativeness has a positive impact on reputation, and
- The fit perception additionally is positively influencing reputation transfer success.

6.4.8 Pharmacists

Hospital pharmacists are involved in the prescription of drugs; their advisory role is becoming more dominant regarding the choices of treatments and desire for information of doctors and nurses (Wright and Fill 2001). The results of this study show that for this stakeholder group,

- Relationship quality is the most important influencing factor and that
- This construct has a very strong impact on reputation, reputation transfer and WOM

These findings are in line with the results of the UK study of Wright and Fill (2001, p. 102), claiming that pharmacists quote their relationship towards sales representatives and the attribute "company offers value for money" as important and "key to the contribution of the overall image of a pharmaceutical company". According to the results of Wright and Fill (2001), sales representatives are the main source of marketing communications with the companies. As the use of direct marketing media varies significantly among the countries, no significant paths were found regarding the use of personal direct marketing. Nevertheless, Hofstede's cultural dimensions of the UK are similar to the Australian data-set regarding the dimensions of IDV, PDI and MAS. The Australian data-set indicates the impact of personal direct marketing media on reputation transfer (personal direct marketing media also include visits of sales representatives). Additionally, in Australia the importance of trust in the recommendations of sales representatives of certain suppliers show much high rates of importance. Therefore, a transfer of the findings of Wright and Fill (2001) regarding the importance of personal direct marketing in countries having the same cultural dimensions like Australia and the UK, is quite likely.

The construct of reputation is also influenced by a company's perceived innovativeness. This is also in line with the study of Wright and Fill (2001) discussing the importance of a high level of research and development investments, which is also closely linked to the perceived innovativeness of a company.

Therefore, to strengthen a company's reputation in the relationship towards pharmacists, the author recommends

- To invest in activities impacting relationship quality ("this company offers value for money" or "takes my concerned seriously") and
- The perceived innovativeness of the company ("this company offers leading/ innovative products")

As far as reputation transfer is concerned, WOM and perceived fit are strongly influencing this construct. As stated above, WOM is influenced by relationship quality. Therefore, putting the focus on the latter, seems to be the one decisive link to reputation transfer success. As far as the direct marketing media are concerned, the related country results need to be referred to.

6.4.9 Doctors and Nurses

The stakeholder group of doctors and nurses is the one with the smallest number of significant paths. Interestingly,

- The perceived innovativeness of a company does not have an impact either on reputation and WOM, or on reputation transfer.
- For the user group of doctors and nurses, to focus on innovativeness in direct marketing media is not a way to success.

On the other hand, relationship quality impacts directly on WOM as well as on reputation:

- The products of a company seem to be often recommended directly by other users having a positive attitude towards the company.
- A good reputation of the supplier is cross-culturally important (see Fig. 6.15, indicating the high scores of doctors and nurses on the importance of a good reputation of the supplier)
- Perceived fit of the new products range impacts positively on reputation transfer and thus is an important feature in this stakeholder group

Regarding all other constructs, no recommendations can be given, due to a lack of significant relationship between the constructs.

6.5 Discussion of Research Questions

The hypotheses listed in Table 6.56 were developed to answer on certain research questions presented in Sect. 4.6. Thus, based on the evaluation of research data and hypotheses, the following statements shall be made:

1. Is reputation transfer influenced by reputation? Is this relationship between reputation and reputation transfer significant across all countries and stakeholder groups or related to market leadership?

An impact of reputation on reputation transfer was found. This effect turned out to be twofold: negative and positive. While evaluating the moderating effects, regarding the Finnish data-set the impact of reputation on reputation transfer was positively moderated through WOM, although there was no direct impact. The Spanish data-set shows a negative relationship between reputation and reputation transfer. Interestingly, the most important stakeholder group involved in the buying decision process-the organizational purchasers-indicates the only direct positive path correlation between reputation and reputation transfer. Obviously, in this study, market leadership does not have an impact on the link between reputation and reputation transfer.

2. In B-to-B relationships, what factors further influence reputation and reputation transfer? Are the factors identical across countries and stakeholder groups?

A very strong influencing factor on reputation is WOM, this construct is also serving as a moderator variable. Additionally, relationship quality is the only construct which indicates strong positive impact on reputation throughout all countries and stakeholder groups. Suprisingly, except for the stakeholder group of pharmacists, relationship quality shows no impact at all on the construct of reputation transfer.

The same pattern holds for the construct of innovativeness: Strong impact on reputation,and-except for Finland-no impact on reputation transfer. Impact factors on reputation transfer are differ significantly across countries and stakeholder groups. Except for the use of direct marketing media, impact factors on reputation are more similar across the countries and stakeholder groups.

3. What role do the media play with regard to CR, reputation transfer and perceived fit of the new product or product range? Is there a difference regarding countries and stakeholder groups in use of personal direct marketing media and media-enabled direct marketing?

Except for Australia (which uses both types of direct marketing media) and Spain (which prefers personal direct marketing media), all countries prefer media-enabled direct marketing like the Internet, brochures and mailings to inform themselves about new products.

Due to the significant differences in the use of direct marketing media, no significant paths are achieved, before splitting up the data-set by countries. This finally led to the conclusion that, based on the results of this study, the use of direct marketing media is strongyl influenced by different cultural values. This result corresponds to the findings of Hofstede (2001), claiming that cultures scoring low in uncertainty avoidance (in this survey: Australia, Finland and Germany) rely more on advertisements than others, which score high in uncertainty avoidance (Russia and Spain).

4. The use of media varies across the countries. Is there a relationship between the e-readiness score of the different countries and media-enabled direct marketing?

A positive relationship can be confirmed in all countries under consideration. The use of media-enabled direct marketing in different countries and across stakeholder groups is influenced by the criteria evaluated in the e-readiness construct.

5. Is it really true that purchase decision involvement plays no role in B-to-B buying behavior? Is there a relationship between purchase decision involvement and WOM in cultures with low scores in PDI?

The study results show that purchase decision involvement is not influencing a company's reputation, although, referring to the German data-set, the positive impact of purchase decision involvement on reputation is moderated through WOM.

In Australia, Finland, and Spain purchase decision involvement has a positive impact on WOM. Findings of this study lead to the conclusion that purchase decision involvement plays a role in B-to-B buying behavior-but the impact is only visible, if the data is split-up by countries. It is not visible, if the data-set is split up by stakeholder groups. Therefore, this impact is also influenced by cultural differences.

Nevertheless, in line with the conclusions of von Wangenheim (2003) no impact of purchase decision involvement on B-to-B buying behavior can be confirmed for Germany. Therefore, before generally denying an impact of one certain construct on another, a possible cultural influence can strongly be recommended.

6. What kind of impact does WOM have on reputation and reputation transfer? Which factors influence WOM across countries and stakeholder groups?

A direct impact of WOM on reputation was exclusively found in the German data-set, this cross-cultural relationship seems to be only weak. Except for Australia, Spain and the stakeholder group of purchasers, WOM has a strong positive impact on reputation transfer. Except for organizational purchasers, all countries and stakeholder groups show a strong influence between relationship quality and WOM. Relationship quality therefore is considered to be an important influencing factor on WOM.

7. In the B-to-B context, does the perceived innovativeness have an impact on both, reputation and reputation transfer? Can new products take advantage of the perceived brand characteristics of the parent brand? What about the relationship between perceived innovativeness and WOM?

Perceived innovativeness is an important factor on reputation, but has hardly no direct influence on reputation transfer success. Thus, perceived innovativeness indirectly impacts reputation transfer through WOM: Except for Spain, all countries show a strong relationship between perceived innovativeness and WOM. As no stakeholder group shows any significant correlation, the influence of innovativeness within this structural model is only visible while separating the main data-set by country.

New products may take advantage of the brand characteristics of the parent brand-strongly influenced directly by WOM and indirectly influenced by relationship quality.

8. How important is the perceived fit of the new product or product range with regard to reputation transfer success? Does CR influence this fit across all countries and stakeholder groups? Is perceived fit also influenced in all countries by both direct marketing media?

According to the results of this study, the perceived fit is a key influencing variable on reputation transfer. This enhances the findings of Keller (2003), who claims that the perceived fit is important with brand extension projects. Except for market-leader country Germany, all countries and stakeholder groups confirm a strong positive relationship between both constructs, the perceived fit and reputation transfer. Also, besides Australia, all countries show significant impact of reputation on perceived fit. With reference to the different stakeholder groups, this impact is also very strong towards pharmacists. This leads to the conclusion that CR has a strong impact on the perceived fit of new products.

In Australia, Finland and Russia, media-enabled direct marketing is able to influence the perceived fit of the new product, although this relationship is negative in Russia. This result is in line with the findings of Hofstede (2001), arguing that cultures scoring high in UAI do not trust in advertisements.

9. Is there a positive relationship between relationship quality and reputation? Does the attitude towards the company also influence reputation transfer?

Study results show that relationship quality by far is the most substantial impact factor on reputation. All countries and stakeholder groups show significant path correlations between both constructs, additionally, relationship quality is also strongly influencing WOM in most of the countries. Thus, the author suggests that within this survey relationship quality as well as the perceived fit are the only constructs which are obviously not influenced by the national culture of buyers.

The findings of this research work also confirm that, surprisingly, relationship quality influences reputation transfer only indirectly though WOM. The attitude towards the company influences reputation transfer success in an indirect way.

10. What about the impact of the national culture of buyers on the factors influencing reputation and reputation transfer? Does national culture influence the impact of a company's reputation on organizational buying decisions?

Some of the constructs are considered to be more related to cultural impacts than others.

- Relationship quality, the perceived fit, perceived innovativeness and WOM mostly play an important role in almost all countries and stakeholder groups. These constructs strongly correlate with reputation or reputation transfer.

- The use and the importance of direct marketing media as well as the impact of purchase decision involvement on WOM varies significantly from country to country and is not visible at all regarding the stakeholder groups.
- Data evaluation leads to the result that reputation, perceived fit and reputation transfer matter more in uncertainty avoiding cultures scoring high in PDI. In these countries, reputation is more important than trust in the supplier and will surely impact organizational buying decisions: A positive reputation may reduce the risk of chosing the wrong supplier (uncertainty avoiding cultures have great fear of failure).

Results of this study show that perceived fit of new products generally has a strong impact on reputation transfer success. Uncertainty avoiding cultures like Russia and Spain show much stronger coefficients than cultures scoring low in this dimension (Australia, Finland).

Chapter 7
Conclusions, Implications and Research Suggestions

This empirical study is motivated by the research question of whether and how national culture influences the way organizational buyers of different countries perceive a company's reputation and whether the impact factors on CR and reputation transfer are identical to all stakeholders and countries.

The relevance of the findings of this study is both theoretical and practical:

- Theoretically, this study increases our understanding of distinctions in impact factors on CR and reputation transfer among stakeholders of different countries in the B-to-B context.
- It also provides further empirical support to the idea that different cultures base their evaluations on different subsets of dimensions of a company's reputation or, in other words, on different subsets of perceived corporate actions and features.
- In practical terms, the findings of this study provide communication managers and marketing managers with general indications about the drivers of CR, and information on the use of direct marketing media by organizational stakeholders.
- This study also indicates that there are countries where it is possible to enter new markets by transferring a company's (positive) reputation on new products.
- Remarkably, for the German market, study results show that there is no significant correlation between the constructs of reputation, perceived fit and reputation transfer. A more exact examination of the survey data indicated that the German customers do not believe that the new transfer product of generic pharmaceuticals will offer the same high quality standard than the core product range of medical devices. Thus, for this certain company in the field of medical devices and in this certain country (Germany), a transfer of reputation core values on generic pharmaceuticals will possibly not be a success.

Referring to the resource-based view, this study confirms that a company's reputation is a very important intangible asset. Nevertheless, it is literally nothing more than how the organization is perceived by its stakeholders. Scientists, as well as managers, need to bear in mind that stakeholders' perceptions vary cross-culturally. Moreover, referring to the knowledge-based view, in the B-to-B setting, the results

C. Falkenreck, *Reputation Transfer to Enter New B-to-B Markets*, Contributions to Management Science,
DOI 10.1007/978-3-7908-2357-8_7, © Springer-Verlag Berlin Heidelberg 2010

of this study show that organizational customers cross-culturally value the fact that a supplier takes their concerns and requests seriously and shares expertise as a partner. Surprisingly, this is applicable cross-culturally and important not only in countries which are said to be relationship-oriented.

To compose "one valid construct of reputation" is a daunting challenge. As suggested by Gatewood et al. (1993), inconsistent perceptions across stakeholder groups might be attributed to different correlates of reputation, whereas consistent perceptions indicate that reputation is a general construct. The findings of this study prove that reputation is influenced by inconsistent perceptions across stakeholder groups and countries, which leads to the conclusion that reputation is NOT a general construct. Helm (2006) claims that if not all stakeholder groups are represented among the respondents, the study results are biased and do not validly represent the collective construct of a company's reputation.

The author wishes to add that an "overall reputation" encompassing several different stakeholder group perceptions (investors, customers, suppliers, employees, general public) does not yet exist, and in the light of the different reputations of countries and stakeholders, is not scientifically reasonable. Taking into consideration the different impact factors on CR, one construct including all stakeholder-specific features is hard to analyze, and to compare the results of different stakeholder groups and countries, the datasets need to be separated.

The above comments surely include some of the reasons why up to now neither researchers nor practitioners have yet found a cross-nationally validated instrument to measure reputation (Fombrun and Wiedmann 2001; Fombrun and Gardberg 2002; Helm 2007; Eberl 2006; Money and Hillenbrand 2006). This work has tried a completely different approach. It focuses on the development and cross-cultural testing of a construct of reputation rooted in resource-based theories. With regard to the strong cultural impact on reputation, future reputational research approaches should bear in mind the following: Before composing the construct of reputation by using indicators related to trust, one should take into consideration the fact that the importance of trust and reputation are discussed controversially in different cultures (see evaluation of Hypotheses 16 and 17). As already concluded by Hofstede (2001), we can confirm the following:

- This study shows that trust is significantly more important in countries where people have low hierarchy levels, fewer laws and regulations and relationship orientation is stronger. According to Hofstede (2001), these countries score low in UAI and PDI (in this study: Australia and Finland).
- On the other hand, trust is less important in cultures where people have more fear of failing, believe in specialists and expertise, and have high hierarchy levels. Following the results of Hofstede (2001), these countries score high in UAI and PDI (in this study: Russia and Spain).

Up to now, no study has ever asked organizational customers to rate the importance of a supplier's positive reputation on their buying decision. CR is said to be important for a company's success (Fombrun et al. 2000; Eberl 2006, MacMillan et al. 2005; Helm 2007), although the importance of CR clearly differs across the countries.

In addition, this study is able to extend Hofstede's (2001) findings by presenting the empirical proof of the cultural influence on reputation.

- CR is significantly more important in cultures where company loyalty is a virtue and where people prefer clarity and structure and are afraid of wrong decisions and failure. This refers to countries scoring high in UAI and PDI (in this study: Russia and Spain).
- CR is less important in cultures where people are open to changes and innovations and are willing to take unknown risks. These professional characteristics refer to countries scoring low in UAI and PDI (in this study: Australia and Finland).

This study shows that a company's reputation in the B-to-B context is influenced by different factors. Nevertheless, some criteria are also influence CR positively across all countries and stakeholder groups. Coming back to the research objectives in Chap. 1, the following conclusions can be made:

- No doubt, companies have many reputations, simply due to the fact that just one stakeholder group will evaluate its reputation cross-culturally and therefore see it in various ways. In general terms, this study shows that reputation may also be negative. This may be a serious issue in those countries where reputation is more important than trust.
- Stakeholder groups use different criteria to evaluate a company. Across all countries and stakeholder groups, relationship quality and perceived innovativeness impact positively on CR.
- Stakeholder groups also use the same criteria to evaluate a company. In Germany, WOM and media-enabled direct marketing activities have a strong influence on CR. In contrast, in Australia, both constructs have no impact at all on CR.
- Also, with reference to the indicators forming the construct of reputation, different outer loadings indicate different evaluations of a company's reputation. Thus, these differences are only obvious while splitting the dataset: Referring to the complete dataset of 250 respondents, the outer loading, of all three indicators are virtually identical.
- In line with the findings of Gardberg (2006), the dimension "vision and leadership" has not been included in the measurement model of CR in this study. B-to-B customers, especially organizational buyers, have only very limited knowledge about their suppliers' "vision and leadership". Similarly, for B-to-C customers, the international adaptability of the dimensions "vision and leadership" and "financial performance" is discussed controversially (Gardberg 2006; Fombrun et al. 2000; Helm 2006; Waldman et al. 2004).

One of the reasons why these features are difficult to adapt globally can be found in the results of Hofstede (2001), claiming that the way leadership is conducted within a nation is also strongly influenced by culture.

This, again, is one indicator of the strong cultural impact on a company's reputation. Also, by transferring the American-based measurement concept of Fombrun's RQ cross-culturally, these differences were obvious and discussed by Gardberg (2006), Walsh and Wiedmann (2004), Dunbar and Schwalbach (2000) and Aperia, et al. (2004), but none of these authors traced the problems of transferring the RQ measures back to cultural differences across the countries.

7.1 Scientific Implications

This research is the first to highlight the cross-link between reputation, reputation transfer and culture, and argues that to develop one cross-culturally valid construct of reputation, which can be used in both B-to-B and B-to-C contexts is neither useful nor appropriate.

However, the chosen set of variables and moderators do not exhaust the list of possible determinants. Although the structural model suggests several important determinants, mediators and moderaors, other variables were omitted. Some determinants, such as "financial performance", "vision and leadership" and "social responsibility", were omitted as the impact of these determinants on reputation is not clearly verifiable in the B-to-B context. Others, like "customers" attitude toward sales representatives", "propensity to leave", "service quality" and "years of experience with product or company" were left out to avoid an overburdening of the existing structural model.

This research addresses the important issue of whether or not purchasing behavior in B-to-B relationships differs across countries. However, purchasing decisions in the B-to-B domain are highly complex and often involve multiple decision makers.

The results of this study are not in line with the conclusions of Helm (2007), who claims that reputation and trust interact and that reputation is a consequence of trust, and that trust may only develop based on a positive reputation. Although it is generally assumed that a positive CR is an important asset, up to now, the significance of reputation in different countries has not yet been empirically investigated.

This research highlights several cross-cultural differences in customers' perception of reputation and in the feasibility of reputation transfer. In the light of these cross-cultural differences, we make the following scientific propositions:

- Generally, a company's reputation is influenced by national culture and may differ by stakeholder groups.
- In cultures scoring high in uncertainty avoidance, a company's positive CR is a valuable asset, as the transfer of reputation is possible.
- Surprisingly, CR is not as important as trust in countries scoring low in uncertainty avoidance. These countries value a trustful relationship with a supplier over a company's reputation, and therefore reputation transfer is virtually impossible.

- The influencing factors on CR differ significantly. Thus, this study argues for a broader perspective on reputation and reputational resources.
- Negative reputations impact negatively on reputation transfer. Only positive reputations offer the feasibility of reputation transfer success.
- Regarding reputation transfer, the fit perception of the new product or product range is essential. Furthermore, different reputations in different cultures impact on perceived fit.

This research was limited to fifty participants of five different countries. Nevertheless, it was obvious how much the single country datasets varied in almost every aspect. Therefore, regarding the theory of commitment and trust and bearing in mind the global relationship-enhancing activities of international companies, recommendations on the treatment of certain stakeholder groups may not be given without evaluating the country-related data.

In this study, the findings regarding media-enabled and personal direct marketing activities differ impressively. Consequently, it is impossible to recommend one direct marketing tool, cross-culturally, to influence CR.

7.2 Managerial Implications

In practice, the definitions of reputation and brand identity are still closely related or mixed up, this until today leads to serious problems in comparing research results on CR. Corresponding to this, Harris and Chernatony (2001, p. 445) adopt their definition of "brand reputation" as "a collective representation of a brand's past actions and results that describes the brand's ability to deliver valued outcomes to multiple stakeholders." From a managerial point of view, this work provides several important insights:

- Suppliers may use their customers' nationality as a customer segmentation element, analyze their customer structure carefully and identify cross-cultural differences.
- Possessing knowledge about the media used in certain cultures increases direct marketing effectiveness. This knowledge helps suppliers in B-to-B markets to position their products exactly in the media most frequently used by their target groups.
- It is often suggested that companies should strive for one consistent reputation among stakeholder groups (e.g., Nguyen and Leblanc 2001). This goal may be reached more easily by extending knowledge on the user habits of direct marketing media as reputation-influencing tools.
- With respect to relationship commitment, positive links have been found between relationship quality, WOM, perceived innovativeness and reputation.
- If a company is planning to introduce new products by transferring its positive reputation, countries should be selected where reputation is more important than

relationship commitment, and where people are afraid of wrong decisions and failure. This refers to countries scoring high in UAI and PDI (in this study: Russia and Spain) In addition, all Latin American countries fall into this category.
- To improve customer relationships in the B-to-B context, trust enhancing actions are recommended in countries having low hierarchy levels, and fewer laws and regulations. In these countries, relationship orientation is stronger. This refers to countries scoring low in UAI like the US, Australia and Finland.

A discussion is currently gaining ground concerning the impact of Internet network communities on CR, not only in the B-to-C setting, but also regarding supplier rankings in B-to-B. Therefore, to learn about the direct marketing communication tools in certain countries and to use them properly will surely be more important in the future. Also, the impact of customer Internet clubs and consumer magazines on CR in countries valuing media-enabled direct marketing can clearly be recommended without restriction.

Two of the constructs, WOM and innovativeness, have been identified in earlier studies carried out on the general population (Fombrun et al. 2000; Fombrun and van Riel 2004). Unlike what was observed for the general population, however, these dimensions, as well as relationship quality, seem central in affecting the overall disposition of the stakeholders in the B-to-B setting. Therefore, all measures enhancing a company's perceptions regarding "It offers value for money", "It takes my concerns seriously" can be recommended cross-culturally. In line with the findings of Morgan and Hunt (1994), this leads neatly to the following conclusion: Relationship commitment and relationship quality are still a very important global issue. Their impact on CR is significant.

7.3 Conclusions and Outlook

In general, the most important contribution of this study is that it improves our basic understanding of how differently the same company's reputation is evaluated by its cross-cultural customers. Consistent with the findings of Hofstede (2001), this work confirms that the use of direct marketing media is influenced by national culture and varies significantly.

The construct of reputation transfer has never been observed empirically before, and seems to be more relevant in some cultures or within certain stakeholder groups. The influence of purchase decision involvement on reputation has never been investigated either. Cross-culturally, does not seem to have an impact on this construct. Nevertheless, the author is able to confirm the relationship between purchase decision involvement and WOM in the B-to-B context. This impact is denied in the literature (e.g., von Wangenheim 2003; Feick and Price 1987).

In general, the results of this study are in line with the findings of Gabbioneta et al. (2007) and Meffert and Bierwind (2002), who suggest that while some dimensions of CR tend to overlap across different countries and groups of stakeholders, different stakeholders may focus their evaluation on different sets of attributes. The results of cross-cultural testing in five countries indicate that a unique cultural influence on reputation and reputation transfer exists: The impact of all constructs integrated in the structural model on reputation and reputation transfer differs significantly across the countries.

Thus, the findings of this study do not support the conclusions of Newman and Nollen (1996), who argue that UAI may not be a useful dimension for comparative research, and Denison and Mishra (1995), who generally deny the impact of culture on the perceptions of policies and good management practices.

Inconsistent perceptions across stakeholder groups might be attributed to different correlates of reputation (Gatewood et al. 1993). Reputational analysis, therefore, should be limited to specific roles of a company:

The findings of Homburg et al. (2004) indicate that countries scoring high in UAI care more for tangible relationship resources, whereas intangibles play a more important role in cultures scoring low in UAI. Trust as well as CR are intangible relationship resources, and cross-culturally important. Thus, this study argues that it is not possible to separate cultures based on the importance of tangible or intangible relationship resources, but to distinguish between the importance of trust (in cultures scoring low in UAI) and the importance of reputation (related to cultures scoring high in UAI) in relationships.

To the author, general reputation can only exist as well as the specific role-confined reputations, as long as the company is known to the general public, i.e., with B-to-C companies. To date, cross-cultural studies located in the B-to-B setting of different stakeholder groups' perceptions of reputation have rarely been published. They are, of course, necessary to gain further insights into stakeholder-specificity or country-specificity of reputational perceptions.

This research approach is limited to five countries. With regard to the Russian context, further research should focus on a larger number of Russian participants, and by geographical regions. This fast-growing economy comprises a diversity of Western and Eastern cultural areas. Also, to investigate the "Asian view of CR" will surely enhance our knowledge of important impact factors on CR and the possibility of reputation transfer in this region.

In addition, to compare the impact factors on CR in a B-to-B and B-to-C setting directly, a replication of this research may be focused on some "most visible companies" in the five countries included in this survey.

A company's reputation may still be one of the key drivers of corporate competitiveness and profitability, provided that the company is aware of the various impact factors on its CR and uses the suitable direct marketing media to influence it. Bearing in mind the economic importance of companies in the B-to-B context and the changes taking place in Russia and China, to repeat this study after a period of 10 years could offer additional insights into the importance of media-enabled direct marketing activities in global expansion and possible changes regarding the impact factors on corporate reputation.

Annex

Outer loadings of reflective constructs: Referring to Sect. 6.2.5

Table A1 Outer loadings of reflective constructs

Constructs	Indicators	Purchasers	Pharmacists	Users
Innovativenes	Innovative prod.	0.8824	0.9359	0.9283
	Leading prod.	0.8970	0.7897	0.9035
Reputation	Cares for cust. opinion	0.8557	0.7539	0.8306
	Shares expertise	0.8381	0.8144	0.8311
	I trust in products	0.8365	0.7088	0.8393
WOM	Would recommend medical dev.	0.9150	0.9545	0.9382
	Would recommend Pharma	0.8879	0.9790	0.9195
RepTransfer	Would purchase it	0.9018	0.9006	0.9239
	Expect same quality	0.8717	0.8149	0.8300

Fornell–Larcker Criterion, Data of Stakeholders: Referring to Sect. 6.2.8, Fornell–Larcker Criterion, Data of Stakeholders

Table A2 Fornell–Larcker criterion, data of purchasers

Purchasers	Perceived innovativeness	Reputation transfer	Reputation	Word of mouth
Perc. innovativeness	1.0000	0.0203	0.4107	0.0529
Reputation transfer	0.0203	1.0000	0.0409	0.3845
Reputation	0.4108	0.0409	1.0000	0.2283
Word of mouth	0.0529	0.3845	0.2283	1.0000
AVE	0.7915	0.7376	0.5779	0.9349

Table A3 Fornell–Larcker criterion, data of pharmacists

Pharmacists	Perceived innovativeness	Reputation transfer	Reputation	Word of mouth
Perc. innovativeness	1.0000	0.2900	0.4554	0.0882
Reputation transfer	0.2900	1.0000	0.4128	0.5941
Reputation	0.4554	0.4128	1.0000	0.2656
Word of mouth	0.0882	0.5941	0.2656	1.0000
AVE	0.7498	0.7376	0.5779	0.9349

Table A4 Fornell–Larcker criterion, data of doctors and nurses

Doctors and nurses	Perceived innovativeness	Reputation transfer	Reputation	Word of mouth
Perc. innovativeness	1.0000	0.2622	0.2481	0.3494
Reputation transfer	0.2622	1.0000	0.2978	0.3928
Reputation	0.4281	0.2978	1.0000	0.4520
Word of mouth	0.3494	0.3928	0.4520	1.0000
AVE	0.8390	0.7713	0.6950	0.8628

Cross-Loadings of Reflective Constructs of Stakeholders: Referring to Sect. 6.2.7 Cross-Loadings of Reflective Constructs of Stakeholders)

Table A5 Cross-loadings of reflective constructs: purchasers

Crossloadings purchasers	Perceived innovativeness	Reputation transfer	Reputation	Word of mouth
innovative products	0,8820	0,1136	0,5581	0,1843
cares for cust. opinions	0,4851	0,2087	0,8546	0,1651
shares expertise	0,5370	0,0763	0,8346	0,1041
trust in products	0,5902	0,2179	0,8404	0,2910
leading products	0,8973	0,1398	0,5817	0,2240
recommend Med. Dev.	0,2607	0,5150	0,3086	0,9219
recommend Pharma	0,1428	0,6150	0,0805	**0,8799**
would purchase it	0,2102	**0,9018**	0,0936	0,6221
expect same quality	0,0323	**0,8717**	0,2770	0,4691

Table A6 Cross-loadings of reflective constructs: pharmacists

Crossloadings Pharmacists	Perceived innovativeness	Rep transfer	Reputation	Word of mouth
innovative products	0,9359	0,3345	0,4520	0,1060
cares for cust. opinions	0,4725	0,2994	0,7517	0,2661
shares expertise	0,3543	0,3710	0,8146	0,1212
trust in products	0,2080	0,2581	0,7108	0,2471
leading products	0,7897	0,1191	0,3123	0,0287
recommend Med. Dev.	0,0441	0,4956	0,1763	0,9549
recommend Pharma	0,1140	0,6310	0,3132	0,9788
would purchase it	0,3340	0,9007	0,4033	0,5992
expect same quality	0,1393	0,8149	0,2943	0,3987

Table A7 Cross-loadings of reflective constructs: doctors and nurses

Crossloadings Doctors, Nurses	Perceived innovativeness	Reputation transfer	Reputation	Word of mouth
Innovative products	0,9283	0,2323	0,4064	0,3724
Cares for cust. opinions	0,3331	0,3207	0,8305	0,3047
Shares expertise	0,3777	0,1068	0,8308	0,3250
Trust in products	0,3640	0,2819	0,8396	0,4810
Leading products	0,9035	0,2468	0,3766	0,2602
Recommend med. dev.	0,3268	0,3830	0,4285	0,9386
Recommend pharma	0,3223	0,3409	0,4103	0,9191
Would purchase it	0,3268	0,9214	0,3472	0,4761
Expect same quality	0,0944	0,8336	0,1408	0,1610

Tables of Multicollinearity, Stakeholders: Tables referring to Sect. 6.2.10 Multicollinearity

Table A8 Mulitcollinearity of formative constructs: purchasers

Purchasers formative	Indicators	Weights, unstandardized	Std. Error	t-values	VIF < 10
Purchase decision involvement	Same features	0.090		0.226	
	Brand imp.	1.014		2.011	
	Purc dec,	−0.183		0.505	
Relationship quality	Value money	0.386		1.249	
	Concerns	0.599		1.981	
	Satisfied	0.387		1.102	
Personal DM	Fairs	−0.386		0.627	
	Symposia	1.228		1.992	
	Visits sr	−0.042		0.138	
Media-enabled DM	Brochures	0.639		1.033	
	Internet	−0.910		1.088	
	Mailings	0.215		0.495	

Table A9 Mulitcollinearity of formative constructs: pharmacists

Pharmacists formative	Indicators	Weights, unstandardized	Std. Error	t-values	VIF < 10
Purchase Decision Involvement	Same features	−0.116		0.476	
	Brand imp.	0.607		3.072	
	Purc dec,	0.639		3.099	
Relationship Quality	Value money	0.657		4.879	
	Concerns	0.227		1.421	
	Satisfied	0.466		3.721	
Personal DM	Fairs	−0.833		1.066	
	Symposia	0.342		0.611	
	Visits sr	0.760		1.168	
Media-enabled DM	Brochures	0.044		0.184	
	Internet	−0.544		1.432	
	Mailings	0.945		2.619	

Table A10 Mulitcollinearity of formative constructs: doctors and nurses

Doctors, Nurses formative	Indicators	Weights, unstandardized	Std. Error	t-values	VIF < 10
Purchase decision involvement	Same features	0.780		1.150	
	Brand imp.	−0.572		1.010	
	Purc dec,	−0.074		0.235	
Relationship quality	Value money	0.294		2.763	
	Concerns	0.589		2.859	
	Satisfied	0.392		4.341	
Personal DM	Fairs	−1.050		0.775	
	Symposia	0.413		1.486	
	Visits sr	0.441		0.845	
Media-enabled DM	Brochures	0.739		1.429	
	Internet	0.637		1.298	
	Mailings	−0.680		1.046	

Data Bonferroni–Holm's Procedure: Data Related to Sect. 4.4

Table A11 Bonferroni–Holm's procedure, related path: Rel. quality – WOM

Paths significant on a p = 0.05 level: Rel.Quality – WOM	t-value	p-value, in ascending order, p-value must be < values of Bonferroni–Holm's	Values based on Bonferroni–Holms procedure
Doctors, Nurses	5.296	0.0	0.00625
Russia	4.553	0.0	0.00714
Germany	7.885	0.0	0.00833
Spain	4.088	0.001	0.01
Pharmacists	3.170	0.0013	0.0125
All countries	2.915	0.0017	0.01666
Australia	2.384	0.0105	0.025
Finland	1.963	0.0276	0.05

Table A12 Bonferroni–Holm's procedure, path: Innovativeness– reputation

Paths significant on a p = 0.05 level: Innovativeness– reputation	t-value	p-value, in ascending order, p-value must be < values of Bonferroni–Holm's	Values based on Bonferroni–Holms procedure
Fin	5.253	0.0	0.00833
Russia	4.530	0.0	0.01
Purchaser	4.455	0.0	0.0125
Pharmacists	4.301	0.0	0.01666
Spain	3.136	0.0014	0.025
All	2.994	0.0015	0.05

Table A13 Bonferroni–Holm's procedure, related path: Rel. quality – WOM

Paths significant on a p = 0.05 level: Innovativeness-Rep. Transfer	t-value	p-value, in ascending order, p-value must be < values of Bonferroni–Holm's	Values based on Bonferroni–Holms procedure
Finland	3.521	0.0005	0.05

Table A14 Bonferroni–Holm's procedure, related path: Innovativeness – WOM

Paths significant on a p = 0.05 level: Innovativeness – WOM	t-value	p-value, in ascending order, p-value must be < result of Bonferroni–Holms procedure	Values based on Bonferroni–Holms procedure
Ger	2.866	0.003	0.0125
Fin	2.625	0.0057	0.01666
Russia	2.153	0.0181	0.025
Aus	1.959	0.0279	0.05

Table A15 Bonferroni–Holm's procedure, related path: Purch. dec. inv. – WOM

Paths significant on a p = 0.05 level: Purch. dec. inv. – WOM	t-value	p-value, in ascending order, p-value must be < values of Bonferroni–Holm's	Values based on Bonferroni–Holms procedure
Spain	3.184	0.0013	0.01666
Fin	3.133	0.0014	0.025
Aus	2.337	0.0117	0.05

Table A16 Bonferroni–Holm's procedure, related path: Rel. Qual.– Reputation

Paths significant on a p = 0.05 level: Rel. Quality– Reputation	t-value	p-value, in ascending order, p-value must be < values of Bonferroni–Holm's	Values based on Bonferroni–Holms procedure
Pharmacists	6.552	0.0	0.00555
Spain	6.140	0.0	0.00625
All	3.963	0.0	0.00714
Doctors, Nurses	3.664	0.0003	0.00833
Purchaser	2.920	0.0023	0.01
Fin	2.750	0.0041	0.0125
Aus	2.377	0.0107	0.01666
Russia.	1.994	0.0258	0.025
Ger	1.931	0.0296	0.05

Table A17 Bonferroni–Holm's procedure, related path: Rel. Qual.– Rep. transfer

Paths significant on a p = 0.05 level: Rel. Quality– Rep. Transfer	t-value	p-value, in ascending order, p-value must be < values of Bonferroni–Holm's	Value based on Bonferroni–Holms procedure
Pharmacists	2.593	0.0057	0.05

Table A18 Bonferroni–Holm's procedure, related path: Rel. Qual.– Rep. transfer

Paths significant on a p = 0.05 level: WOM-Reputation	t-value	p-value, in ascending order, p-value must be < values of Bonferroni–Holm's	Value based on Bonferroni–Holms procedure
Ger	2.913	0.0027	0.05

Table A19 Bonferroni–Holm's procedure, path: WOM-Rep. transfer

Paths significant on a p = 0.05 level: WOM-Rep. Transfer	t-value	p-value, in ascending order, p-value must be < values of Bonferroni–Holm's	Values based on Bonferroni–Holm's procedure
Fin	3.529	0.0005	0.00833
Ger	3.205	0.0012	0.01
Doctors, Nurses	2.877	0.0028	0.0125
All	2.553	0.0056	0.01666
Pharmacists	2.433	0.0086	0.025
Russia	1.980	0.0266	0.05

Table A20 Bonferroni–Holm's procedure, path: Perc. Fit-Rep. Transfer

Paths significant on a p = 0.05 level: Perc. Fit-Rep. Transfer	t-value	p-value, in ascending order, p-value must be < values of Bonferroni–Holm's	Result based on Bonferroni–Holms procedure
Aus	8.705	0.0	0.00625
All	7.277	0.0	0.00714
Doctors, Nurses	6.647	0.0	0.00833
Pharmacists	3.832	0.0	0.01
Purchaser	17.901	0.0	0.0125
Russia	15.570	0.0	0.01666
Fin	12.899	0.0	0.025
Spain	11.703	0.0	0.05

Table A21 Bonferroni–Holm's procedure, path: Reputation-Perc. Fit

Paths significant on a p = 0.05 level: Reputation-Perc. Fit	t-value	p-value, in ascending order, p-value must be < values of Bonferroni–Holm's	Result based on Bonferroni–Holms procedure
Pharmacists	4.415	0.0	0.00833
Russia	3.430	0.0006	0.01
Spain	2.882	0.0029	0.0125
Fin	2.544	0.007	0.01666
All	2.058	0.0203	0.025
Ger	1.916	0.0305	0.05

Data of Pearson's Chi-Square test

Table A22 Chi-Square test on trustful relationship and reputation, data set "All Countries"

All country data-set, n = 250	Trustful relationship	Reputation
Chi-square	92.997	108.812
5% error level	7.814	9.488
5% error level exceeded	Yes	Yes
Degrees of freedom	3	4
Asymptotic significance	0.001	0.001
φ-coefficient	0.6089	0.6597

Table A23 Chi-Square test on direct marketing media, data set "All Countries"

All country data-set, n = 250	Fairs	Symposia	Internet	Brochures	Mailings	Visits of SR's
Chi-square	7.048	11.957	35.986	45.728	31.664	82.145
5% error level	11.070	9.488	9.488	9.488	9.488	9.488
5% error level exceeded	No	Yes	Yes	Yes	Yes	Yes
Degrees of freedom	5	4	4	4	4	4
Asymptotic significance	0.217	0.018	0.001	0.001	0.001	0.001
φ-coefficient	0.1670	0.2186	0.3793	0.4276	0.3558	0.5732

Table A24 Chi-square test on trustful relationship and reputation, data set "Germany"

German data-set, n = 50	Trustful relationship	Reputation
Chi-square	10.667	5.542
5% error level	3.841	9.487
5% error level exceeded	Yes	No
Degrees of freedom	1	4
Asymptotic significance	0.001	0.236
φ-coefficient	0.4619	0.3328

Table A25 Chi-square test on direct marketing media, data set "Germany"

German data-set, n = 50	Fairs	Symposia	Internet	Brochures	Mailings	Visits of SR's
Chi-square	24.160	9.760	59.760	31.120	14.560	32.400
5% error level	11.070	11.070	7.814	11.070	11.070	7.814
5% error level exceeded	Yes	No	Yes	Yes	Yes	Yes
Degrees of freedom	5	5	3	5	5	3
Asymptotic significance	0.001	0.082	0.001	0.001	0.001	0.012
φ-coefficient	0.695	0.4418	1.093	0.7889	0.5396	0.8498

Table A26 Chi-square test on trustful relationship and reputation, data set "Russia"

Russian data-set, n = 50	Trustful relationship	Reputation
Chi-square	3.053	25.872
5% error level	7.814	9.487
5% error level exceeded	No	Yes
Degrees of freedom	3	4
Asymptotic significance	0.384	0.001
φ-coefficient	0.2471	0.7193

Table A27 Chi-square test on direct marketing media, data set "Russia"

Russian data-set, n = 50	Fairs	Symposia	Internet	Brochures	Mailings	Visits of SR's
Chi-square	9.118	7.837	9.491	6.683	30.471	18.167
5% error level	11.070	9.487	9.487	9.487	9.487	9.487
5% error level exceeded	No	No	Yes	No	Yes	Yes
Degrees of freedom	5	4	4	4	4	4
Asymptotic significance	0.104	0.098	0.051	0.154	0.001	0.001
φ-coefficient	0.4270	0.3959	0.4345	0.3656	0.7806	0.6028

Table A28 Chi-square test on trustful relationship and reputation, data set "Finland"

Finnish data-set, n = 50	Trustful relationship	Reputation
Chi-square	19.613	19.806
5% error level	5.991	9.487
5% error level exceeded	Yes	Yes
Degrees of freedom	2	4
Asymptotic significance	0.001	0.001
φ-coefficient	0.6263	0.6293

Table A29 Chi-square test on direct marketing media, data set "Finland"

Finnish data-set, n = 50	Fairs	Symposia	Internet	Brochures	Mailings	Visits of SR's
Chi-square	34.600	18.800	48.857	33.108	89.238	26.600
5% error level	9.487	7.815	7.815	3.841	7.815	5.991
5% error level exceeded	Yes	Yes	Yes	Yes	Yes	Yes
Degrees of freedom	4	3	3	1	3	2
Asymptotic significance	0.001	0.001	0.001	0.001	0.001	0.001
φ-coefficient	0.6028	0.8318	0.6131	0.8137	1.3359	0.7294

Table A30 Chi-square test on trustful relationship and reputation, data set "Spain"

Spanish data-set, n = 50	Trustful relationship	Reputation
Chi-square	15.500	34.320
5% error level	5.991	7.815
5% error level exceeded	Yes	Yes
Degrees of freedom	2	3
Asymptotic significance	0.001	0.001
φ-coefficient	0.5568	0.8285

Table A31 Chi-square test on direct marketing media, data set "Finland"

Spanish data-set, n = 50	Fairs	Symposia	Internet	Brochures	Mailings	Visits of SR's
Chi-square	39.600	36.600	1.172	38.667	37.800	4.818
5% error level	9.487	9.487	9.487	9.487	9.487	9.487
5% error level exceeded	Yes	Yes	No	Yes	Yes	Yes
Degrees of freedom	4	4	4	4	4	4
Asymptotic significance	0.001	0.001	0.883	0.001	0.001	0.306
φ-coefficient	0.8899	0.8555	0.1531	0.8793	0.8695	0.3104

Table A32 Chi-square test on trustful relationship and reputation, data set "Spain"

Australian data-set, n = 50	Trustful relationship	Reputation
Chi-square	6.533	23.000
5% error level	3.841	7.814
5% error level exceeded	Yes	Yes
Degrees of freedom	1	3
Asymptotic significance	0.11	0.0
φ-coefficient	0.3615	0.6782

Table A33 Chi-square test on direct marketing media, data set "Australia"

Australian data-set, n = 50	Fairs	Symposia	Internet	Brochures	Mailings	Visits of SR's
Chi-square	15.520	19.105	28.312	9.296	26.571	12.304
5% error level	11.070	9.487	9.487	7.814	9.487	7.814
5% error level exceeded	Yes	Yes	Yes	Yes	Yes	Yes
Degrees of freedom	5	4	4	3	4	3
Asymptotic significance	0.008	0.001	0.001	0.26	0.001	0.006
φ-coefficient	0.5571	0.6181	0.7524	0.4312	0.7290	0.4961

Original Questionnaire in English Language

According to Hofstede (2001), organizations are

Questionnaire to Customers

Country: ______________________
(AUS=1, ; GER=3; FIN=2, SP=4;RUS=5)

Town: ______________________

Name of Hospital: ______________________ Part of Purchasing Group yes (1) ☐ no (2) ☐

1. Public hospital ☐
2. Private hospital
3. University Hospital
4. Military Hospital

1. What is your exact position? ☐
1. Person in Charge, Purchasing Department
2. Head of Purchasing Dept.
3. Head Pharmacist
4. Anesthetist
5. Head Nurse
6. ICU Doctor
7. Expert Group Member (Devices)
8. ICU Nurse
9. Others, please specify ______________________

2. Your nationality is ______________________ US= 6, Austria= 7, Turkish= 8
Asian Countries= 9,
others= 0, please specify

Male (1) ☐ Female (2) ☐

Questionnaire to customers on product perception and positioning

3a. In which kind of product purchase are you involved?

Medical Devices =1
Pharmaceuticals= 2
Pumps= 3
others= 4

☐

b) Since how many years? ☐

c) How many people are part of your purchasing dept? ☐

1= up to two
2= three or four
3= five or six
4= seven or eight
5= more than eight

4. When looking at your purchasing decision, different features can be taken into account. I am now going to read out some of these features. Could you please tell me whether these features are to you

decisive	**4**
important	**3**
less important	**2**
not important	**1**

a) Safety features ☐
b) Environmental friendliness of products ☐
c) Personal relationship to sales reps. ☐
d) Reliability of delivery terms ☐
e) Prompt problem solving by suppliers staff ☐
f) Known name of supplier ☐
g) The offer of useful benefits beyond the basic product needs ☐

5. In your opinion – how would you score the importance of a trustful relationship with your suppliers for your work.

Please use a scale from 1 to 5 (1 meaning not important, 5 meaning of most importance). ☐

6. Suppose you have two suppliers. Supplier A is your current supplier, supplier B is an unkown supplier offering products at a lower price. How likely is it that you will shift from your current supplier A to the unknown supplier B ...

	Certainly	Likely	Unlikely	Certainly not
	4	3	2	1
a) if it offers comparable features	☐	☐	☐	☐
b) if other incentives are offered (stock replenishment, return of goods after shelf life expiry, training ...)	☐	☐	☐	☐
c) if the quality is absolutely the same	☐	☐	☐	☐
d) there is no time left to get informed about new suppliers or products	☐	☐	☐	☐

Questions on features influencing customers to change

12. In your opinion, what are the most important facts to buy pharmaceutical generics instead of original products. I will now read out a list of six features. Please rate their importance on a 1 to 4 scale (1 is absolutely not important, 4 is decisive) :

OPEN COMMENTS

a) Bio-equivalent (similar to the original product) ☐

b) better unit price ☐ ____________________

d) supplier with a good reputation on the market ☐ ____________________

e) better safety features ☐ ____________________

f) handling of the medicine has not changed ☐ ____________________

g) volume discount at the end of the year ☐

k) Is an important feature missing from the list that I just mentioned?

____

not applicable= 0 ☐

Questionnaire Products and Positioning

Explanations concerning Company X is involved in this survey, short second introduction

12.a Do you know Company X?

(yes= 1, no = 2) ☐

13. Do you agree or disagree to the following statements on Company X...

	agree 4	3	2	disagree 1	don't know
a) is known for innovative products	☐	☐	☐	☐	☐
b) cares about customer opinions	☐	☐	☐	☐	☐
c) shares expertise as a partner	☐	☐	☐	☐	☐
d) I trust in products of Company X	☐	☐	☐	☐	☐
e) is known for leading products	☐	☐	☐	☐	☐
f) I am satisfied with this company	☐	☐	☐	☐	☐

14. Which of the Company X product ranges do you

1: know/purchase: **2** I don't know them **0**

a) Clinical Nutrition ☐
b) Generic Injectable Drugs ☐
c) Regional Anesthesia ☐
d) IV Sets ☐
e) Small Volume Infusion Solutions ☐
f) Large Volume Infusion Solutions ☐
g) Infusion Pumps ☐
h) others ____________

i) How much experience do you have in Company X products? Rank 1 to 5, 1 is not having long experience) ☐

j) From which year on have you started using Company X products?__________

15. According to your personal opinion: To what extend is Company X related to the following product ranges?

	agree 4	3	2	disagree 1	never thought about this
a) Pumps	☐	☐	☐	☐	☐
b) Standard Infusion Solutions	☐	☐	☐	☐	☐
c) Generic Injectable Medicine	☐	☐	☐	☐	☐
d) Regional Anesthesia	☐	☐	☐	☐	☐
e) Clinical Nutrition	☐	☐	☐	☐	☐
f) Disposable Medical Devices	☐	☐	☐	☐	☐
g) Proprietary Drugs	☐	☐	☐	☐	☐

16. In your opinion which of the following products would fit in the future product range of Company X? (please rank form 5= very important to be included to 1= of little importance) Note: Compounding Services: patient tailored nutrition, antibiotic admixture, chemotherapy

1. General Compounding Services ☐
2. IT Consulting Hospital Services ☐
3. Oncology Drugs ☐
4. Enteral Nutrition ☐
5. Prefilled Syringes ☐
6. Pediatric Products ☐
7. others, like ____________

Questionnaire Trust/Reliability/Recommendation

17. To what extent do you agree that Company X is offering value for money.

4	somehow agree	somehow disagree	disagree	Don't know
☐	☐	☐	☐	☐

18. In your opinion, to which extend do you agree or disagree with the following statements on Company X

a) Company X takes my concerns and requests seriously

4 agree	somehow agree	somehow disagree	1 disagree	Don't know
☐	☐	☐	☐	☐

b) Even if competitors offer the same features as Company X, I would prefer to buy Company X products

4 agree	somehow agree	somehow disagree	1 disagree	Don't know
☐	☐	☐	☐	☐

19. To which extend would you recommend **Company X medical devices/ products?** Note examples are pumps, IV sets…

4 ☐ ☐ ☐ ☐ 1

1= I don't recommend

not applicable ☐ 0

4= I will surely recommend

20. To which extend would you recommend **Company X pharmaceutical products?** Note: examples are clinical nutrition, large volume infusion solutions, generic injectable

4 ☐ ☐ ☐ ☐ 1

1= I don't recommend

not applicable ☐ 0

4= I will surely recommend

Questions on Direct Marketing, Sales & Services

21. Company X is also supplying injectable drugs to more than 80 countries. Knowing that, what is your opinion on purchasing these injectable drugs?

	4 agree	somehow agree		1 dis-agree
a) You would purchase them because you trust in the products of Company X	☐	☐	☐	☐
b) You would expect the same high product quality standard as with other Company X products	☐	☐	☐	☐
c) You think that this fits to the Company X product range	☐	☐	☐	☐

22. What is your opinion on Company X sales reps.? Please indicate on which extend you agree or disagree on the following statements

	4 agree	somehow agree		1 disagree
a) He or she visits me too often	☐	☐	☐	☐
b) He or she is always friendly and helpful	☐	☐	☐	☐
c) He or she is not a product specialist	☐	☐	☐	☐
d) Sales reps. of competitors are much better trained on products	☐	☐	☐	☐

23. In your opinion, who would you recommend to present Company X products to a) in terms of medical devices and b) in terms of pharmaceuticals. Please rank the following potential contact persons from five (first to contact) to one (less decisive).

Medical devices		Pharmaceuticals
☐ a)	Pharmacists	f) ☐
☐ b)	Purchasing Organizations	g) ☐
☐ c)	Physicians	h) ☐
☐ d)	Nurses	i) ☐
☐ e)	Management & Administration	j) ☐

24. Is there something you want Company X to know? Some additional remarks?

____

____

References

Aaker DA (1989) Managing asset and skills: the key to sustainable competitive advantage. Calif Manage Rev Winter:91–106

Aaker DA (1991) Managing brand equity: capitalizing on the value of a brand name. Free Press, New York

Aaker DA, Keller KL (1990) Consumer evaluations of brand extensions. J Market 54:27–42

Abdul-Muhmin AG (2005) Instrumental and Interpersonal determinants of relationship satisfaction and commitment in industrial markets. J Bus Res 58:619–628

Adler P (2002) Market, hierarchy, and trust: the knowledge economy and the future of capitalism. In: Choo CW, Bontis N (eds) The strategic management of intellectual capital and organizational knowledge. Oxford University Press, Oxford, pp 23–34

Ahlert D, Hesse J, Jullens J, Smend P (2003) Multikanal-strategien: konzepte, methoden und erfahrungen, wiesbaden. Gabler Verlag, Germany

Albert N, Merunka D, Valette-Florence P (2008) When consumers love their brands: exploring the concept and its dimensions. J Bus Res 61(10):1062–1075

Alden DL, Hoyer WD, Lee C (1993) Identifying global and culture-specific dimensions of humor. J Market 57(April):64–75

Allen N, Meyer J (1990) The measurement and antecedents of affective, continuance and normative commitment to the organization. J Occup Psychol 63:1–18

Amato S, Esposito Vinzi V, Tenenhaus M (2004) A global goodness-of-fit index for PLS structural equation modeling. Oral communication to PLS Club, HEC School of Management, France, March 24

American Marketing Association (2008). What are the definitions of marketing and marketing research. Available at http://www.marketingpower.com/_layouts/Dictionary.aspx

Anderson JC, Gerbing DW (1988) Structural equation modeling in practice: a review and recommended two-step approach. Psychol Bull 103(3):411–423

Anderson EW, Mittal V (2000) Strengthening the satisfaction-profit-chain. J Serv Res 3(2): 107–120

Anderson JC, Narus JA (1990) A model of distributor firm and manufacturer firm working partnership. J Market 54:42–58

Anderson JC, Narus JA (2004) Business market management: understanding, creating and delivering value, 2nd edn. Prentice Hall, Upper Saddle River, NJ

Anderson EW, Weitz B (1992) The use of pledges to build and sustain commitment in distribution channels. J Market Res 29(1):18–34

Aperia T, Bronn PS, Schultz M (2004) A reputation analysis of the most visible companies in the scandinavian countries. Corp Reputation Rev 7:218–230

Argenti PA, Druckenmiller B (2004) In practice: reputation and the corporate brand. Corp Reputation Rev 6(4):368–374

Arndt J (1967) The role of product-related conversations in the diffusion of a new product. J Market Res 4(August):291–295

Atamer T, Calori R (1993) Diagnostic et Décision Stratégiques. Dunod, Paris

Aumann RJ (1987) Game theory. In: Eatwell J, Milgate M, Newman P (eds) The new Palgrave: a dictionary of economics, vol 2. Macmillan, London, pp 460–482

Backhaus K, Voeth M (2007) Industriegütermarketing, 8th edn. Vahlen Verlag, München

Backhaus K, Erichson B, Plinke W, Weiber R (2003) Multivariate Analysemethoden – eine anwendungsorientierte Einführung, 10th edn. Springer-Lehrbuch, Berlin

Bagozzi RP, Baumgartner H (1994) The evaluation of structural equation models and hypothesis testing. In: Bagozzi R (ed) Principles of marketing research. Blackwell, England, pp 386–422

Bagozzi RP, Fornell C, Larcker DF (1981) Canonical correlation analysis as a special case of a structural relations model. Multivariate Behav Res 16(4):437–454

Balmer JM (1998) Corporate identity and the advent of corporate marketing. J Market Manage 14:963–996

Barnett ML, Jermier JM, Lafferty B (2006) Corporate reputation: the definitional landscape. Corp Reputation Rev 9:26–38

Barney JB (1991) Firm resources and sustained competitive advantage. J Manage 17:99–120

Barney JB (1996) The resource-based theory of the firm. Organ Sci 7(5):469–469

Baron RM, Kenny DA (1986) The moderator-mediator variable distinction in social psychological research: conceptual, strategic, and statistical considerations. J Pers Soc Psychol 6:1173–1182

Bartels R (1968) The general theory of marketing. J Market 32(January):29–33

Basu A, Lal R, Srinivasan V, Staelin R (1985) Sales force compensation plans: an agency theoretic perspective. J Market Sci 4:267–291

Batra R, Ray ML (1985) How advertising works at contact. In: Linda A, Mitchall AA (eds) Psychological processes and advertising effects: theory, research, and applications. Eribaum, Hillsdale, NJ, pp 13–43

Beatty R, Ritter JR (1986) Investment banking, reputation and underpricing of initial public offerings. J Financ Econ 17:213–232

Beck BE, Moore LF (1985) Linking the host culture to organizational variables. In: Frost PJ et al (eds) Organizational culture. Sage, Beverly Hills, CA, pp 335–354

Benjamin BB, Podolny JM (1999) Status, quality, and social order in california wine industry. Admin Sci Q 44:563–589

Bennett R, Kottasz R (2000) Practitioner perceptions of corporate reputation: an empiric investigation. Corp Commun 5(4):224–234

Berens G, Van Riel CBM (2004) Corporate associations in the academic literature: three main streams of thought in the reputation measurement literature. Corp Reputation Rev 7(2): 161–178

Bergkvist L, Rossiter JR (2007) The predictive validity of multiple-item versus single item measures of the same constructs. J Market Res 44(May):175–184

Bergstrom A, Blumenthal D, Crothers S (2002) Why internal branding matters: the case of Saab. Corp Reputation Rev 5(2/3):133–142

Bernstein D (1986) Company image and reality, a critique of corporate communications. Cassell Ltd, London

Berry LL (1983) Relationship marketing. In: Berry LL, Shostock GL, Upah GD (eds) Emerging perspectives on service marketing. American Marketing Association, Chicago, pp 25–28

Berry LL, Parasuraman L (1991) Marketing services: competing through quality. The Free Press, New York

Bevis M (1967) quoted by Bernstein D (1984) Company image and reality. Reinhart and Winston, Eastbourne

Bhagat RS, Kedia BL, Harveston PD, Triandis HC (2002) Cultural variations in the cross-border transfer of organizational knowledge: an integrative framework. Acad Manag Rev 27(2): 204–219

Biehal G, Sheinin D (2007) The influence of corporate messages on the product portfolio. J Market 71:12–25
Bishop M (2008) A bigger world-a special report on globalisation. The Economist 388(8598): 57–65
Blalock HM (1968) The measurement problem: a gap between the languages of theory and research. In: Blalick HM, Blalock AB (eds) Methodology in social reseach. McGraw-Hill, New York, pp 5–27
Blau PM (1960) A theory of social integration. Am J Sociol 65:550–553
Blau PM (1964) Exchange and power in social life. Wiley, New York
Blichfeldt BS (2005) On the development of brand and line extensions. J Brand Manag 12(3): 177–190
Bollen KA (1984) Multiple indicators: internal consistency or no necessary relationship? J Qual Quant 18:377–385
Bollen KA (1989) Structural equations with latent variables. John Wiley, New York
Bollen KA, Lennox R (1991) Conventional wisdom on measurement: a structural equation perspective. Psychol Bull 110(2):305–314
Bollen KA, Ting KF (2000) A tetrad test for causal indicators. Psychol Methods 5(1):3–22
Bond R, Smith PB (1996) Culture and conformity: a meta-analysis of studies using asch's (1952b, 1965) line judgement task. Psychol Bull 119(1):113–137
Borsboom D, Mellenbergh GJ, Heerden JV (2003) The theoretical status of latent variables. Psychol Rev 110(2):203–219
Borsboom D, Mellenbergh GJ, Heerden JV (2004) The concept of validity. Psychol Rev 111(4): 1061–1071
Bower JL (2005) Breakthrough ideas for 2005: the velcro organization. Harv Bus Rev 83(2): 6–7
Boyacigiller N, Adler NJ (1991) The parochial dinosaur: the organizational sciences in a global context. Acad Manag Rev 16(2):262–291
Brammer SJ, Pavelin S (2006) Corporate reputation and social performance: the importance of fit. J Manag Stud 43(3):435–456
Brislin RW (1980) Translation and content analysis of written materials. In: Triandis HC, Berry JW (eds) Handbook of cross-cultural psychology, vol 2. Allyn & Backon, Boston, pp 389–444
Brislin RW, Lonner WJ, Thorndike RH (1973) Cross cultural research methods. John Wiley, New York
Bristol LH (1960) Developing the corporate image, a management guide to public relations. Scribner, New York
Brock JK, Zhou Y (2005) Organizational use of the internet – scale development and validation. Internet Res 15(1):67–87
Bromley DD (1993) Reputation, image and impression management. John Wiley, Chichester, Sussex
Bromley DD (2000) Psychological aspects of corporate identity, image and reputation. Corp Reputation Rev 3(3):240–252
Bromley DD (2002) Comparing corporate reputations: league tables, quotients, benchmarks or case studies. Corp Reputation Rev 5(1):35–51
Brown B, Perry S (1994) Removing the financial performance halo from fortune's most admired companies. Acad Manage J 37:1347–1359
Brown SP, Peterson RA (1993) Antecedents and consequences of salesperson job satisfaction: meta-analysis and assessment of causal effects. J Market Res 30:63–77
Browne MW, Cudeck R (1993) Alternative ways of assessing model fit. In: Bollen K, Long A, Scott J (eds) Testing structural equation models. Sage, Newbury Park, London, New Delhi, pp 136–162
Bruhn M (2003) Relationship marketing. Management of Customer Relationships, Prentice Hall
Bruhn M (2004) Handbuch Markenführung, Book 1, 2nd edn. Gabler Verlag, Wiesbaden

Bruhn M (2005) Unternehmens- und Marketingkommunikation - Handbuch für ein integriertes Kommunikationsmanagement. Vahlen Verlag, München

Burgess SM, Steenkamp JB (2006) Marketing renaissance: research in emerging markets advanced marketing science and practice. Int J Res Market 23(4):1–25

Burke T (1998) Risk and reputations: the economics of transaction costs. Corp Commun 3(1):5–10

Burmann C, Schaefer K, Maloney P (2008) Industry image: its impact on the brand image of potential employees. J Brand Manag 15(3):157–176

Calhoun KJ, Teng JTC, Cheon MJ (2002) Impact of national culture on information technology usage behaviour: an exploratory study of decision making in Korea and the USA. Behav Information Technol 21(4):293–302

Carter SM, Deephouse DL (1999) 'Tough talk'and 'soothing speech': managing reputations for being tough and for being good. Corp Reputation Rev 2(4):308–332

Caruana A (1997) Corporate reputation: concept and measurement. J Product Brand Manage 6:109–118

Caves RE, Porter ME (1977) From entry barriers to mobility barriers. Q J Econ 91:421–434

Chatelin YM, Vinzi VE, Tenenhaus M (2002) State of the art on PLS path modeling through the available software. Available at http://www.sinopai.com/sinopai2/index.html

Chien P-H, Cornwell TB, Stokes R (2005) A theoretical framework for analysis of image transfer in multiple sponsorships. In: Purchase S (ed.) ANZMAC 2005 Conference Proceedings: Broadening the Boundaries. Australia & New Zealand Marketing Academy Conference (ANZMAC), Fremantle, Western Australia, 5–7 December, 2005

Chin WW (1998) The Partial least square approach to structural equation modeling. In: Marcoulides G (ed) Modern methods for business research. Erlbaum, Mahwah/London, pp 295–336

Chin WW, Newsted PR (1999) Structural equation modeling analysis with small samples using partial least squares. In: Hoyle RH (ed) Strategies for small sample research. Sage, Thousand Oaks, CA, pp 307–341

Chin WW, Marcolin BL, Newsted PR (1996) A partial least squares latent variable modeling approach for measuring interaction effects: results from a Monte Carlo simulation study and voice mail emotion/adoption study. Paper presented at the 7th International Conference on Information Systems, Cleveland, Ohio

Churchill GA (1979) A paradigm for developing better measures of marketing constructs. J Market Res 16(3):64–73

Cliffe SJ, Motion J (2005) Building contemporary brands: a sponsorship-based strategy. J Bus Res 58(8):1068–1077

Cohen JB, Basu K (1987) Alternative models of categorization: toward a contigent processing framework. J Consum Res 13(March):455–472

Coleman R (1990) Foundations of social theory. Belknap Press, Cambridge, MA

Collier JE, Bienstock CC (2006) Measuring service quality in E-Retailing. J Serv Res 8(3): 260–275

Coltman T, Devinney M, Midgley D, Venaik S (2008) Formative versus reflective measurement models: two applications of formative measurement. J Bus Res 61(12):1250–1262

Conner KR, Prahalad CK (1996) A resource-based theory of the firm: knowledge vs opportunism. Organ Sci 7(5):477–501

Cook J, Wall T (1980) New work attitude measure of trust, organisational commitment, and personal need fulfilment. J Occupied Psychol 53:39–52

Cordeiro J, Schwalbach J (2000) Preliminary evidence on the structure and determinants of global corporate reputations. Institut für Management – Humbold Universität Berlin, Diskussionspapier 2000–4

Cornwell TB, Weeks C, Roy D (2005) Sponsorship-linked marketing: opening the blackbox. J Advert 34(2):23–45

Costner HL (1969) Theory, deduction, and the rules of correspondence. Am J Sociol 75:245–263

Coviello N, Brodie R, Danaher PJ, Johnston WJ (2002) How firmes relate to their markets: an empirical examination of contemporaty marketing practices. J Market 66(July):33–46
Cronbach LJ (1951) Coefficient alpha and the internal structure of tests. Psychometrika 16(3): 297–334
Cropanzano R, Mitchell MS (2005) Social exchange theory: an interdisciplinary review. J Manag 31(6):874–900
Cutler BD, Erdem AS, Javalgi RG (1997) Advertiser's relative reliance on collectivism-individualism appeals: a cross-cultural study. J Int Consum Market 9(3):43–55
Czellar S (2003) Consumer attitude toward brand extensions: an integrative model and research propositions. Int J Res Market 20(1):97–115
Dacin PA, Brown TJ (2002) Corporate identity and corporate associations: a framework for future research. Corp Reputation Rev 5(1/2):254–263
Dacin PA, Smith DC (1994) The effect of brand portfolio characteristics on customer evaluation of brand extensions. J Market Res 31(May):229–242
Darby MR, Karni E (1973) Free competition and the optimal amount of Fraud. J Law Econ 16 (April):67–88
Dasgupta P (1988) Trust as a commodity. In: Gambetta D (ed) Trust: making and breaking cooperative relations. Basil Blackwell, New York, pp 47–72
Davies G, Chun R, da Silva R, Roper S (2002) Corporate reputation and competitiveness. Routledge, London
Day GS, Montgomery DB (1999) Managing marketing relationships. J Acad Market Sci 28(1): 24–30
de Mooij M (1998) Masculinity/femininity and consumer behavior. In: Hofstede G et al (eds) Masculinity and femininity: the taboo dimension of national cultures. Sage, Thousand Oaks, pp 55–73
de Mooij M, Hofstede G (2002) Convergence and divergence in consumer behavior: implications for international retailing. J Retailing 78:61–69
de Ruyter K, Moorman L, Lemmink J (2001) Antecedents of commitment and trust in customer-supplier relationships in high technology markets. Ind Market Manag 30:271–286
Decarolis DM, Deeds DL (1999) The impact of stocks and flows of organizational knowledge on firms performance: an empirical investigation of the biotechnology industry. Manag Sci 20:953–968
Deephouse D (2000) Media reputation as a strategic resource: an integration of mass communication and resource-based theories. J Manag 26:1091–1112
Dellarocas C (2002) The digitization of word-of-mouth: promise and challenges of online reputation mechanisms. Paper of Sloan School of Management, http://dspace.mit.edu/bitstream/handle/1721.1/7346/4296-03.pdf.txt?sequence=3
Denison DR, Mishra AK (1995) Toward a theory of organizational culture and effectiveness. Organ Sci 6:204–223
Dentchev N, Heene A (2004) Managing the reputation of restructuring corporations: send the right signal to the right stakeholder. J Publ Aff 4(1):56–72
Deshpande R (1983) Paradigms lost: on theory and method in research in marketing. J Market 47(3):101–110
Deshpandé R, Farley JU (2004) Organizational culture, market orientation, innovativeness, and firm performance: an international research odyssey. Int J Res Market 21(1):3–22
Deshpandé R, Farley JU, Webster FE (2000) Triad lessons: generalizing results on high performance firms in five business-to-business markets. Int J Res Market 17(4):353–374
Dholakia UM (2001) A motivational process model of product involvement and consumer risk perception. Eur J Market 35(11/12):1340–1360
Diamantopoulos A (1999) Viewpoint-export performance measurement: reflective versus formative indicators. Int Market Rev 16(6):444–457
Diamantopoulos A (2005) The C-OAR-SE procedure for scale development in marketing: a comment. Int J Res Market 22:1–9

Diamantopoulos A, Siguaw JA (2006) Formative versus reflective indicators in organizational measure development: a comparison and empirical illustration. Br J Manag 17:263–282

Diamantopoulos A, Winklhofer HM (2001) Index construction with formative indicators: an alternative to scale development. J Market Res 38(5):269–277

Diamantopoulos A, Riefler P, Roth KP (2008) Advancing formative measurement models. J Bus Res 61:1066–1200

Dick A, Basu K (1994) Customer loyalty: toward an integrated conceptual framework. J Acad Market Sci 22(2):99–113

Dierickx I, Cool K, Barney JB (1989) Asset stock accumulation and sustainability of competitive. Manag Sci 35(12):1504–1511

Donaldson T, Preston LE (1995) The stakeholder theory of the corporation: concepts, evidence and implication. Acad Manag Rev 20(1):65–91

Doney P, Cannon J (1997) An examination of the nature of trust in buyer-seller relationships. J Market 61(2):35–51

Doney P, Cannon J, Mullen M (1998) Understanding the influence of national culture on the development of trust. Acad Manag Rev 23(3):601–620

Dorfman PW, Howell JP (1988) Dimensions of national culture and effective leadership patterns: hofstede revisited. In: Farmer RN, McGoun EG (eds) Advances in international comparative management. JAI, New York, pp 127–150

Dowling G (2001) Creating corporate reputation: identity, image and performance. Oxford University Press, New York

Dowling G (2004) Journalists' evaluation of corporate reputations. Corp Reputation Rev 7(2): 196–205

Doyle SX, Roth GT (1992) Selling and sales management in action: the use of insight coaching to improve relationship selling. J Personal Selling Sales Management 12:59–64

Dozier DM (1993) Image, reputation and mass communication effects. In: Armbrecht W, Avenarius H, Zabel U (eds) Image und PR. Westdeutscher Verlag, Opladen, pp 227–250

Drolet A, Morrison DG (2001) Do we really need multiple-term measures in service research? J Serv Res 3:196–204

Dunbar R, Schwalbach J (2000) Corporate reputation and performance in Germany. Paper no. 2000-1, Humboldt Universität Berlin, Wirtschaftswissenschaftliche Fakultät, Institut für Management

Dutton JE, Dukerich JM (1996) Keeping an eye on the mirror: image and identity in organizational adaptation. Acad Manag J 34:517–554

Dyer JH, Singh H (1998) The relational view: cooperative strategy and sources of interorganizational competitive advantage. Acad Manag Rev 23(4):660–679

East R, Hammond K, Lomax W (2008) Measuring the impact of positive and negative word of mouth on brand purchase probability. Int J Res Market 25(3):215–224

Eberl M (2006) Unternehmensreputation und Kaufverhalten. Deutscher Universitäts-Verlag, Wiesbaden

Edwards JR, Bagozzi RP (2000) On the nature and direction of relationships between constructs and measures. Psychol Methods 5(2):155–174

Efron B, Gong G (1983) A leisurely look at the bootstrap, the jackknife, and cross-validation. Am Stat 37(1):36–48

Efron B, Tibshirani RJ (1993) An introduction to the bootstrap (monographs on statistics and applied probability), vol 57. Chapman and Hall, New York

Eggert A, Fassott G, Helm S (2005) Identifizierung und Quantifizierung mediierender und moderierender Effekte in komplexen Kausalstrukturen. In: Bliemel F, Eggert A, Fassott G, Henseler J (eds) Handbuch PLS-Pfadmodellierung: Methode, Anwendung, Praxisbeispiele. Schäfer-Poeschel Verlag, Stuttgart, pp 101–116

Eisenhardt KM (1985) Control: organizational and economic approaches. J Manag Sci 31:134–149

Eisenhardt KM (1989) Agency theory: an assessment and review. Acad Manag Rev 14(1): 57–74
Eisenhardt KM, Santos FM (2001) Knowledge-based view: a new theory of strategy? In: Pettigrew A, Thomas H, Wittington R (eds) Handbook of strategy and management. Sage, London, pp 139–165
EIU (2007) The 2007 e-readiness rankings. Economist Intelligence Unit. Available at http://graphics.eiu.com/files/ad_pdfs/2007Ereadiness_Ranking_WP.pdf. Accessed 27 Feb 2008
Falkenreck C, Wagner R (2008) Modeling culture's impact on reputation transfer in direct marketing. In: Proceedings of the 2008 AMS Cultural Perspectives in Marketing Conference, Academy of Marketing Science, New Orleans, pp 115–120
Falkenreck C, Wagner R (forthcoming) Impact of direct marketing activities on company reputation transfer success: empirical evidence from five different cultures. Corporate Reputation Review
Farrelly F, Quester P (2003) The effects of market orientation on trust and commitment. Eur J Market 37(3/4):530–553
Fassott G, Eggert A (2005) Zur Verwendung formativer und reflektiver Indikatoren in Strukturgleichungsmodellen: Bestandsaufnahme und Anwendungsempfehlungen. In: Bliemel F, Eggert A, Fassott G, Henseler J (eds) PLS-Pfadmodellierung – Methode, Anwendung, Praxisbeispiele. Schäfer-Poeschel Verlag, Stuttgart, pp 31–47
Finn A, Kayande U (2004) How fine is C-OAR-SE? A generalizability theory perspective on Rossiter's procedure. Int J Res Market 19:305–335
Firth-Cozens J (2004) Organisational trust: the keystone to patient safety. Qual Saf Health Care 13:56–61
Fishbein M, Ajzen I (1975) Belief, attitude, intention and behavior. Addison-Wesley, Reading, MA
Fiske ST (1982) Schema-triggered affect: application to social perception. In: Clark MS, Fiske ST (eds) Affect and cognition: the 17th annual carnegie symposium on cognition. Erlbaum, Hillsdale, NJ, pp 55–78
Fombrun CJ (1996) Realizing value from the corporate image. Harvard Business School Press, Boston, MA
Fombrun CJ (1998) Indices of corporate reputation: an analysis of media rankings and social monitors' ratings. Corp Reputation Rev 1(4):327–340
Fombrun CJ (2001) Corporate reputation – its measurements and management. Thexis 18(4): 327–340
Fombrun CJ (2007) List of list: a compilation of international corporate reputation ratings. Corp Reputation Rev 10(2):144–153
Fombrun CJ (2008) Reputation Systems. Available at http://www.reputationinstitute.com/about/news#systems
Fombrun CJ, Gardberg NA (2002) The global reputation quotient project: first steps towards a cross-nationally valid measure of corporate reputation. Corp Reputation Rev 4(4): 303–307
Fombrun CJ, Rindova V (1998) Reputation management in 1000 global firms, a benchmarking study. Corp Reputation Rev 1(3):205–214
Fombrun CJ, Rindova V (2000) The road to transparency: reputation management at royal dutch/shell. In: von Schultz M, Hatch M (eds) The expressive organization – linking identity, reputation and the corporate brand. Oxford University Press, Oxford, pp 77–96
Fombrun CJ, Shanley M (1990) What's in a name? Reputation building and corporate strategy. Acad Manag J 33(2):233–258
Fombrun CJ, van Riel CBM (1997) The reputational landscape. Corp Reputation Rev 1(1):5–13
Fombrun CJ, van Riel CBM (2004) Fame & fortune. How successful companies build winning reputations. FT Prentice Hall, Upper Saddle River, NJ

Fombrun CJ, Wiedmann K-P (2001) "Reputation Quotient" – Analyse und Gestaltung der Unternehmensreputation auf Basis fundierter Erkenntnisse, Schriftenreihe Marketing Management des Lehrstuhls für ABWL und Marketing II. University of Hanover, Germany

Fombrun CJ, Gardberg NA, Sever J (2000) The reputation quotient: a multi-stakeholder measure of corporate reputation. J Brand Manag 7(4):241–255

Foreman P, Whetten DA (1994) An identity theory perspective on multiple expectations in organizations. Paper presented at the Academy of Management Meetings in Dallas, TX: Reducing Barriers to Understanding

Forman J, Argenti P (2005) How corporate communication influences strategy implementation, reputation and the corporate brand: an exploratory qualitative study. Corp Reputation Rev 8(3): 245–264

Fornell C (1987) A second generation of multivariate analysis: classification of methods and implications for marketing research. In: Houston M (ed) Review of marketing. American Marketing Association, Chicago, IL, pp 407–450

Fornell C, Bookstein FL (1982) Two structural equation models: LISREL and PLS applied to consumer exit-voice theory. J Market Res 14(6):440–452

Fornell C, Larcker DF (1981) Evaluating structural equation models with unobservable variables and measurement error. J Market Res 18:39–50

Fornell C, Lorange P, Roos J (1990) The cooperative venture formation process: a latent variable structural modeling approach. Manag Sci 36(10):1246–1255

Fournier S (1998) Consumers and their brands: developing relationship theory in consumer research. J Consum Res 24:343–353

Freeman R (1984) Strategic management: a stakeholder approach. Pitman, Boston

Friman M, Gärling T, Millett B, Mattson J (2002) An analysis of international business-to-business relationships in the commitment-trust theory. Ind Market Manag 31:403–409

Fryxell G, Wang J (1994) The fortune corporate reputation index: reputation for what? J Manag 20(1):1–14

Fullerton G (2003) When does commitment lead to loyalty? J Serv Res 5(4):333–344

Gabbioneta C, Ravasi D, Mazzola P (2007) Exploring the drivers of corporate reputation: a study of italian securities analysts. Corp Reputation Rev 10:99–123

Gaines-Ross L (2000) CEO reputation: a key factor in shareholder value. Corp Reputation Rev 3(4):366–370

Ganassali S, Didellon L (1996) Le Transfer come Principe Central du Parrainage. Recherche et Applications en Marketing 11(1):37–48

Ganesan S (1994) Determinants of long-term orientation in buyer-seller relationships. J Market 58(2):1–18

Gardberg N (2001) How do individuals construct corporate reputations? Dissertation, New York University, New York

Gardberg N (2006) Reputatie, reputation, réputation, reputazione, ruf: a cross-cultural qualitative analysis of construct and instrument equivalence. Corp Reputation Rev 9:39–61

Gatewood R, Gowan M, Lautenschlager G (1993) Corporate image, recruitment image and initial job choice decisions. Acad Manag J 36:414–427

Geisser S (1975) The predictive sample reuse method with applications. J Am Stat Assoc 70:320–328

Genasi C (2001) Act Now to guard your reputation. Financial Times, July 13, 2001

Gensch DH, Javalgi RG (1987) The influence of involvement on disaggregate attribute choice models. J Consum Res 14(1):71–82

Giering A (2000) Der Zusammenhang zwischen Kundenzufriedenheit und Kundenloyalität: Eine Untersuchung moderierender Effekte. Gabler, Wiesbaden

Gilliand DI, Bello DC (2002) Two sides to attitudinal commitment: the effect of calculative and loyalty commitment on enforcement mechanisms in distribution channels. J Acad Market Sci 30(1):24–43

Gioia DA, Thomas JB (1996) Identity, image and issue interpretation: sensemaking during strategic changes in academia. Adm Sci Q 41:370–403
Gordon GL, Calantone RJ, di Benedetto CA (1993) Brand equity in the business-to-business sector: an exploratory study. J Product Brand Manage 2(3):4–16
Gotsi M, Wilson AM (2001) Corporate reputation: seeking a definition corporate communications. Int J 6(1):24–30
Grant RM (1996) Toward a knowledge-based theory of the firm. Strat Manag J 17(Winter Special Issue):24–43
Grant RM (2002) The knowledge-based view of the firm. In: Choo CW, Bontis N (eds) The strategic management of intellectual capital and organizational knowledge. Oxford University Press, Oxford, pp 133–145
Gray ER, Balmer JM (1998) Managing corporate reputation and corporate Image. Long Range Plann 31:695–702
Greenspan A (1999) Remarks by Chairman Alan Greenspan Maintaining Economic Vitality Millennium Lecture Series, sponsored by the Gerald R. Ford Foundation and Grand Valley State University, Grand Rapids, Michigan http://www.federalreserve.gov/boarddocs/speeches/1999/19990908.htm Accessed 8th Sept 1999
Grewal D, Krishnan R, Baker J, Borin N (1998) The effect of store name, brand name and price discounts on consumers' evaluations and purchase intentions. J Retailing 74(3):331–352
Griffin K (1975) The contribution of studies of source credibility to a theory of interpersonal trust in the communication department. Psychol Bull 68:104–120
Griffith DA, Harvey MG (2001) A resource perspective of global dynamic capabilities. J Int Bus Stud 32(3):597–606
Griffith DA, Myers M, Harvey MG (2006) An investigation of national culture's influence on relationship and knowledge resources in interorganizational relationships between Japan and the United States. J Int Market 14(3):1–32
Grimes I, Diamantopoulos A, Smith G (2002) Consumer evaluation of extensions and their effects on the core brand: key issue and research propositions. Eur J Market 36(11/12):1415–1438
Groenland EA (2002) Qualitative research to validate the RQ-Dimensions. Corp Reputation Rev 4(4):308–317
Grönroos C (2000) Service management and marketing, 2nd edn. John Wiley, Chichester
Gruen T, Summers J, Acito F (2000) Relationship marketing activities commitment and membership behaviors in professional associations. J Market Sci 26(2):101–114
Gudykunst WB, Matsumoto Y, Ting-Toomey S, Nishida T, Kim K, Heyman S (1996) The influence of cultural individualism-collectivism, self construals, and individual values on communication styles across cultures. Hum Commun Res 22(4):510–543
Gummesson E (1995) Focus shifts in marketing: a new agenda for the third millenium. In: Presentation at the Twentieth Anniversary Program of the Marketing Technology Center, Stockholm, Sweden
Gustafson LT, Reger RK (1999) Beyond collective organizational identity: empirical evidence for multiple subidentities. Paper presented at the 1999 Academy of Management meeting, Chicago, Illinois
Gwinner K (1997) A model of image creation and image transfer in event sponsorship. Int Market Rev 14(3):145–158
Håkansson H, Snehota I (1989) No business is an island: the network concept of business strategy. Scand J Manag 5:187–200
Håkansson H, Snehota I (2000) The IMP perspective, assets and liabilities of relationships'. In: Sheth J, Parvatiyar A (eds) Handbook of relationship marketing. Sage, Thousand Oaks, CA, pp 69–93
Håkansson H, Snehota I (2006) No Business is an Island: The Network Concept of Business Strategy. Scand J Manag 22(3):256–270
Hall E (1976) Beyond culture. Anchor, New York
Hall R (1992) The strategic analysis of intangible resources. Strat Manag J 13:153–144

Harris F, de Chernatony L (2001) Corporate branding and corporate brand performance. Eur J Market 35(3/4):441–456

Heider F (1958) The psychology of interpersonal relations. Wiley, New York

Helfat C, Finkelstein S, Mitchell W, Peteraf M, Singh H, Teece D, Winter S (2007) Dynamic capabilities: understanding strategic change in organisations. Blackwell, Malden

Helgenson GJ, Kluge EA, Mager J, Taylor C (1984) Trends in consumer behaviour literature: a content analysis. J Consum Res 10:449–54

Helm S (2006) Common grounds in the perception of corporate reputation? A comparison of three stakeholder groups. Paper presented at the 10th Reputation Institute Conference. New York, USA, May 25–28, 2006

Helm S (2007) Unternehmensreputation und Stakeholder-Loyalität, Neue Betriebswirtschaftliche Forschung, Bd. 356, Deutscher Universitätsverlag

Hem L, de Chernatony L, Iversen N (2003) Factors influencing successful brand extension. J Market Manag 19:781–806

Henderson R, Cockburn I (1994) Measuring competence? Exploring firm effects in pharmaceutical research. Strat Manag J 15:63–84

Hennig-Thurau T, Hansen U (2001) Kundenartikulation im Internet. Die Betriebswirtschaft 61(5): 3–38

Herbig P, Milewicz J (1993) The relationship of reputation and credibility to brand success. J Consum Market 10(3):18–24

Herrmann A, Huber F, Kressmann F (2006) Varianz- und kovarianzbasierte Strukturgleichungsmodelle – Ein Leitfaden zu deren Spezifikation, Schätzung und Beurteilung. Zeitschrift für Betriebswirtschaft 58(2):34–66

Hewett K, Money BR, Sharma S (2006) National culture and industrial buyer-seller relationships in the US and Latin America. J Acad Market Sci 32(1):9–22

Ho S-C, Kauffman RJ, Liang T-P (2007) A growth theory perspective on B2C E-commerce growth in Europe: an exploratory study. Electron Commer Res Appl 6(3):237–259

Hochberg Y (1988) A sharper bonferroni procedure for multiple tests of significance. Biometrika 75:800–802

Hofstede G (1980) Culture's consequences: international differences in work-related values. Sage, Beverly Hills

Hofstede G (1983) Dimensions of national cultures in fifty countries and three regions. In: Deregowski J, Dziurawiec S, Annis RC (eds) Expiscations in cross-cultural psychology. Swats and Zeitlinger BV, The Netherlands, pp 335–355

Hofstede G (1986) Cultural differences in teaching and learning. Int J Intercult Relat 10: 301–320

Hofstede G (1991) Cultures and organizations. McGraw-Hill, London

Hofstede G (1997) Lokales Denken, globales Handeln, 2nd edn. Deutscher Taschenbuch Verlag, Munich

Hofstede G (2001) Culture's consequences: comparing values, behaviors, institutions and organizations across nations, 2nd edn. Sage, California

Hofstede G et al (1998) Masculinity and femininity: the taboo dimension of national cultures. Sage, Thousand Oaks

Holm S (1979) A simple sequentially rejective multiple test procedure. Scand J Stat 6:65–70

Homans GC (1958) Human behavior as exchange. Am J Sociol 63:597–606

Homans GC (1961) Social behavior: its elementary forms. Harcourt, Brace $ World, New York

Homans GC (1974) Social behavior: its elementary forms, Revisedth edn. Harcourt Brace Jovanovich, New York

Homburg C, Baumgartner H (1995) Die Kausalanalyse als Instrument der Marketingforschung: Eine Bestandsaufnahme. Zeitschrift für Betriebswirtschaft 65(10):1091–1108

Homburg C, Giering A (2001) Personal characteristics as moderators of the relationship between customer satisfaction and loyalty-an empirical analysis. Psychol Market 18(1):43–66

Homburg C, Krohmer H (2006) Marketingmanagement. Gabler Verlag, Wiesbaden

Homburg C, Krohmer H, Workman J (2004) A strategy implementation perspective of market orientation. J Bus Res 57:1331–1340
Homburg C, Kuester S, Beutin N, Menon A (2005) Determinants of customer benefits in business-to-business markets: a cross-cultural comparison. J Int Market 13(3):1–31
Hoopes DG, Madsen TL, Walker G (2003) Guest editors' introduction to the special issue: why is there a resource-based view? toward a theory of competitive heterogeneity. Strat Manag J 24(10):889–902
House RJ, Hanges PJ, Ruis-Quintanilla SA, Dorfman PW, Javidan M, Dickson M, Gupta V (1999) Cultural influences on leadership and organizations, advances in global leadership. JAI Press, Stanford, CT
Houston MJ, Rothschild ML (1978) Conceptual and methodological perspectives in involvement". In: Jain SC (ed) Research frontiers in marketing: dialogues and directions. American Marketing Association, Chicago, IL, pp 184–187
Huff L, Kelley L (2003) Levels of organizational trust in individualist versus collectivist societies: a seven-nation study. Organ Sci 14(1):81–90
Hulland J (1999) Use of partial least squares (PLS) in strategic management research: a review of four recent studies. Strat Manag J 20(4):195–204
Hunt SD (2000) A general theory of competition. Sage, Thousand Oaks, London
Hunt SD (2002) Foundations of marketing theory. M.E. Sharpe, Armonk, NY
Hunt ST, Lambe CJ (2000) Marketing's contribution to business strategy: market orientation, relationship marketing and resource-advantage theory. Int J Manag Rev 2(1):17–43
Hunt ST, Morgan R (1995) The comparative advantage theory of competition. J Market 59(2): 1–15
Hunt ST, Morgan R (1997) Resource-advantage theory: a snake swallowing its tail or a general theory of competition? J Market 61:74–84
Jackson BB (1984) Winning and keeping industrial customers. Lexington Books, Lexington, KY
Jacobson R, Aaker DA (1985) Is market share all that it's cracked up to be? J Market 49:11–22
Jaeger AM (1986) Organization development and national culture: where's the fit. Acad Manag Rev 11:178–190
Jarvis CB, Mackenzie SB, Podsakoff PM (2003) A critical review of construct indicators and measurement model misspecification in marketing and consumer research. J Consum Res 30(3):199–218
John DR, Loken B, Joiner C (1998) The negative impact of extensions: can flagship products be deluted? J Market 62:19–32
Johnson D, Grayson K (2005) Cognitive and affective trust in service relationships. J Bus Res 58:500–507
Johnson MD, Selnes F (2004) Customer portfolio management: toward a dynamic theory of exchange relationships. J Market 68(April):1–17
Johnson M, Herrmann A, Huber F (2006) The evolution of loyalty intentions. J Market 70 (April):122–132
Jöreskog KG (1993) Testing structural equation models. In: Bollen KA, Long JS (eds) Testing structural equation models. Sage, Newbury Park, CA, pp 294–316
Jöreskog KG, Wold H (1982) The ML and PLS techniques for modeling with latent variables: historical and comparative aspects. In: Wold H, Jöreskog K (eds) Systems under indirect observation: causality, structure, prediction , vol 1. North-Holland, Amsterdam, pp 263–270
Kaas K-P (1990) Langfristige Werbewirkung und Brand Equity. Werbeforschung und Praxis 3:48–51
Kanter R (1968) Commitment and social organization: a study of commitment mechanisms in utopian communities. Am Sociol Rev 33:499–517
Karaosmanoglu E, Melewar TC (2006) Corporate communications, identity and image: a research agenda. Corp Reputation Rev 14(1/2):196–206

Kaufmann G, Sattler H, Völckner F (2006) Markenstrategische Optionen. Die Betriebswirtschaft (DBW) 66(2):245–249
Kay J (1993) Foundations of corporate success. Oxford University Press, Oxford
Keaveney SM (1995) Customer switching behavior in service industries: an exploratory study. J Market 59(2):71–82
Keller KL (1993) Conceptualizing, measuring and managing customer-based brand equity. J Market 57(1):1–22
Keller KL (1998) Strategic brand management. Prentice-Hall, Upper Saddle River, NJ
Keller KL (2003) Building, measuring, and managing brand equity, 2nd edn. Prentice Hall, Upper Saddle River, NJ
Keller KL, Aaker D (1992) The effects of sequential introduction of brand extensions. J Market Res 29:35–40
Keller KL, Sood S (2003) Brand equity dilution. MIT Sloan Manage Rev 45(1):12–15
Keller N, Stolper M (2006) Messung der Kundenbeziehungs-qualität im B2B Marketing-eine Studie im industriellen Großhandel. Working Paper no. 15, University of Dortmund, Germany
Kiesler C (1971) The psychology of commitment. Academic Press, New York
Kirkman BL, Lowe KB, Gibson CB (2006) A quarter century of culture's consequences: a review of empirical research incorporating hofstede's cultural values framework. J Int Bus Stud 37(3):285–370
Klein B, Leffler K (1981) The role of market forces in assuring contractual performance. J Polit Econ 89:615–641
Kleinaltenkamp M (2000) Einführung in das business-to-business marketing. In: Kleinaltenkamp M, Plinke W (eds) Technischer Vertrieb: Grundlagen des Business-to-Business Marketing, 2nd edn. Springer, Berlin, pp 171–247
Klink RR, Smith DC (2001) Threats to the external validity of brand extension research. J Market Res 38:326–335
Kluckhohn F, Strodtbeck F (1961) Variations in value orientations. Row, Peterson, Evanston, IL
Ko J-W, Price JL, Mueller CW (1997) Assessment of meyer and allen's three-component model of organizational commitment in South Korea. J Appl Psychol 82(6):961–973
Kogut B, Singh H (1988) The effect of national culture on the choice of entry mode. J Int Bus Stud 19:411–432
Kogut B, Zander U (1992) Knowledge of the firm, combinative capabilities, and the replication of technology. Organ Sci 3:383–397
Kotler P, Keller KL (2006) Marketing-management, 12th edn. Pearson education, Upper Saddle River, NJ
Kracher B, Marble RP (2007) The significance of gender in predicting the cognitive moral development of business practitioners using the sociomoral reflection objective measure. J Bus Ethics 78(4):503–526
Krafft M, Götz O, Liehr-Gobbers K (2005) Die Validierung von Strukturgleichungsmodellen mit Hilfe des Partial-Least-Square (PLS)-Ansatzes. In: Bliemel F, Eggert A, Fassott G, Henseler J (eds) Handbuch PLS-Pfadmodellierung. Schäffer-Poeschel, Stuttgart, pp 71–86
Krafft M, Hesse J, Höfling J, Peters K, Rinas D (eds) (2007) International direct marketing. Springer, Berlin
Krathwohl DR (1985) Social and behavioral science research, Jossey bass social and behavioral science series. Wiley, New York
Kristensen K, Eskildsen JK (2005) PLS structural equitation model for customer satisfaction management: some empirical and theoretical results. In: Bliemel F, Eggert A, Fassott G, Henseler J (eds) Handbuch PLS Pfadmodelierung-Methode, Anwendung, Praxisbeispiele. Schäfer-Poeschel Verlag, Stuttgart, pp 117–134
Kroeber AL, Kluckhohn C (1952) Culture: a critical review of concepts and definitions. In: Harvard University Papers of the Peabody Museum of American Archeology and Ethnology, vol 47(1). Harvard University Press, Cambridge
Kroeber-Riel W, Weinberg P (1996) Konsumentenverhalten, 6th edn. Franz Vahlen, München

Kroeber-Riel W, Weinberg P (2003) Konsumentenverhalten, 8th edn. Franz Vahlen, München
Krugman HE (1965) The impact of television advertising: learning without involvement. Public Opin Q 29(3):349–356
Kuhn K, Alpert F (2004) Applying Keller's brand equity model in a B2B Context: limitations and an empirical test. Paper presented at the 2004 ANZMAC Australian and New Zealand Marketing Academy Conference. Available at http://www.anzmac.org/Default.aspx?page=2080
Kumar P (2005) Brand counterextensions: the impact of brand extension success versus failure. J Market Res 62(May):183–194
Kumar N, Scheer LK, Steenkamp JB (1995) The effect of perceived interdependence on dealer attitudes. J Market 32(August):348–356
Lafferty B, Goldsmith R (1999) Corporate credibility's role in consumers' attitudes and purchase intentions when a high versus a low credibility endorser is used in the Ad. J Bus Res 44(2): 109–116
Landon S, Smith CE (1997) The use of quality and reputation indicators by consumers: the case of bordeaux wine. J Consum Policy 20:289–323
Lane PJ, Lubatkin M (1998) Relative absorptive capacity and interorganizational learning. Strat Manag J 19:461–477
Larkin J (2003) Strategic reputation risk management. Basingstoke, New York
Law KS, Wong C (1999) Multidimensional constructs in structural equation analysis: an illustration using the job perception and job satisfaction constructs. J Manag 25:143–160
Lee N, Lings I (2007) Doing business research-a guide to theory and practice. Sage, London
Leung K, Bhagat RS, Buchan NR, Erez M, Gibson CB (2005) Culture and national business: recent advantages and their implications for future research. J Int Bus Stud 36(4):357–378
Levitt T (1983) The globalization of markets. Harv Bus Rev 61(5):87–91
Lewellyn PG (2002) Corporate reputation: focusing the zeitgeist. Bus Soc 41(4):446–455
Lewis S (2001) Measuring corporate reputation. Corp Commun 6(1):31–35
Lin CH, Sher PJ, Shih HY (2005) Past progress and future directions in conceptualizing customer perceived value. Int J Serv Industry Manag 16(4):318–336
Little P, Little B (2000) Do perceptions of corporate social responsibility contribute to explaining differences in corporate price-earnings rations? A research note. Corp Reputation Rev 3:137–142
Lok P, Crawford J (2004) The effect of organizational culture an leadership style on job satisfaction and organisational commitment: a cross-national comparison. J Manag Dev 23(4): 321–338
Loken B, John DR (1993) Diluting brand beliefs: when do brand extensions have a negative impact. J Market 57(July):71–84
Longsdon JM, Wood DJ (2002) Reputation as an emerging construct in the business and society field: an introduction. Bus Soc 41(4):365–370
Lord R, Maher KJ (1991) Leadership and information processing: linking perceptions and performance. Unwin-Everyman, Boston
Lord FM, Novick MR (1968) Statistical theories of mental test scores. Addison-Wesely, Reading, MA
Low J, Blois K (2002) The evolution of generic brands in industrial markets: the challenges to owners of brand equity. Ind Market Manag 31(5):385–392
Lu L, Rose G, Blodgett J (1999) The effects of cultural dimensions on ethical decision making in marketing. J Bus Ethics 18:91–105
Lutz RJ (1985) Affective and cognitive antecedents of attitude toward the Ad: a conceptual framework. In: Linda FA, Andrew AM (eds) Psychological processes and advertising effects: theory, research, and applications. Lawrence Erlbaum, Hillsdale, NJ, pp 45–63
MacKinnon DP, Krull JL, Lockwood CM (2000) Equivalence of the mediation, confounding and suppression effect. Prev Sci 1(4):173–181

MacMillan K, Money K, Downing S, Hillenbrand C (2004) Giving your organisation SPIRIT: an overview and call to action for directors on issues of corporate governance, corporate reputation and corporate responsibility. J Gen Manag 30(2):15–42

MacMillan K, Money K, Downing S, Hillenbrand C (2005) Reputation in relationships: measuring experiences, emotions and behaviors. Corp Reputation Rev 8(3):214–233

Madrigal R (2000) The role of corporate associations in new product evaluations. Adv Consum Res 27(1):80–86

Mahon JF (2002) Corporate reputation. Bus Soc 41(4):415–445

Mahon JF, Wartick SL (2003) Dealing with stakeholders: how reputation, credibility and framing influence to game. Corp Reputation Rev 6(1):19–35

Maio E (2003) Managing brand in the new stakeholder environment. J Bus Ethics 44(4):235–246

Mann A (2004) Dialogmarketing: Konzeption und empirische Befunde. Gabler Verlag, Wiesbaden

Marques PA (2009) Ethical ideology and ethical judgments in the portuguese accounting profession. J Bus Ethics 86(2):227–242

Mayer A, Mayer RM (1987) Imagetransfer. Spiegel Verlagsreihe, Hamburg

McCort DJ, Malhotra NK (1993) Cultural and consumer behaviour, toward an understanding of cross-cultural consumer behaviour in international marketing. J Int Consum Market 6(2): 91–127

McCranken G (1989) Who is the celebrity endorser? Cultural foundations of the endorsement process. J Consum Res 16:310–321

McDowell Mudabi S, Doyle P, Wong V (1997) An exploration of branding in industrial markets. Industrial Marketing Management 36(3):433–46

McEnally MR, de Chernatony L (1999) The evolving nature of branding: consumer and managerial considerations. Acad Market Sci Rev 1999(2):1–24

McGuire J, Schneeweis T, Branch B (1990) Perceptions of firm quality: a cause or a result of firm performance. J Manag 16(1):167–180

McKnight DH, Cummings LL, Cervany NL (1998) Initial trust formation in new organizational relationships. Acad Manag Rev 23(3):473–490

Meffert H, Bierwirth A (2002) Corporate Branding-Führung der Unternehmensmarke im Spannungsfeld unterschiedlicher Zielgruppen. In: Meffert H, Burmann C, Koers M (eds) Markenmanagement. Gabler, Wiesbaden, pp 181–200

Meyer JP, Stanley DJ, Herscovitch L, Topolnytsky L (2002) Affective, continuance, and normative commitment to the organization: a meta-analysis of antecedents, correlates, and consequences. J Vocat Behav 61:20–52

Miller RG (1981) Simultaneous statistical inference. Springer, New York

Miller K (2001) Communication theories: perspectives, processes, and contexts. McGraw-Hill, Boston

Milner LM, Fodness D, Speece MW (1993) Hofstede's research on cross-cultural work-related values: implications for consumer behavior. In: van Raaij WF, Barnossy G (eds) European advances in consumer research, , vol 1. Association for Consumer Research, Provo, UT, USA, pp 70–76

Mittal B (1989) A theoretical analysis of two recent measures of involvement. In: Thomas KS (ed) Advances in consumer research association for consumer research, vol 16. Provo, UT, pp 697–702

Mittal B, Lee M (1989) A causal model of consumer involvement. J Econ Psychol 12(17):363–389

Money K, Hillenbrand C (2006) Beyond reputation measurement: placing reputation within a model of value creation by integrating existing measures into the theoretical framework. Paper presented at the 10th International Conference on Corporate Reputation, New York

Money BR, Gilly MC, Graham JL (1998) Explorations of national culture and word-of-mouth referral behavior in the purchase of industrial services in the United States and Japan. J Market 62:76–87

Moon CJ, Woolliams P (2000) Managing cross cultural business ethics. J Bus Ethics 27(1–2): 105–115

Moorman C, Zaltman G, Deshpandé R (1992) Relationship between providers and users of marketing research: the dynamics of trust within and between organizations. J Market Res 29:314–329
Moorman C, Deshpandé R, Zaltman G (1993) Factors affecting trust in market research relationship. J Market 57:81–101
Moran MD (2003) Arguments for rejecting the sequential bonferroni in ecological studies. Oikos 100(2):403–405
Morgan RM, Hunt SD (1994) The commitment-trust theory of relationship marketing. J Market 58:20–38
Morgan NA, Zou S, Vohries DW, Katsikeas CS (2003) Experiental and informational knowledge, architectural marketing capabilities, and the adaptive performance of export ventures: a cross-national study. Decis Sci 34(2):287–253
Mowday RT, Steers RM, Porter LW (1979) The measurement of organizational commitment. J Vocat Behav 14:224–247
Mowday RT, Porter LW, Steers RM (1982) Employee-organizational linkages: the psychology of commitment, absenteeism, and turnover. Academic Press, New York
Mudambi S, Doyle P, Wong V (1997) An exploration of branding in industrial marketing management. 26:433–446
Nakata C, Sivakumar K (1996) National culture and new product development: an integrative review. J Market 60:61–72
Naudé P, Holland C (1996) Business-to-business marketing. In: Buttle F (ed) Relationship marketing theory and practice. Paul Chapman, London
Negandhi AR (1983) Cross-cultural management research, trend and future directions. J Int Bus Stud 14(2):17–28
Newburry W, Yakova N (2006) Standardization preferences: a function of national culture, work interdependence and local embeddedness. J Int Bus Stud 37(1):44–60
Newman KL, Nollen SD (1996) Culture and congruence: the fit between management practices and national culture. J Int Bus Stud 27:753–779
Nguyen N, Leblanc G (2001) Image and reputation of higher education institutions in students' retention decisions. Int J Educ Manag 15:165–171
Nonaka I (1990) Redundant, overlapping organization: a japanese approach to managing the innovation process. Calif Manag Rev 32(3):27–38
North DC (1990) A transaction cost theory of politics. J Theor Polit 2(4):355–367
Nunally JC (1978) Psychometric theory, 2nd edn. McGraw-Hill, New York
O'Cass A (2000) An assessment of consumers product purchase decision, advertising and consumption involvement in fashion clothing. J Econ Psychol 21:343–370
Oliver R (1999) Whence consumer loyalty. J Market 63(Special Issue):33–44
Palmatier RW, Dant R, Grewal D, Evans K (2006) Factors influencing the effectiveness of relationship marketing: a meta-analysis. J Market 70:136–153
Palmatier RW, Scheer LK, Evans KR, Arnold TJ (2008) Achieving relationship marketing effectiveness in business-to-business exchanges. J Acad Market Sci 36:174–190
Parasuraman A, Zeithaml VA, Berry LL (1988) SERVQUAL: a multiple item scale for measuring consumer perceptions of service quality. J Retailing 64(1):12–40
Park CW, Lawson R, Milberg S (1989) Memory structure of brand names. In: Srull T (ed) Advances in consumer research, vol 16. Association for Consumer Research, UT, pp 726–731
Park CW, Milberg S, Lawson R (1991) Evaluation of brand extension: the role of product feature similarity and brand concept consistency. J Consum Res 18:185–193
Parwoll M, Wagner R (forthcoming) Direct marketing for best-agers: In dialogue with challenging customers. In: Bornemeyer C (ed.) Aging society and its implications on service marketing approaches in the Tourism and Hospitality Industry, Bad Honnef, Bock

Pearson K (1900) On the criterion that a given system of deviations from the probable in the case of a correlated system of variables is such that can be reasonably supported to have arisen from random sampling. Philosophy Magazine 50:157–172

Penrose E (1959) The theory of the growth of the firm. Oxford University Press, New York

Peter S (1997) Kundenbindung als Marketingziel: Identifikation und Analyse zentraler Determinanten, Wiesbaden

Peter S (1999) Kundenbindung als Marketingziel, 2nd edn. Gabler Verlag, Wiesbaden

Peteraf MA (1993) The cornerstones of competitive advantage: a resource-based view. Strat Manag J 14(3):179–191

Petty RE, Cacioppo JT (1981) Attitudes and persuasion: classic and contemporary approaches. William C. Brown, Dubuque, IA

Petty RE, Cacioppo JT (1983) Central and peripherial routes to persuasion: application to advertising, advertising and consumer psychology. In: Percy L, Woodside AG (eds) Lexington. Lexington Books, MA, pp 3–23

Petty RE, Cacioppo JT (1986) Communication and persuasion: central and peripheral routes to attitude change. Springer, New York

Plinke W (1999) Grundzüge des industriellen Marketing, unpublished manuscript, Berlin

Podolny JM (1993) A status-based model of market competition. Am J Sociol 98:829–872

Porac JF, Thomas H (1990) Taxonomic mental models in competitor definition. Acad Manage Rev 15:224–240

Porter ME (1980) Competitive advantage. The Free Press, New York

Porter ME (1985) Competitive strategy. The Free Press, New York

Porter LW, Steers RM, Mowday RT, Boulian PV (1974) Organizational Commitment Job Satisfaction, and Turnover Among Psychiatric Technicians. J Appl Psychol 59:603–609

Powell WW, Koput KW, Smith-Doerr L (1996) Interorganizational collaboration and the locus of innovation: networks of learning in biotechnology. Admin Sci Q 41:116–145

Prahalad CK, Hamel G (1990) The core competence of the corporation. Harv Bus Rev 33:79–91

Price L, Arnould E (1999) Commercial friendship: service provider-client relationships in context. J Market 63(4):38–56

Priem R, Butler J (2001) Is the resource-based "view" a useful perspective for strategic management research. Acad Manag Rev 26(1):57–66

Pritchard M, Havitz M, Howard D (1999) Analyzing the commitment-loyalty link in service contexts. J Acad Market Res 27(3):333–348

Ranaweera C, Prabhu J (2003) Customer satisfaction and trust as determinants of customer retention and positive word of mouth. J Target Meas Anal Market 12(1):82–90

Rauyruen P, Miller K (2005) Relationship quality as a predictor of B2B customer loyalty. J Bus Res 60:21–31

Reynolds T, Westberg S, Olson J (1994) A stratecic framework for developing and assesing political, social issue and corporate image advertising. Working Papers in Marketing, No. 186, The Mary Jean and Frank P. Smeal College of Business Administration, Pensylvania State University

Rice WR (1989) Analyzing tables of statistical tests. J Evolution 43:223–225

Richins ML, Bloch PH (1991) Post-purchase product satisfaction: incorporating the effect of involvement and time. J Bus Res 23:145–158

Rindova V, Fombrun C (1999) Constructing competitive advantage: the role of firm-constituent interactions. Strat Manag J 20:691–710

Rindova V, Williamson I, Petkova A (2005) Being good or being known: an empirical examination of the dimensions, antecedents, and consequences of organizational reputation. Acad Manag J 48(6):1033–1049

Ringle CM, Spreen F (2007) Beurteilung der Ergebnisse von PLS-Pfadanalysen. WISU – Das Wirtschaftsstudium 42:211–216

Ringle CM, Wende S Will S (2005) SmartPLS 2.0 (M3) Beta, Hamburg, http://www.smartpls.de.

Ringle CM, Boysen N, Wende S, Will A (2006) Messung von Kausalmodellen mit Partial-Least-Squares-Verfahren. Das Wirtschaftsstudium 35:81–87
Roberts PW, Dowling GR (2002) Corporate reputation and sustained superior financial performance. Strat Manag J 23:1077–1093
Ronen S (1986) Comparative and multinational management. Wiley, New York
Rosenzweig PM (1994) When can management science reseach be generalized internationally? Manag Sci 40:28–39
Rossiter J (2002) The C-OAR-SE procedure for scale development in marketing. Int J Res Market 19:305–335
Rossiter J (2005) Reminder: a horse is a horse, international. J Res Market 22(1):23–25
Roth MS (1995) The effects of culture and socioeconomics on the performance of global brand image strategies. J Market Res 32:163–175
Rothchild ML, Houston MJ (1977) The consumer involvement matrix: some preliminary findings. In: Greenberg B, Bellenger D (eds) Contemporary marketing thought. American Marketing Association, Chicago, pp 95–98
Rousseau DM (1978) Characteristics of departments positions, and individuals: contexts for attitudes and behavior. Admin Sci Q 23:521–538
Rowley TJ (1997) Moving beyond dyadic ties: a network theory of stakeholder influences. Acad Manag Rev 22:887–910
Salter SB, Niswander F (1995) Cultural influence on the development of accounting systems internationally: a test of gray's (1988) theory. J Int Bus Stud 26(2):379–395
Sanchez-Pérez M, Iniesta-Bonillo M (2004) Consumers felt commitment towards retailers: index development and validations. J Bus Psychol 19(2):141–159
Sandig C (1962) Der Ruf der Unternehmung. Veröffentlichung der Wirschaftshochschule Mannheim, Reihe 2: Reden, booklet 8, Stuttgart
Santala M, Parvinen P (2007) From strategic fit to customer fit. Manag Decis J 45(3):582–601
Saparito P, Chen C, Sapienza H (2004) The role of relational trust in bank-small firm relationships. Acad Manag J 473:400–410
Saxton K (1998) Understanding and Evaluating Reputation. Reputation Management May/June
Saxton MK (1998) Where do reputations come from? in: Corporate Reputation Review 4:393–399
Schmitt N (1996) Uses and abuses of coefficient alpha. Psychol Assess 8(4):350–353
Schneider SC, DeMeyer A (1991) Interpreting and responding to strategic issues: the impact of national culture. J Cross Cult Psychol 21:109–118
Schulz M, Mouritsen J, Gabrielsen G (2001) Sticky reputation: analyzing a ranking system. Corp Reputation Rev 4:24–41
Schwager JH (2004) Markenerweiterung, Working Paper No. 145, FGM Verlag, Munich
Schwaiger M (2004) Components and parameters of corporate reputation-an empirical study. Schmalenbach Bus Rev 56:46–71
Schwalbach J (2002) Unternehmensreputation als Erfolgsfaktor. In: Rese M, Söllner A, Utzig B (eds) Relationship Marketing – Standortbestimmung und Perspektiven. Springer, Berlin, pp 225–238
Schwartz SH, Bilsky W (1990) Toward a theory if the universal content and structure of values: extensions and cross-cultural replications. J Pers Soc Psychol 58(5):878–891
Schwartz SH, Boehnke K (2004) Evaluating the structure of human values with confirmatory factor analysis. J Res Pers 38(3):230–255
Schweizer T, Wijnberg N (1999) Transferring reputation to the corporation in different cultures: individuals, collectives, systems and the strategic management of corporate reputation. Corp Reputation Rev 2(3):249–266
Seltin N, Keeves JP (1994) Path analysis with latent variables. In: Husén T, Postlethwaite TN (eds) The international encyclopedia of education, 2 edn. Oxford, pp 4352-4359
Shapiro SD, Macinnis DJ, Heckler SE (1997) The effect of incidental and exposure on the formation of consideration sets. J Consum Res 24(1):94–104

Sharpiro C (1982) Consumer information product quality and seller reputation. Bell J Econ 13:20–35

Sheppard JP, Young M (2007) The routes of moral development and the impact of exposure to the milgram obedience study. J Bus Ethics 75(4):315–333

Sheth JN, Sisodia RS (1999) Revisiting marketing's lawlike generalizations. J Acad Market Sci 27(1):71–87

Shimp TA (1982) Thoughts on the concept of involvement. Unpublished Working Paper, University of South Carolina, Columbia, SC

Shrout PE, Bolger N (2002) Mediation in experimental and nonexperimental studies: new procedures and recommendations. Psychol Meth 7(4):422–445

Simon HA (1991) Bounded rationality and organizational learning. Organ Sci 2:125–134

Singelis TM, Brown WJ (1995) Culture, self, and collectivist communication linking culture to individual behavior. Hum Commun Res 21(3):354–389

Singh J (1995) Measurement issues in cross-national research. J Int Bus Stud 26:597–618

Sjödin H (2007) Financial assessment of brand extensions. J Brand Manag 14:223–231

Sjovall AM, Talk AC (2004) From actions to impressions: cognitive attribution theory and the formation of corporate reputation. Corp Reputation Rev 7(3):269–281

Skowronski JJ, Carlston DE (1989) Negativity and extremity biases in impression formation: a review of explanations. Psychol Bull 105(1):131–142

Smith B (2007) Excellence in medical marketing: origins, definition and precursors. J Med Market 7(1):25–32

Smith JB, Barclay DW (1997) The effects of organizational differences and trust on the effectiveness of selling partner relationships. J Market 61:3–21

Smith DC, Park CW (1992) The effects of brand extensions on market share and advertising efficiency. J Market Res 29(3):296–313

Smith RE, Swinyard WR (1982) Information response models: an integrated approach. J Market 46:81–93

Smith RE, Swinyard WR (1983) Attitude-behavior consistency: the impact of product trial versus advertising. J Market Res 20:257–267

Sobol M, Farelly G, Taper J (1992) Shaping the corporate image – an analytical guide for executive decision makers Quorum Book, New York

Spender J-C (1996) Making knowledge the basis of a dynamic theory of the firm. Strat Manag J 17(Special Issue):45–62

Spiller LD, Baier M (2005) Contemporary direct marketing. Pearson Prentice Hall, Upper Saddle River, New Jersey, USA

Srite M, Karahanna E (2006) The role of espoused national cultural values in technology acceptance. MIS Q 30(3):679–704

Srivastava R, Fahey L, Christensen K (2001) The resource-based view and marketing: the role of market-based assets in gaining competitive advantage. J Manag 27:777–802

Stedham Y, Yamamura JH, Beekun RI (2007) Gender differences in business ethics: justice and relativist perspectives. Bus Ethics A Eur Rev 16(2):163-174

Steenkamp J-B, ter Hofstede F, Wedel M (1999) A cross-national investigation into the individual and national cultural antecedents of consumer innovativeness. J Market 63(2):55–69

Stigler G (1962) Information in the labor market. J Political Econ 70:49–73

Stone M, Woodcock N, Wilson M (1996) Managing the change from marketing planning to customer relationship management. Long Range Planing 29(5):675-683

Sutton RI, Rousseau DM (1979) Structure technology, and dependence on a parent organization: organizational and environmental correlates of individual responses. J Appl Psychol 64:675–687

Swaminathan V, Reddy SK (2000) Affinity partnering: conceptualisation and issues. In: Sheth JN, Parvatiyar A (eds) Handbook of relationship marketing. Sage Publications, Thousand Oaks, pp 381–405

Swedberg R (2000) The social science view of entrepreneurship: introduction and practical applications. In: Swedberg R (ed) Entrepreneurship the social science view. Oxford University Press, Oxford

Tauber EM (1981) Brand franchise extension: new product benefits from existing brand names. Bus Horiz 24:36–41

Tenenhaus M, Vinzi VE, Chatelin Y-M, Lauro C (2004) PLS path modeling. Comput Stat Data Anal 48:159–205

Triandis HC (1994) Culture and social behavior. McGraw-Hill, New York

Trompenaars F, Hampden-Turner C (2007) Nicholas brearley riding the waves of culture. 2 edn. First published 1997 by Nicholas Brealey Publishing, London

Tversky A (1977) Features of similarity. Psychol Rev. 84:327–352

van Recom J, van Riel CBM (2000) Operational measures of organizational identity: a review of existing methods. Corp Reputation Rev 3(4):334–350

van Riel CBM (1995) Principles of corporate communications. Prentice Hall, Eaglewood Cliffs, London

van Riel CBM, Fombrun C (2002) Which company is most visible in your country? An Introduction to the Special Issue on the Global RQ-Project Nominations. Corp Reputation Rev 4:296–302

van Riel CBM, Stroeker NE, Maathuis OJM (1998) Measuring corporate images. Corp Reputation Rev 1(4):313–326

Vanderveer RB, Pines NM (2007) Customer-driven positioning: the next generation approach to pharmaceutical product positioning. J Med Market 7:71–76

Vergin RC, Qoronfleh MW (1998) Corporate reputation and the stock market. Business Horizons 1:19–26

Völckner F, Sattler H (2006) Drivers of brand extension success. J Market 70:18–34

von Wangenheim F (2003) Weiterempfehlung und Kundenwert. Deutscher Universitätsverlag, GWV Fachverlage GmbH, Wiesbaden

von Wangenheim F, Bayón T (2007) The chain from customer satisfaction via word-of-mouth referrals to new customer acquisition. J Acad Market Sci 35:233–249

Waddock S (2003) Stakeholder performance implications of corporate reputation in germany. Int J Perform Manag 5(2–3):114–124

Wagner R, Klaus M (2008) Mobile direct marketing. In: Unhelkar B (ed.) Handbook of research on mobile business, 2nd edn, IGI, Hershey, pp 269–281

Wagner R, Klaus M (2008) Cultural impacts on the spread of mobile commerce: an international comparison. In: Unhelkar B (ed) Handbook of research on mobile business, 2nd edn. IGI, Hershey, pp 245–259

Waldman DA, de Luque MS, Washburn N, House R (2004) Cultural and leadership predictors of corporate social responsibility values of top management: a globe study of 15 countries. J Int Bus Stud 37:823–837

Walsh G, Beatty SE (2007) Customer-based corporate reputation of a service firm: scale development and validation. J Acad Market Sci 35(1):127–143

Walsh G, Wiedmann K-P (2004) A conceptualization of corporate reputation in germany: an evaluation and extension of the RQ. Corp Reputation Rev 6(4):304–312

Wartick SL (2002) Measuring corporate reputation: definition and data. Bus Soc 41(4):371–393

Webster FE (1992) The changing role of marketing in the corporation. J Market 56:1–17

Webster FE, Wind Y (1972) Organizational buying behavior-foundations of marketing, Prentice-Hall

Weigelt K, Camerer C (1988) Reputation and corporate strategy: a review of recent theory and applications. Strat Manag J 9:443–454

Wernerfelt B (1984) A resource-based view of the firm. Strat Manag J 5(2):171–180

Werts CE, Linn RL, Jöreskog KG (1974) Intraclass reliability estimates: testing structural assumptions. Educ Psychol Measur 34:25–33

Whetten DA, Mackey A (2002) A social action conception of organizational identity and its implications for the study of organizational reputation. Bus Soc 41(4):393–414

Wiedmann K-P (2004) RQ Deutschland 2004, erste Ergebnisse und Einschätzungen sowie relevante Kontaktdaten. Universität Hannover, Arbeitspapier

Wiedmann K-P, Buxel H (2005) Corporate reputation management in germany: results of an empirical study. Corp Reputation Rev 8(2):145–163

Wiedmann K-P, Prauschke C (2005) How do stakeholder alignment concepts influence corporate reputation? the role of corporate communication In: Reputation Building, paper presented at the 10th Conference on Reputation, Image, Identity & Competitiveness, May 25–28, New York

Wieseke J, Homburg C, Lee N (2008) Understanding the adoption of new brands through salespeople: a multilevel framework. J Acad Market Sci 36:278–291

Williams MR (1998) The influence of salesperson's customer orientation on buyer-seller relationship development. J Bus Ind Market 13(3):271–287

Williams RJ, Schnake ME, Fredenberger W (2005) The impact of corporate strategy on a firm's reputation. Corp Reputation Rev 8(3):187–197

Windsperger J (1994) The evolution of the vertically integrated firm: a transaction cost analysis. In: Aiginger K, Finsinger J (eds) Applied industrial organization. Kluwer Academic Publishers, Dordrecht, Boston, London, pp 111–132

Witt K, Witt F-J (2008) Managers Methodenwind. Controller Magazin, May/June, pp 18–22

Witzel R (2006) Relationship marketing in der pharmazeutischen industrie. Deutscher Universitätsverlag, Wiesbaden

Wold H (1981) The fix-point approach to interdependent systems: review and current outlook. In: Wold H (ed) The fix-point approach to interdependent systems. North-Holland, Amsterdam, pp 1–35

Wold H (1982) Systems under indirect observation using PLS. In: Fornell C (ed) A second generation of multivariate analysis, booklet 1, New York, pp. 325–347

Wold H (1989) Introduction to the second generation of multivariate analysis. In: Wold H (ed) Theoretical empiricism. Paragon House, New York, pp 71–101

Wright H, Fill C (2001) Corporate images, attributes and the UK pharmaceutical industry. Corp Rep. Rev 4(2):99–110

Zabala I, Panadero G, Amate GLM, CM Sanchez-Galindo M, Tena I, Villalba I (2005) Corporate reputation in professional service firms: reputation management based on intellectual capital management. Corp Rep Rev 8(1):59–71

Zaheer A, McEvily B, Perrone V (1998) Does trust matter? exploring the effects of interorganizational and interpersonal trust on performance. Organ Sci 9(2):141–159

Zahra SA, Sapienza HJ, Davidsson P (2006) Entrepreneurship and dynamic capabilities: a review, model and research agenda. J Manag Stud 43(4):917–955

Zaichkowsky JL (1985) Measuring the involvement construct. J Consum Res 12(3):341–352

Zaichkowsky JL (1994) The personal involvement inventory: reduction, revision, and application to advertising. J Adv 23(4):59–70

Zaykin DV, Zhivotovsky LA, Westfall PH, Weir BS (2002) Truncated product method for combining p-values. Genet Epidemiol 22(2):170–185

Zinkham GM, Munderrisoglu A (1985) Involvement, familiarity, cognitive differentiation, and advertising recall: a test of convergent and discriminant validity. Adv Consum Res 12(1): 356–361

http://www.reputationinstitute.com/members/nyc06/Wiedmann_Prauschke.pdf, last access date: 09.09.2009

Index

GPSR Compliance

The European Union's (EU) General Product Safety Regulation (GPSR) is a set of rules that requires consumer products to be safe and our obligations to ensure this.

If you have any concerns about our products, you can contact us on ProductSafety@springernature.com

In case Publisher is established outside the EU, the EU authorized representative is:

Springer Nature Customer Service Center GmbH
Europaplatz 3
69115 Heidelberg, Germany

Batch number: 10725802

Printed by Printforce, the Netherlands